PHILIP JODIDIO

CH
ARCHITECTURE
IN
SWITZERLAND

TASCHEN

KÖLN LONDON LOS ANGELES MADRID PARIS TOKYO

#2/7/9

#6/11/14

#17

#14   #10

#4

#17

#8

#13

#3/3

INTRODUCTION

Imagine a landlocked country less than twice the size of New Jersey, with a population even smaller than that of the American state (7 489 370–July 2005 est.). It shares borders with its larger and more powerful neighbors, France, Germany or Italy. This country has four official languages and a history that goes back to the year 1291. These might not seem to be ideal circumstances for the creation of a culture of contemporary architecture, and yet Switzerland appears to be more convinced of its often austere modernity than most other European countries. It is no accident that the ten-franc bill of the country carries a portrait of Le Corbusier. Often thought to be French, Charles-Édouard Jeanneret was of course born in La Chaux-de-Fonds, Switzerland, in 1887. The unusual mixture of strong and ancient national traditions with a fascination for structural innovation has also been expressed in Switzerland through its engineers. Robert Maillart (born in Bern in 1872–died in 1940) is best known for his elegant and radically innovative bridges, based on the use of flat and curved slabs of reinforced concrete. Maillart's education and career offer one answer to the enigma of the creativity of modern Swiss architecture and engineering. He obtained his degree from the Federal Polytechnic Institute (ETH) in Zurich in 1894, and taught there for several years after 1912.

ETH Zurich was founded in 1854 by the Confederation and opened its doors the following year as the Eidgenössisches Polytechnikum (Federal Polytechnic Institute). At that time, it was the only Swiss national university and included six sections: architecture, civil engineering, mechanical engineering, chemistry, forestry, and a department grouping mathematics, natural sciences, literature, social and political sciences. The main building of the ETH, designed by Gottfried Semper, who was a professor for architecture there, was built from 1861 to 1864. Semper (1803–79) was a German architect, art critic, and professor of architecture, who designed the Semper Oper in Dresden (1838–41 and 1871–78 respectively). He is also known for his writing, in particular, the 1851 book *The Four Elements of Architecture,* and the later *Style in the Technical and Tectonic Arts* (1860–63). With such prestigious roots, the ETH has established itself today as one of the foremost schools of engineering and architecture in Europe. Most of the leading architects and engineers of contemporary Switzerland, and such considerable foreign figures as Santiago Calatrava, are graduates of the ETH Zurich.

The only other Swiss school of comparable status is the École Polytechnique Fédérale (EPFL) in Lausanne. Founded in 1853 as the École Spéciale de Lausanne, it became the technical department of the Académie de Lausanne in 1869. Part of a university reorganization carried out in 1890, the faculty became the École d'Ingénieurs de l'Université de Lausanne. In 1946, it was again renamed École Polytechnique de l'Université de Lausanne (EPUL). Finally, in 1969, the EPUL, like the ETH, came under the direct control of the Swiss government and assumed its current name. Since the promulgation of a law in 1991, the ETH Zurich, the EPFL and four associated research institutes were put under joint administration as the ETH Bereich.

Aside from these two federal universities, Switzerland boasts a number of other excellent architecture schools, such as the recently created Accademia di Architettura di Mendrisio located in the Italian-speaking canton of Ticino. Part of the Università della Svizzera Italiana (USI), this faculty was created along lines suggested by Mario Botta in 1996. With such prestigious faculty members as Botta, Peter Zumthor or Kenneth Frampton, Mendrisio has also taken a place in the constellation of architecture schools serving what remains a small country. Indeed, an architect like Mario Botta, perhaps because of his Swiss Italian origin, does not fit into the ETH background that has come to be considered typical of the country. Born in Mendrisio in 1943, Botta became an apprentice in a Lugano architectural office at the age of 15, before completing his studies in Milan and Venice. Having worked in the entourage of Le Corbusier, Louis Kahn and Luigi Snozzi, Botta has surely done more than other contemporary Swiss architects to affirm the viability and strength of a southern tradition within the confines of Switzerland, 65 percent of whose citizens speak German (only 10 percent speak Italian as a first language). "In a political sense, I am Swiss," says Botta, "but I belong to a minority. The residents of Ticino are marginalized within their country. But the fact that we live on the border of a larger country is also an advantage. Being on the fringe of an economic and political system is, in my opinion, very positive. I would have had great difficulty working in Zurich. Italian culture has nourished me, it is even in my chromosomes in a sense. The history of architecture that I know is that of churches from the Romanesque to Ronchamp." Botta has called on a geometric, modernist vocabulary since designing his first houses, but there are deep historical roots in his work, linked as he suggests to the Romanesque. In materials and plan, in his sense of a site, and above all in the power of his gestures, Botta at his best represents southern Switzerland with an original voice.

Although, there are other considerable figures in the architectural world of Ticino, two young protégés of Botta are represented in this book—Davide Macullo, who was born in Giornico in 1965, and worked in Botta's office in Lugano beginning in 1990, and the even younger Aldo Celoria, who is a product of Botta's school in Mendrisio. A different sensibility, surely more in tune with the Mediterranean south than the darker north, is expressed by these architects, and even if they do not form the mainstream of the country's creativity, they do enrich and broaden its horizons. Another architect of southern origin who has marked the country, despite having been born in Valencia, is Santiago Calatrava. He obtained a doctorate in engineering at the ETH Zurich in 1981 and created his own architecture and civil engineering office the same year in Zurich. Although Calatrava has worked recently more outside of the country, designing the stadiums for the 2004 Athens Summer Olympics, or the current Transportation Hub for the new World Trade Center in New York, he created the very interesting Stadelhofen train station in Zurich, as well as the more recent Law Faculty at the University of Zurich (2004). Although his frequently anthropomorphic designs are far from the more typical austerity of Swiss contemporary architecture, it is significant that Calatrava is a product of the ETH, where, in his case, architecture and engineering came together in a unique way.

In the case of this brief and naturally subjective survey of Swiss contemporary architecture, engineers play a larger role than they might in other countries, where the limits between professions may be more strictly defined. Jürg Conzett, born in 1956 in the Graubünden area of the country, studied civil engineering at the EPFL and the ETH, before working in the office of Peter Zumthor. The Pùnt da Suransuns he designed in the late 1990s for a site in the Viamala Gorge demonstrates that the tradition of modern, innovative Alpine bridges so brilliantly represented early in the century by Robert Maillart is not dead. Conzett works in Chur with two other engineers, Gianfranco Bronzini and Patrick Gartmann. Gartmann, born in Chur in 1968, worked as an assistant of Valerio Olgiati at the ETH before creating the partnership. Gartmann's own rather ample house in Chur shows a mixture of intelligent architecture and respect for a natural setting, with technical innovation. Like much contemporary Swiss architecture, Gartmann's house is well built and detailed. In this it differs greatly from much of the production in neighboring countries, such as Italy and France.

French-speaking architects are not quite as rare in Switzerland as their Italian-speaking counterparts, but French nonetheless remains a minority language in the country (18 %). The long dominance of the ETH Zurich has also left more of a mark on the country perhaps than the rising star of the EPFL. The architects Patrick Devanthéry and Inès Lamunière, both born in 1954, are products of the EPFL (1980). They have taught at the EPFL but also at the ETH or at Harvard for example. Their Primary School in Rolle, published in this volume, shows an acute sense of contextual use of modern forms, since they were called on to enlarge a 1930s facility. Cheerful and clever, their addition does keep to the type of strict lines that are often expected of Swiss architects.

Another young graduate of the EPFL selected for this book is Philippe Rahm, who was born in 1967 and is at the conceptual forefront of a very different idea of architecture. He has chosen with his former partner Gilles Décosterd to look into the physiological aspects of the built environment, imagining, as they did for the Hormonorium, the Swiss Pavilion at the 2002 Venice Architecture Biennale, what would happen if oxygen were reduced or light increased in a typical exhibition environment. Some of their work has been even more radical, as was the case of the ND Cult, a work that borders on the morbid. Imagine a roomy glass coffin with piped-in gas. Oxygen is reduced to six percent and one enters "a space on the borderline of death, where perception and consciousness are modified in a way probably close to that of mystical states. Under these extreme physical conditions, the space is extremely dangerous, irreversible brain damage is possible and the risk of death is real." ND stands for "Near Death." Experimenting with light, humidity and the air we breathe, Philippe Rahm promises to bring entirely new dimensions in architecture into focus. What makes this effort fascinating is that, in a sense, the architect is going back even beyond the fundamentals of the built environment to question the physiological roots of any building.

Just as Rem Koolhaas/OMA strides beyond his country on the world stage, Switzerland, too, boasts native architects of truly international significance, such as the Basel office Herzog & de Meuron. Both born in Basel in 1950, Jacques Herzog and Pierre de Meuron obtained their degrees from the ETH Zurich in 1975. They emerged on the international scene with their dramatic remake of London's Bankside Power Station into the Tate Modern. Their recent work, from the Allianz Arena in Munich to the Walker Art Center in Minneapolis, Minnesota, has confirmed their capacity to approach architecture in a truly innovative manner. As Alejandro Zaera Polo of the London firm Foreign Office Architects (FOA), who cleverly called Herzog & de Meuron "The Alchemical Brothers," has written, "Unlike patronized and patronizing artists, their trade came from their operative engagement with an open world rather than by exploiting their own subjective obsessions or their patrons' representations. The focus of their discipline allowed them to pierce many more strata—physical, social, political, psychological—than artists ever could ... Herzog & de Meuron work ranges also from the mystic to the kinky: Gerhard Richter or the Spice Girls, Helmut Federle or Manchester United, Prada cool or Versace kitsch—anything goes as long as it yields excitement."[1] Basel, as their occasional collaborator artist Rémy Zaugg points out, is a real cultural crossroads of Europe. "Swiss German is spoken here," he says, "but France is nearby, and there are exchanges between French and German speakers ... Between 1960 and 1970, Basel was one of the main centers of contemporary art ... During those years and in that city, complexity and the clash between minimalism and Beuys could very well have been important for Jacques and Pierre as well."[2]

The office of Herzog & de Meuron, like that of Rem Koolhaas in the Netherlands, has produced numerous other talents, like Annette Gigon, who worked in their office from 1985 to 1988 before creating her own office in Zurich. In fact her partner, Mike Guyer, worked for Koolhaas during almost the same period. Gigon/Guyer recently completed the Museum for the Alberts/Honegger Collection in Mouans-Sartoux, France (2003), showing their ability to use an unexpected combination of a minimalist vocabulary with colors to very positive effect. Gigon/Guyer is not on the same scale of international fame as Herzog & de Meuron, but their talent, also formed at the ETH, is definitely such that they will continue to build extensively inside and outside their native country.

In the book *Herzog & de Meuron, Natural History*, Kurt Forster recalls that the architect Karl Friedrich Schinkel (1781–1841) had a passionate interest in mountain architecture. He wrote, "Alpine buildings, the small and insignificant ones as well as the handsome residence of a patrician in a small village, are works of architecture like ancient Greek temples, that were certainly built in this way already during

[1] Alejandro Zaera Polo, "The Alchemical Brothers" in *Herzog & de Meuron, Natural History*, Canadian Centre for Architecture, 2002.

[2] "Architecture in itself doesn't interest me." Interview of Rémy Zaugg by Philip Unsprung, in *Herzog & de Meuron, Natural History*, Canadian Centre for Architecture, 2002.

the time of Pericles." The strong connections of contemporary Swiss architecture to its ancestral roots may not always be evident in the minimal forms that often prevail. And yet what people call the "Swiss box" in a sometimes derogatory way can be a much more sophisticated and rich form of architecture than it first appears to be. Two architects who have confronted the past of Switzerland in different ways might illustrate this point. Valerio Olgiati was born in Chur in 1958. He studied at the ETH and created his own office in Zurich in 1986. One of his emblematic projects is the so-called Yellow House, located in the Graubünden town of Flims. By stripping off the old plaster to reveal the old building's original stone, painting it entirely white, and rebuilding its interior in wood, Olgiati brought forth what he calls "childlike archaism and animal substance" of the structure. Intended to display a collection of artifacts united by his own father, Olgiati's Yellow House is a study in the deep connections that can exist between modernity and the past in Switzerland.

The real master of Swiss tradition in a modern context might be Peter Zumthor, whose relatively rare built work has been amply published the world over. Born in 1943 in Basel, Zumthor worked first as an apprentice carpenter before studying at the Pratt Institute in New York. A former architect for the preservation of historic buildings in the Graubünden region, his Thermal Baths in Vals (1996) are an ode to the power of the mountains. Using locally quarried gneiss, his "geometric cave system" of green stone feels as though it might have been carved from the earth centuries ago. Located in a steep valley with difficult access, Vals is in a sense located at the very heart of Swiss tradition and spirit. It can't be said that these baths quote any specific Swiss architecture—they are more like a geological emergence, something related to a time before time, when the Alps were already there, and so too was the natural reality of today's Switzerland. So, too, Zumthor has taken on the delicate task of building a local house in wood, using careful local craftsmanship to hone a truly modern building from the depths of a past whose name is not uttered here. He literally builds on the past to create a specific and quite Swiss form of modern architecture. Zumthor has also shown in such works as his glass and concrete Bregenz Kunsthalle (1997) that he is by no means limited in his vocabulary to the interpretation of Swiss tradition or its natural environment as in Vals.

Switzerland's strong natural presence, in the form of mountains, and its architectural tradition have also recently inspired some of the best foreign architects, as is the case of the Italian Renzo Piano at the Paul Klee Center in Bern (2005), which assumes the form of rolling hills, or even more obviously of Lord Norman Foster, who finished the Chesa Futura in St. Moritz in 2002. The English architect openly sought to ally computer-assisted design and "indigenous building techniques." Covered in larch like many mountain chalets, the Chesa Futura also shows something of its digital origins in a "bubble-like form." This might be a case of an obviously foreign point of view on Swiss traditions, but it does show the vivacity of those past forms, much as Schinkel suggested long ago.

As small and landlocked as it may be, Switzerland has affirmed its modernity even as its mountain communities often recycle traditional chalet forms to the point of over-consumption. Where cow bells and chocolate occupy the tourist's superficial vision of a charming kitsch universe, an even cursory overview of Switzerland's contemporary architecture reveals a commitment to a strong but perhaps austere vision of new buildings. Inclined to quality construction, perhaps because of its combination of wealth and a harsh winter climate, Switzerland's contemporary architecture occupies a place apart in Europe. Though currents from France, Germany or Italy flow strongly through its designs, Swiss architecture schools, the ETH Zurich and the EPFL in particular, assure that locally produced talent will continue to form the core of its population of designers and engineers. Like a bridge by Robert Maillart, it may be expected that Swiss architecture will nurture its very special combination of audacity and innovation, allied to solidity.

Philip Jodidio

EINLEITUNG

Man stelle sich ein Land vor, etwa doppelt so groß wie das Bundesland Hessen und mit einer Bevölkerung, die deutlich kleiner ist als die von Bayern. Es grenzt an größere, mächtigere Nachbarn wie Frankreich, Deutschland oder Italien. In diesem Land werden vier Sprachen gesprochen, und seine Geschichte reicht bis in das Jahr 1291 zurück. Man könnte meinen, dies seien keine idealen Voraussetzungen für das Entstehen einer wirklichen Kultur zeitgenössischen Bauens, und doch ist die Schweiz anscheinend von ihrer oft asketischen Moderne überzeugter, als die meisten anderen europäischen Länder. Es ist kein Zufall, dass der Zehn-Franken-Schein ein Porträt von Le Corbusier zeigt. Der häufig für einen Franzosen gehaltene Charles-Édouard Jeanneret wurde tatsächlich 1887 in La Chaux-de-Fonds in der Schweiz geboren. Die ungewöhnliche Mischung aus vitalen, uralten Nationaltraditionen und der Begeisterung für konstruktive Innovation kam in der Schweiz auch durch ihre Ingenieure zum Ausdruck. Robert Maillart (1872–1940) ist am bekanntesten durch seine eleganten, radikal innovativen Brückenbauten, die auf der Verwendung von flachen und gebogenen Stahlbetonplatten basieren. Maillarts Ausbildung und Laufbahn sind vielleicht ein Schlüssel für das Rätsel der Kreativität moderner schweizerischer Architektur und Ingenieurkunst. Er wurde 1894 am Eidgenössischen Polytechnikum in Zürich diplomiert und war dort nach 1912 einige Jahre als Lehrender tätig.

Die Eidgenössische Technische Hochschule (ETH) in Zürich wurde 1854 gegründet und öffnete ihre Türen im folgenden Jahr als Eidgenössisches Polytechnikum. Damals war sie die einzige Universität der Schweiz und umfasste sechs Abteilungen: Architektur, Bauingenieurwesen, Maschinenbau, Chemie, Forstwirtschaft sowie ein Institut, in dem Mathematik, Naturwissenschaften, Literatur sowie Sozial- und Politikwissenschaften zusammengefasst waren. Der von Gottfried Semper entworfene Hauptbau der ETH entstand zwischen 1861 und 1864. Semper (1803–79) war ein deutscher Architekt, Kunstkritiker und Architekturprofessor, der u. a. die Semperoper in Dresden (1838–41 bzw. 1871-78) erbaute. Er ist darüber hinaus für seine Schriften bekannt, insbesondere das 1851 erschienene Buch *Die vier Elemente der Baukunst* und später *Der Stil in den technischen und tektonischen Künsten* (1860–63). Nach ihren ruhmreichen Anfängen konnte sich die ETH als eine der führenden technischen Universitäten Europas etablieren. Die große Mehrheit der renommierten Architekten und Ingenieure der heutigen Schweiz und einige bedeutende auswärtige Persönlichkeiten wie Santiago Calatrava sind Absolventen der ETH Zürich.

Die einzige andere schweizerische Ausbildungsstätte von vergleichbarer Bedeutung ist die École Polytechnique Fédérale in Lausanne (EPFL). Die 1853 als École Spéciale de Lausanne gegründete Institution wurde 1869 zum technischen Institut der Académie de Lausanne. Als Teil einer 1890 durchgeführten Umgestaltung der Universität wurde das Institut zur École d'Ingénieurs de l'Université de Lausanne. 1946 wurde sie erneut umbenannt in École Polytechnique de l'Université de Lausanne (EPUL). 1969 schließlich kam die EPUL, ebenso wie die ETH, unter die direkte Kontrolle der schweizerischen Regierung und führt seither ihren heutigen Namen. Mit der Verkündung eines Gesetzes im Jahr 1991 kamen die ETH Zürich, die EPFL sowie vier beigeordnete Forschungsinstitute als ETH-Bereich unter eine gemeinsame Verwaltung.

Abgesehen von diesen beiden eidgenössischen Universitäten gibt es in der Schweiz eine Reihe weiterer ausgezeichneter Architekturschulen, so die vor einigen Jahren im italienischsprachigen Tessin gegründete Accademia di architettura di Mendrisio. Sie entstand 1996 als Teil der Università della Svizzera Italiana (USI) nach einem Konzept, das Mario Botta lancierte. Dank solch renommierter Fakultätsmitglieder wie Botta, Peter Zumthor oder Kenneth Frampton nahm auch Mendrisio bald einen herausragenden Platz im Reigen der Architekturschulen dieses kleinen Landes ein. Vielleicht aufgrund seiner Herkunft aus der italienischen Schweiz passt ein Architekt wie Mario Botta nicht recht in die von der ETH geprägten Szenerie, die inzwischen als typisch für die Schweiz gilt. Der 1943 in Mendrisio geborene Mario Botta begann im Alter von 15 eine Lehre in einem Architekturbüro in Lugano, ehe er sein Studium in Mailand und Venedig abschloss. Botta, der im Gefolge von Le Corbusier, Louis Kahn und Luigi Snozzi tätig war, hat mit Sicherheit mehr als andere zeitgenössische Schweizer Architekten zur Vitalität und Stärke der südeuropäischen Bautradition innerhalb der Grenzen der Schweiz beigetragen, deren Einwohner zu 65 % deutschsprachig sind und nur 10 % Italienisch als Muttersprache haben. „Im politischen Sinn bin ich Schweizer", sagt Botta, „aber ich gehöre einer Minderheit an. Die Bewohner des Tessin werden im eigenen Land an den Rand gedrängt. Andererseits ist der Umstand, dass wir an der Grenze zu einem größeren Land leben, auch von Vorteil. Am Rand eines politischen und ökonomischen Systems zu leben, ist für meinen Begriff äußerst positiv. In Zürich zu arbeiten, wäre für mich sehr schwierig gewesen. Die Kultur Italiens hat mich genährt, sie ist in gewissem Sinn sogar in meinen Chromosomen. Die Architekturgeschichte, die ich kenne, reicht von den Kirchen der Romanik bis Ronchamp." Seit seinen ersten Entwürfen bediente sich Botta einer geometrischen, modernistischen Formensprache, aber es gibt in seinem Œuvre auch tiefreichende, historische Wurzeln, die, wie Botta andeutet, auf die Romanik Bezug nehmen. Mit der Wahl der Materialien und Grundrisse, mit seinem Gespür für den jeweiligen Standort und vor allem mit der Überzeugungskraft seiner Bauten, vertritt Botta die südliche Schweiz mit einer außergewöhnlichen Stimme.

Obgleich es andere beachtliche Persönlichkeiten in der Tessiner Architekturszene gibt, werden in diesem Buch zwei junge Protégés von Botta vorgestellt – Davide Macullo, der 1965 in Giornico geboren wurde und ab 1990 in Bottas Büro in Lugano arbeitete, und der noch jüngere Aldo Celoria, ein Absolvent von Bottas Schule in Mendrisio. Diese Architekten bringen eine andere Empfindsamkeit zum Ausdruck, die sich eher in Einklang mit dem mediterranen Süden befindet als mit dem dunkleren Norden. Obwohl sie nicht den Mainstream der Kreativität des Landes prägen, bereichern und erweitern sie doch seine Horizonte. Ein weiterer Architekt südlicher Herkunft, der in diesem Land Zeichen gesetzt hat, ist der in Valencia geborene Santiago Calatrava. Er promovierte 1981 an der ETH Zürich im Fach Ingenieurwesen und gründete im selben Jahr in Zürich sein eigenes Architektur- und Bauingenieurbüro. Calatrava, der in jüngerer Zeit mehr außerhalb der Landesgrenzen tätig ist und z. B. die Stadien für die Olympischen Sommerspiele 2004 in Athen plante und aktuell den Verkehrsknotenpunkt für das neue World Trade Center in New York konzipiert, entwarf den höchst interessanten Bahnhof Stadelhofen in Zürich sowie unlängst das Gebäude der Juristischen Fakultät der Universität Zürich (2004). Obwohl sich seine häufig anthropomorphen Entwürfe von der für die zeitgenössische Architektur der Schweiz typischeren Kargheit deutlich unterscheiden, ist Calatrava doch von seiner Ausbildung an der ETH geprägt, wo sich in seinem Fall Architektur und Bauingenieurwesen in einzigartiger Weise zusammenfügten.

In diesem kurzen und naturgemäß subjektiven Überblick über die heutige Architektur der Schweiz spielen Ingenieure eine größere Rolle, als sie das vielleicht in anderen Ländern täten, in denen die Grenzen zwischen den Berufen genauer festgelegt sind. Der 1956 im Kanton Graubünden geborene Jürg Conzett studierte an der EPFL und der ETH Ingenieurwesen, ehe er im Büro Peter Zumthors arbeitete. Der Pùnt da Suransuns, den er Ende der 1990er Jahre für die Viamala-Schlucht entwarf, beweist, dass die Tradition moderner, innovativer Alpenbrücken weiterlebt, die Robert Maillart zu Beginn des Jahrhunderts so glänzend vertrat. Conzett arbeitet in Chur mit Gianfranco Bronzini und Patrick Gartmann, zwei weiteren Ingenieuren, zusammen. Der 1968 in Chur geborene Gartmann war als Assistent von Valerio Olgiati an der ETH tätig, ehe er die Partnerschaft einging. Gartmanns eigenes, recht geräumiges Haus in Chur zeichnet sich aus durch eine Mischung aus intelligenter Architektur, Achtung vor der umgebenden Natur und technischer Innovation. Wie ein großer Teil der zeitgenössischen schweizerischen Architektur, ist auch Gartmanns Haus solide gebaut und detailliert ausgeführt. In dieser Hinsicht unterscheidet es sich deutlich von einem Großteil der Neubauten in Nachbarländern wie Italien und Frankreich.

Frankophone Architekten sind in der Schweiz nicht ganz so rar wie ihre italienischsprachigen Kollegen, aber auch Französisch wird nur von einer Minderheit im Land gesprochen (18 %). Die lang anhaltende Dominanz der ETH hat das Land außerdem stärker geprägt als der aufsteigende Stern der EPFL. Die beiden 1954 geborenen Architekten Patrick Devanthéry und Inès Laumunière sind Absolventen der EPFL (1980). Sie haben beide dort auch gelehrt, aber beispielsweise ebenso an der ETH und in Harvard. Die in diesem Band publizierte Grundschule der beiden in Rolle zeigt ein ausgeprägtes Gespür für die kontextuelle Verwendung moderner Formen, da es darum ging, eine in den 1930er Jahren errichtete Schule zu erweitern. Wennmöglich heiter und raffiniert, hält sich ihr Anbau dennoch an die Art von gerader Linienführung, die man häufig von schweizerischen Architekten erwartet.

Ein weiterer junger Absolvent der EPFL, der für dieses Buch ausgewählt wurde, ist der 1967 geborene Philippe Rahm. Er vertritt eine deutlich andere Vorstellung von Architektur. Mit seinem früheren Partner Gilles Décosterd untersuchte er die physiologischen Aspekte der gebauten Umwelt. Für den Hormonorium genannten Pavillon der Schweiz auf der Architekturbiennale 2002 in Venedig

stellten sie Überlegungen an, was passiert, wenn man in einem typischen Ausstellungsambiente den Sauerstoff reduziert oder das Licht verstärkt. Ein Teil ihres Œuvres ist noch radikaler, wie „ND Cult", ein Werk, das ans Morbide grenzt. Man stelle sich einen geräumigen, gläsernen Sarg vor, in den ein Luftgemisch geleitet wird. Der Sauerstoff ist auf 6 % reduziert, und man begibt sich „in einen Raum an der Grenze zum Tod, in dem Wahrnehmung und Bewusstsein auf eine Art verändert sind, die wahrscheinlich der eines mystischen Zustands nahe kommt. Unter diesen extremen physischen Bedingungen ist der Raum äußerst gefährlich, eine irreversible Schädigung des Gehirns möglich und die Gefahr des Sterbens real." ND ist die Abkürzung für „Near Death", dem Tod nahe. Indem er mit Licht, Feuchtigkeit und Atemluft experimentiert, rückt Philippe Rahm völlig neue Dimensionen der Architektur in den Blickpunkt. Das Faszinierende an dieser Arbeit ist, dass der Architekt dabei nicht nur zu den Grundlagen des Bauens zurückgeht, sondern darüber hinaus die physiologischen Wurzeln hinterfragt, die jedem Gebäude zugrunde liegen.

Gerade so wie Rem Koolhaas mit OMA über sein Land hinaus auf der Weltbühne agiert, so kann sich auch die Schweiz einheimischer Architekten von wahrhaft internationaler Bedeutung rühmen, und zwar in Gestalt der Baseler Bürogemeinschaft Herzog & de Meuron. Jacques Herzog und Pierre de Meuron wurden 1950 in Basel geboren und erwarben 1975 an der ETH ihr Diplom. Mit dem spektakulären Umbau des stillgelegten Kraftwerks an der Londoner Bankside zur Tate Modern betraten sie die internationale Szene. Ihre neueren Werke, von der Allianz-Arena in München bis zum Walker Art Center in Minneapolis, bestätigen ihre Fähigkeit, an Architektur in wirklich innovativer Weise heranzugehen. Alejandro Zaera Polo vom Londoner Büro Foreign Office Architects (FOA), der Herzog & de Meuron einmal scharfsinnig „die alchimistischen Brüder" nannte, schrieb: „Im Gegensatz zu herablassenden Auftragskünstlern, ergab sich ihr Gewerbe aus der operativen Einlassung mit einer offenen Welt und nicht, indem sie ihre höchsteigenen Obsessionen oder die Vorstellungen ihrer Auftraggeber ausschlachteten. Der Schwerpunkt ihrer Disziplin gestattete es ihnen, in sehr viel zahlreichere Schichten – seien sie physischer, sozialer, politischer oder psychologischer Art – einzudringen, als es Künstler je könnten … Das Œuvre von Herzog & de Meuron reicht außerdem vom Mystischen bis zum Überdrehten: Gerhard Richter oder die Spice Girls, Helmut Federle oder Manchester United, Prada-Coolness oder Versace-Kitsch – alles ist erlaubt, solange es nur aufregend ist."[1] Der gelegentlich mit ihnen zusammen arbeitende Künstler Rémy Zaugg wies darauf hin, dass Basel in Europa an einer Kreuzung liegt. „Man spricht hier Schwyzerdütsch", sagt er, „aber Frankreich ist nahe, und es gibt einen Austausch zwischen französisch und deutsch sprechenden Anwohnern … Von 1960 bis 1970 war Basel eines der Hauptzentren zeitgenössischer Kunst … Während dieser Zeit und in dieser Stadt könn-

[1] Alejandro Zaera Polo, „The Alchemical Brothers", in: Herzog & de Meuron, Natural History, Canadian Centre for Architecture, 2002.

[2] „Architecture in itself doesn't interest me", Gespräch von Rémy Zaugg mit Philip Ursprung, in: Herzog & de Meuron, Natural History, Canadian Centre for Architecture, 2002.

ten die Komplexität und der Widerspruch zwischen Minimalismus und Beuys für Jacques und Pierre sehr gut von Bedeutung gewesen sein."[2]

Ähnlich wie aus dem OMA von Koolhaas in den Niederlanden gingen auch aus dem Büro von Herzog & de Meuron zahlreiche Begabungen hervor wie Annette Gigon, die, ehe sie in Zürich ihr eigenes Büro eröffnete, von 1985 bis 1988 dort tätig war. Ihr Partner, Mike Guyer, arbeitete fast zeitgleich bei Rem Koolhaas. Gigon/Guyer vollendeten 2003 das Museum für die Albers/Honegger-Sammlung in Mouans-Sartoux, Frankreich, das ihre Fähigkeit demonstriert, minimalistische Formen auf überraschende und höchst überzeugende Weise mit Farben zu kombinieren. Gigon/Guyer, die ebenfalls an der ETH studierten, mögen international noch nicht den Status von Herzog & Meuron haben, werden aber dank ihres Talents sicherlich weiterhin zahlreiche Bauten innerhalb und außerhalb ihres Heimatlandes realisieren können.

In dem Buch *Herzog & de Meuron, Naturgeschichte* erinnert Kurt Forster an Karl Friedrich Schinkels (1781–1841) Passion für Bergarchitektur. Er schrieb: „Die Alphütte, sowohl die kleine und unbedeutende, als die zierlichste große Wohnung eines Patriziers eines kleinen Ortes, ist ein classisches architektonisches Werk, wie ein altgriechischer Tempel, und gewiss war sie zu Perikles Zeit schon ganz ebenso gebaut." Die vitalen Verbindungen der heutigen Architektur der Schweiz zu ihren Wurzeln mögen ihren meist minimalistischen Formen nicht allzu augenfällig sein. Und doch kann hinter der manchmal etwas abfällig so genannten „Swiss Box" viel mehr Raffinesse und Einfallsreichtum stecken, als man auf den ersten Blick meinen sollte. Das zeigt zum Beispiel das Werk von zwei Architekten, die sich jeweils auf unterschiedliche Weise mit der schweizerischen Vergangenheit auseinandersetzen: Valerio Olgiati wurde 1958 in Chur geboren. Nach seinem Studium an der ETH gründete er 1986 in Zürich ein eigenes Büro. Eines seiner emblematischen Projekte ist das so genannte Gelbe Haus in der Stadt Flims in Graubünden. Olgiati entfernte den Verputz, um das ursprüngliche Mauerwerk des alten Gebäudes freizulegen, strich das gesamte Haus weiß an und entwarf ein neues, hölzernes Interieur. So brachte er zum Vorschein, was er als „kindlichen Archaismus und animalische Substanz" des Gebäudes bezeichnet. Gedacht für die Ausstellung einer von seinem Vater zusammengetragenen Sammlung von Artefakten, ist Olgiatis Gelbes Haus ein Musterbeispiel für die tiefgründigen Verbindungen, die in einem Land wie der Schweiz zwischen Moderne und Vergangenheit bestehen können.

Der wahre Meister der schweizerischen Tradition im modernen Kontext ist wohl Peter Zumthor, dessen schmales Œeuvre weltweit publiziert wurde. 1943 in Basel geboren, absolvierte er eine Schreinerlehre, ehe er am Pratt Institute in New York ein Studium aufnahm. Zunächst als Architekt für die Denkmalpflege in Graubünden tätig, lieferte er mit seinem Thermalbad in Vals (1996) eine Ode an die Macht des Gebirges. Das „geometrische Höhlennetz" des Thermalbads aus grünem Stein, für das er vor Ort abgebauten Gneis verwendete, wirkt, als habe man es vor Jahrhunderten aus dem Felsen gehauen. Das in einem schwer zugäng-lichen, tiefen Tal gelegene Vals liegt in gewissem Sinn genau im Herzen von schweizerischer Tradition und Gemüt. Man kann nicht sagen, dieses Bad zitiere irgendeine bestimmte Architektur der Schweiz, es wirkt eher, als sei es geologischen Ursprungs, etwas, das mit Urzeiten zu tun hat, als es die Alpen schon gab und damit auch die Natur der heutigen Schweiz. Außerdem hat sich Zumthor an die heikle Aufgabe gemacht, ein ortsspezifisches Holzhaus zu bauen. Mithilfe der sorgfältigen heimischen Handwerkskunst zauberte er ein modernes Gebäude aus den Tiefen einer diffusen Vergangenheit hervor. Er baut buchstäblich auf der Vergangenheit, um eine spezifische, ganz schweizerische Form der modernen Architektur zu erschaffen. Mit Werken wie seiner aus Glas und Beton errichteten Kunsthalle in Bregenz von 1997 hat Zumthor darüber hinaus bewiesen, dass sein Vokabular sich keineswegs auf die Interpretation der Schweizer Tradition oder, wie in Vals, der natürlichen Gegebenheiten beschränkt ist.

Die eindrucksvolle gebirgige Natur der Schweiz und ihre Architekturtradition haben in jüngster Zeit auch einige der besten auswärtigen Architekten beflügelt – z. B. den Italiener Renzo Piano mit seinem Paul-Klee-Zentrum in Bern von 2005, das die Form sanft gewellter Hügel hat. Noch augenfälliger ist es im Fall von Norman Foster, der 2002 in St. Moritz die Chesa Futura fertig stellte. Er unternahm bei diesem Projekt den Versuch, computergestütztes Entwerfen und „heimische Bauverfahren" miteinander in Einklang zu bringen. Obwohl sie wie viele Chalets in den Alpen mit Lärchenholz verkleidet ist, treten in der runden Form die digitalen Ursprünge der Chesa Futura zutage. Dies mag offensichtlich der Blick eines Ausländers auf die Schweizer Tradition sein, aber es belegt auch – ganz im Sinne Schinkels – die Lebendigkeit von Formen der Vergangenheit.

Dem kleinen Binnenstaat Schweiz ist es in jedem Fall gelungen, seine Modernität unter Beweis zu stellen, selbst wenn in den Alpenorten die traditionellen Chaletformen bis zum Überdruss verwendet werden. Wo Kuhglocken und Schokolade die oberflächliche Sichtweise des Touristen vom idyllischen Kitschuniversum beherrschen, offenbart selbst ein summarischer Überblick über die zeitgenössische Architektur der Schweiz ein kraftvolles, wenn auch eher asketisches Verständnis vom Bauen. Die vielleicht wegen der Kombination aus harschen klimatischen Bedingungen im Winter und Wohlstand bestehende Neigung zu solidem Bauen, verschafft der zeitgenössischen Architektur der Schweiz in Europa eine Sonderstellung. Obgleich sich Strömungen aus Frankreich, Deutschland und Italien in den Entwürfen deutlich bemerkbar machen, stellen die ETH und insbesondere die EPFL sicher, dass heimische Talente auch künftig die Mehrzahl der Designer und Ingenieure ausmachen werden. Man darf erwarten, dass die schweizerische Architektur ihre ganz spezielle Kombination aus Wagemut und Innovation im Verein mit Gediegenheit bewahren wird – gleich einer Brücke von Robert Maillart.

Philip Jodidio

INTRODUCTION

Imaginez un pays enclavé ne mesurant même pas le double de l'État du New Jersey pour une population encore plus faible (7 489 370 habitants, estimation juillet 2005). Il possède des frontières communes avec de plus vastes et plus puissants voisins dont la France, l'Allemagne et l'Italie, quatre langues officielles et une histoire qui remonte à l'an 1291. On pourrait penser que ce ne sont pas là des circonstances idéales pour la création d'une vraie culture architecturale contemporaine et, cependant, la Suisse semble mieux vivre sa modernité – souvent austère – que la plupart des autres pays d'Europe. Ce n'est pas un hasard si le portrait de Le Corbusier figure sur le billet de 10 francs puisque Charles-Édouard Jeanneret est né à La Chaux-de-Fonds, en Suisse, en 1887, même s'il est souvent considéré comme français. Un mélange inhabituel de puissantes et anciennes traditions nationales et de fascination pour les innovations techniques dans le domaine des structures s'est également exprimé à travers de grands ingénieurs suisses, dont Robert Maillart (né à Berne en 1872, mort en 1940), surtout connu pour l'élégance et la nouveauté radicale de ses ponts faits de dalles plates ou incurvées en béton armé. La formation de Maillart et sa carrière apportent une réponse à l'énigme apparente de la créativité de l'architecture et de l'ingénierie suisses modernes : il obtint son diplôme d'ingénieur de l'Institut polytechnique fédéral de Zurich en 1894 et y enseigna plusieurs années après 1912.

L'ETH Zurich a été fondé en 1854 par la Confédération et a ouvert ses portes l'année suivante sous le nom de Eidgenössisches Polytechnikum (Institut polytechnique confédéral). Seule institution universitaire nationale suisse à l'époque, il comprenait six sections : architecture, ingénierie civile, ingénierie mécanique, chimie, sylviculture et un département regroupant mathématiques, sciences naturelles, littérature, sciences sociales et politiques. Son bâtiment principal, conçu par Gottfried Semper (1803–79) qui y enseigna l'architecture, fut édifié entre 1861 et 1864. Semper était un architecte allemand, critique d'art et professeur d'architecture, l'auteur du fameux Semper Oper de Dresde (1838–41 ou bien 1871-78). Il est également célèbre pour ses écrits, en particulier pour un ouvrage publié en 1851, *Les Quatre éléments de l'architecture*, ainsi que *Style dans les arts techniques et tectoniques* (1860-63). À partir de ces bases prestigieuses, l'ETH est aujourd'hui devenu l'une des plus brillantes écoles d'architecture et d'ingénierie d'Europe. La plupart des grands architectes et ingénieurs suisses contemporains et beaucoup de praticiens étrangers de renom comme Santiago Calatrava en sont diplômés.

Le seul autre centre d'enseignement suisse de statut comparable est l'École Polytechnique Fédérale de Lausanne, l'EPFL. Fondée en 1853 sous le nom d'École spéciale de Lausanne, elle devint le département technique de l'Académie de Lausanne en 1869. À l'occasion d'une réorganisation de l'Université en 1890, elle se transforma en École d'Ingénieurs de l'Université de Lausanne avant de prendre le nom d'École Polytechnique de l'Université de Lausanne (EPUL) en 1946. Finalement, en 1969, l'EPUL, comme l'ETH, passa sous le contrôle direct de l'administration confédérale, date à laquelle elle prit son nom actuel. Depuis la promulgation d'une loi de 1991, l'ETH Zurich, l'EPFL et quatre instituts de recherche associés ont été regroupés sous une administration commune appelée Domaine des EPF.

En dehors de ces deux universités confédérales, la Suisse possède un certain nombre d'autres excellentes écoles d'architecture comme la récente Accademia di architecttura di Mendrisio située dans le canton italophone du Tessin. Faculté de l'Università della Svizzera Italiana (USI), elle a été créée en 1996 sur des propositions de Mario Botta. Avec des enseignants aussi prestigieux que Botta, Peter Zumthor ou Kenneth Frampton, Mendrisio s'est fait une place dans la constellation des écoles d'architecture au service de ce qui n'est, somme toute, qu'un petit pays. Il faut savoir qu'un architecte comme Mario Botta, en raison peut-être de ses origines italo-suisses, ne correspond pas vraiment à l'esprit ETH considéré comme typique de celui de la Confédération. Né à Mendrisio en 1943, il a été apprenti dans une agence d'architecture de Lugano dès l'âge de quinze ans avant d'achever ses études à Milan et à Venise. Même s'il a travaillé auprès de Le Corbusier, Louis Kahn et Luigi Snozzi, il a certainement fait plus que d'autres architectes suisses actuels pour affirmer la viabilité et la force d'une tradition méridionale aux confins d'un pays dont 65 % des habitants parlent le suisse-allemand, et 10 % seulement le suisse-italien. « Au sens politique, je suis suisse », explique l'architecte, « mais j'appartiens à une minorité. Les habitants du Tessin sont marginalisés dans ce pays. Cependant, le fait que nous vivions à la frontière d'un pays plus grand est aussi un avantage. Être aux marges d'un système politique et économique est, à mon sens, très positif. J'aurais eu beaucoup de mal à travailler à Zurich. Je suis nourri d'une culture italienne qui figure pratiquement dans mes chromosomes. L'histoire de l'architecture telle que je la connais est d'abord celle des églises, du style roman à Ronchamp. » Dès ses premières réalisations de maisons, Botta a développé un vocabulaire moderniste géométrique, mais on note néanmoins de profondes racines historiques dans son œuvre, liées en effet au style roman. Dans les matériaux comme dans les plans, son sens du site et par-dessus tout la puissance de ses « gestes » font d'un Botta à son sommet une personnalité originale de la Suisse méridionale.

Si l'on trouve d'autres figures architecturales d'importance dans le Tessin, ce livre s'arrête également sur deux jeunes « protégés » de Botta : Davide Macullo, né en 1965 à Gironico, qui a travaillé dans l'agence de Botta à partir de 1990, et Aldo Celoria, plus jeune encore et produit de l'école de Mendrisio. Une sensibilité différente, qui les rattache davantage à l'esprit du Sud méditerranéen qu'à celui des cantons du Nord s'exprime en eux et même s'ils n'appartiennent pas au courant principal de la créativité suisse, ils enrichissent et élargissent ses horizons.

Un autre architecte d'origine méridionale a marqué la création dans ce pays, bien que né en Espagne, à Valence : Santiago Calatrava. Docteur en ingénierie de l'ETH à Zurich en 1981, il a ouvert la même année et dans la même ville son agence d'architecture et d'ingénierie civile. Bien qu'il ait récemment beaucoup travaillé à l'étranger, concevant, entre autres, des stades pour les Jeux olympiques d'Athènes 2004 ou la plate-forme d'échange du nouveau World Trade Center de New York, il a construit à Zurich la très intéressante gare de Stadelhofen ainsi qu'une plus récente faculté de droit. Ses « gestes » anthropomorphiques sont certainement très éloignés de l'austérité caractéristique de l'architecture contemporaine suisse, mais il ne faut pas oublier qu'il est un produit de l'ETH et que, dans son cas, architecture et ingénierie forment une combinaison exceptionnelle.

Dans le cadre de ce bref survol nécessairement subjectif, les ingénieurs jouent un rôle plus important que dans d'autres pays où les frontières entre les professions sont peut-être plus strictement définies. Jürg Conzett, né en 1956 dans la région des Grisons, a étudié l'ingénierie civile à l'EPFL et à l'ETH avant de travailler pour Peter Zumthor. Le Punt da Suransuns, dessiné à la fin des années 1990 pour la gorge de Viamala, prouve que la tradition des ponts alpins modernes et novateurs si brillamment représentée au début du XXᵉ siècle par Robert Maillart n'est pas morte. Conzett travaille à Chur avec deux autres ingénieurs, Gianfranco Bronzini et Patrick Gartmann. Ce dernier, né à Chur en 1968, a été l'assistant de Valerio Olgiati à l'ETH avant de créer son agence. Sa propre et assez grande maison édifiée à Chur illustre un mélange d'architecture intelligente, d'innovations techniques et de respect pour le cadre naturel. Comme beaucoup de réalisations suisses contemporaines, elle est bien construite et réalisée avec un grand soin du détail, ce qui la différencie d'une grande partie de la production de pays voisins comme l'Italie ou la France.

Les architectes francophones ne sont pas aussi rares que leurs confrères italophones, même si le français est lui aussi une langue minoritaire parlée par 18 % de la population seulement. La longue domination de l'ETH Zurich a par ailleurs laissé une marque plus profonde que celle de l'étoile encore montante de l'EPFL. Les architectes Patrick Devanthéry et Inès Lamunière, tous deux nés en 1954, sont des produits de l'EPL (1980). Ils y ont enseigné mais professent également à l'ETH ou à Harvard. Leur école primaire de Rolle, publiée ici, montre un sens aigu de l'utilisation contextuelle des formes modernes, puisqu'il s'agissait d'agrandir un bâtiment des années 1930. Chaleureux et intelligent, ce projet reste dans le cadre des limites strictes de ce que l'on attend généralement des architectes suisses.

Autre jeune diplômé de l'EPFL sélectionné dans cet ouvrage, Philippe Rahm, né en 1967, poursuit des recherches d'avant-garde sur une idée très différente de l'architecture. Son ancien associé, Gilles Décosterd, et lui étudient les aspects physiologiques du bâti. Par exemple, ils ont imaginé pour l'Hormonorium, le pavillon suisse de la Biennale d'architecture de Venise en 2002, ce qui se passerait si la quantité d'oxygène était réduite ou le niveau de lumière accru dans un environnement d'exposition. Certains de leurs travaux sont encore plus radicaux, comme dans ND Cult, une œuvre qui frise le morbide. Imaginez un vaste cercueil de verre dans lequel est injecté un gaz. La présence de l'oxygène est réduite à 6 % du volume normal et on pénètre alors dans « un espace à la limite de la mort, où la perception et la conscience sont modifiées d'une façon probablement proche de celle de certains états mystiques. Dans ces conditions physiques extrêmes, l'espace se charge de dangers, des atteintes irréversibles au cerveau peuvent se produire et le risque de mort est réel ». ND signifie Near Death (presque mort). Par ces expérimentations sur la lumière, l'humidité et l'air que nous respirons Philippe Rahm fait prendre conscience de dimensions entièrement nouvelles de l'architecture.

Ses travaux sont fascinants dans la mesure où l'architecte va ici au-delà des fondamentaux du bâti pour en remettre en question les racines physiologiques.

De même que les activités de Rem Koolhaas/OMA s'étendent bien au-delà de leur pays d'origine, deux architectes d'importance réellement internationale portent les couleurs suisses de par le monde, les Bâlois Herzog & de Meuron. Tous deux nés à Bâle en 1950, Jacques Herzog et Pierre de Meuron sont diplômés de l'ETH (1975). Ils se sont imposés sur la scène internationale à l'occasion de leur spectaculaire transformation de la centrale électrique de Bankside à Londres en un vaste musée d'art moderne et contemporain, la Tate Modern. Leurs réalisations récentes, de l'Allianz Arena à Munich au Walker Art Center à Minneapolis, ont confirmé une approche particulièrement novatrice de leur métier. Comme Alejandro Zaera Polo de l'agence londonienne Foreign Office (FOA) qui les a surnommés « Les frères alchimistes » l'écrit : « À la différence d'artistes protégés et condescendants, leur spécificité vient d'un engagement opérationnel dans un monde ouvert plutôt que de l'exploitation de leurs obsessions subjectives ou des souhaits de représentation de leurs clients. Leur concentration sur leur discipline leur a permis de percer bien davantage de strates – physiques, sociales, politiques, psychologiques – qu'aucun artiste ne l'a jamais fait ... l'œuvre d'Herzog & de Meuron peut aller du mystique ou pervers : Gerhard Richter ou les Spice Girls, Helmut Federle ou Manchester United, le cool de Prada ou le kitsch de Versace, tout est bon dans la mesure où la démarche suscite une excitation intellectuelle et visuelle. »[1] Bâle, comme le fait remarquer leur collaborateur occasionnel, l'artiste Rémy Zaugg, « est un des carrefours culturels de l'Europe : on y parle le suisse-allemand, mais la France est proche et les échanges existent entre germanophones et francophones... Entre 1960 et 1970, la ville fut l'un des principaux centres de l'art contemporain ... Ici, au cours de ces années, la complexité et l'affrontement entre le minimalisme et Beuys ont très bien pu jouer un rôle important dans la formation de Jacques et de Pierre. »[2]

Comme pour Koolhaas aux Pays-Bas, l'agence bâloise a permis l'éclosion de nombreux talents, dont celui d'Annette Gigon qui y a travaillé de 1985 à 1988 avant de créer sa propre structure à Zurich. Son associé Mike Gruyer travaillait, lui, chez Koolhaas à peu près à la même période. Gigon/Gruyer ont récemment achevé le musée qui abrite la collection Albers/Honneger à Mouans-Sartoux, France (2003), projet qui illustre leur capacité à associer couleur et vocabulaire minimaliste pour obtenir un effet très positif. Leur agence n'a pas encore atteint le même degré de notoriété internationale que Herzog & de Meuron, mais leur talent – également formé à l'ETH – les amènera certainement à construire aussi bien en Suisse qu'à l'étranger.

[1] Alejandro Zaera Polo, « The Alchemical Brothers » in *Herzog & de Meuron, Natural History*, Centre Canadien d'Architecture, Montréal, 2002.
[2] « L'architecture en soi ne m'intéresse pas. » Entretien avec Rémy Zaugg, par Philip Unsprung, in *Herzog & de Meuron, Natural History*, Centre canadien d'architecture, 2002.

Dans l'ouvrage *Herzog & de Meuron, Natural History*, Kurt Forster rappelle que l'architecte Karl Friedrich Schinkel (1781-1841) s'intéressait avec passion à l'architecture de montagne et avait écrit : « Les constructions alpines, les plus petites et les plus insignifiantes, comme les élégantes résidences patriciennes de village sont des œuvres d'architecture au même titre que les temples grecs, qui étaient certainement déjà construits de cette façon au temps de Périclès. » Les puissantes connexions entre l'architecture suisse contemporaine et ses racines ancestrales ne sont cependant pas toujours évidentes dans les formes souvent minimales qu'elle semble apprécier. Cependant, ce que certains appellent la « boîte suisse », d'une manière parfois condescendante, se révèle parfois une forme beaucoup plus riche et plus sophistiquée que ce que l'on pourrait penser au premier abord. Deux architectes confrontés au passé de leur pays de façon différente peuvent illustrer ce propos. Valerio Olgiati, né à Chur en 1958, a étudié à l'ETH et créé sa propre agence à Zurich en 1986. L'un de ses projets emblématiques est la « Maison jaune » située dans la petite ville de Flims dans les Grisons. En éliminant le plâtre ancien pour faire apparaître la pierre d'origine de cet ancien bâtiment, en le peignant entièrement en blanc et en reconstruisant son intérieur en bois, il a fait ressortir ce qu'il appelle « l'archaïsme enfantin et la substance animale » de cette construction. Restructurée pour présenter une collection d'objets d'art réunis par le père de l'architecte, la « Maison jaune » est une recherche sur les connexions profondes qui peuvent exister entre passé et modernité dans un pays aussi ancien que la Suisse.

Mais le vrai maître d'une tradition suisse revisitée dans un contexte moderne reste peut-être Peter Zumthor, dont l'œuvre relativement peu abondante a été amplement publiée dans le monde. Né à Bâle en 1943, il a d'abord travaillé comme apprenti charpentier avant d'étudier au Pratt Institute à New York. Les thermes de Vals (1996) conçus par cet ancien architecte pour la préservation des bâtiments historiques des Grisons sont une ode à la puissance des montagnes. Son « système géométrique de caverne » de pierre verte – un gneiss local – donne l'impression d'avoir été sculpté dans les profondeurs de la terre des siècles plus tôt. Situé dans une vallée profonde et d'accès difficile, Vals se trouve en un sens au cœur même de la tradition et de l'esprit suisses. On ne peut pas dire que ces bains citent une quelconque architecture helvète spécifique, car ils sont davantage une émergence géologique, quelque chose d'avant l'histoire qui renverrait à la naissance des Alpes et à la réalité naturelle de la Suisse d'aujourd'hui. Zumthor a également entrepris la tâche délicate de construire une maison en bois, à partir de techniques artisanales de qualité pour tirer une construction authentiquement moderne des profondeurs d'un passé anonyme. Il construit ainsi littéralement à partir du passé pour créer une forme d'architecture moderne spécifique et assez suisse, mais a aussi montré dans des réalisations comme sa Kunsthalle de Bregenz en verre et béton (1997) qu'il ne limite en aucun cas son vocabulaire à des interprétations de la tradition ou de la nature suisses comme à Vals.

La forte présence de la nature en Suisse et la tradition architecturale de ce pays ont aussi inspiré récemment quelques-uns des meilleurs praticiens étrangers comme l'Italien Renzo Piano pour le Centre Paul Klee à Berne (2005), en forme de vallonnement, ou encore plus fortement Norman Foster et sa Chesa Futura (Saint-Moritz, 2002). L'architecte britannique a cherché à allier la conception par ordinateur et les « techniques de construction indigènes ». Habillée de mélèze comme de nombreux chalets de montagne, cette Chesa Futura laisse transparaître ses origines numériques dans sa « forme de bulle ». Ce chantier pourrait être l'exemple d'un point de vue étranger sur les traditions suisses, mais illustre aussi la vitalité des formes du passé, non loin de ce que suggérait Schinkel il y a longtemps.

Petit pays enclavé, la Suisse affirme sa modernité même si ses communautés montagnardes préfèrent souvent recycler la typologie traditionnelle du chalet *ad nauseam*. Alors que les cloches des vaches et le chocolat marquent toujours la vision touristique superficielle d'un univers kitsch et charmant, un survol, même rapide, de l'architecture contemporaine suisse montre une volonté forte, et non dénuée d'austérité, de s'engager en faveur d'une architecture nouvelle. Marquée par son goût pour une construction de qualité (sans doute conséquence de la richesse économique et de conditions climatiques difficiles), l'architecture suisse d'aujourd'hui occupe une place à part en Europe. Même si des courants venus de France, d'Allemagne ou d'Italie alimentent de nombreux projets, les écoles locales, comme l'ETH Zurich et l'EPFL en particulier, font que les talents locaux continuent à former l'essentiel des concepteurs et ingénieurs. À l'image d'un pont de Robert Maillart, on peut penser que l'architecture suisse poursuivra sur la voie de sa combinaison si particulière d'audace, d'innovation et de solidité.

Philip Jodidio

MARIO BOTTA

MARIO BOTTA
Via Ciani 16
6904 Lugano

Tel: +41 91 9 72 86 25
Fax: +41 91 9 70 14 54
e-mail: mba@botta.ch
Web: www.botta.ch

Born in Mendrisio, Switzerland, in 1943, **MARIO BOTTA** left school at 15 to become an apprentice in a Lugano architectural office (Carloni and Camenisch, 1958–61) and designed his first house the following year. After studies in Milan and Venice (Istituto Universitario di Architettura, IUAV, 1964–69), he worked briefly in the entourage of Le Corbusier, Louis Kahn and Luigi Snozzi. More recently, he created the program for the new Academy of Architecture (Mendrisio, 1996) and was Director of the Academy (2002–03). Botta built has private houses in Cadenazzo (1970–71), Riva San Vitale (1971–73); and Ligornetto (1975–76). Major buildings include: Médiathèque, Villeurbanne, France (1984–88); Cultural Center, Chambèry, France (1982–87); Évry Cathedral (1988–95); San Francisco Museum of Modern Art (1992–95); Tamaro Chapel, Monte Tamaro, Switzerland (1992–96); Tinguely Museum, Basel (1993–96); Chapel, Mogno, Switzerland (1986–98); and a design for the renovation of the Presbytery of the Cathedral of Santa Maria del Fiore, Florence (1997). More recently, he has worked on an office building for TCS Tata, Hyderabad, India (1999–2003); the Petra Winery, Suvereto, Italy (1999–2003); the extension and restructuring of the Querini Stampalia Foundation, Venice, (1996–2003); the Church and Pope John XXIII Pastoral Center, Seriate, Bergamo, Italy (1994–2000); the restoration and structuring of the Scala Theater, Milan (2001–04); and the Tour de Moron, Malleray (1998–2004) featured here. He also completed the Leeum, Samsung Museum of Art, Seoul, South Korea, in 2004. Current work includes a Spa and Wellness Center in Ascona.

BODMER LIBRARY AND MUSEUM
COLOGNY 1998-2003

FLOOR AREA: 1280 m², exhibition area 750 m²
CLIENT: Bibliotheca Bodmeriana,
Fondation Martin Bodmer, Cologny
COST: not disclosed

Mario Botta was given the delicate task of extending the prestigious facilities of the Martin Bodmer Foundation in Cologny in 1998. He designed a two-story underground space connecting the two existing eclectic classical-style villas in which the Foundation was housed. As Botta says, "The exceptional nature of the documents preserved here suggested the idea of a buried presentation case with nothing emerging from the ground except five parallelepiped volumes in glass on square bases, rising to about 3,5 meters and aligned with the entrance like a set of perspective screens, which draw the visitor's eye to the lake. These glass shapes rising from the ground act as skylights, letting natural light into the underground exhibition area. Their transparency and their highly geometrical shape combine to change the perception of outside space at the entrance, unexpectedly creating an atmosphere that prompts a different view of the landscape. At the same time they discreetly reveal the presence of the underground exhibition space." The net floor area of the extension is 1280 m², while the exhibition area itself is 750 m² in size. Cast-iron display cases with armored glass give an impression of strength that contrasts with the apparent fragility of the books and documents on display in the Library. The intention of the directors of the Foundation was to extend the appeal of their institution to a broader public. By calling on Mario Botta, they managed to do so without sacrificing the prestige of their facilities. His addition combines discretion with a strong sense of architectural volumes.

Mario Botta wurde 1998 mit der anspruchsvollen Aufgabe betraut, die renommierten Einrichtungen der Fondation Martin Bodmer in Cologny bei Genf zu erweitern. Er entwarf einen zweigeschossigen, unterirdischen Raum, der die beiden, im Stil des Neoklassizismus erbauten Pavillons verbindet, in denen die Stiftung untergebracht ist. Botta führt dazu aus: „Der außergewöhnliche Charakter der hier bewahrten Dokumente legte die Idee eines versenkten Schaukastens nahe, bei dem sich nichts über den Boden erhebt, abgesehen von fünf gläsernen Kuben auf quadratischen Sockeln, die etwa 3,5 m hoch sind und wie perspektivische Projektionsflächen in einer Flucht mit dem Eingang stehen und das Auge des Besuchers zum See lenken. Die sich aus dem Boden erhebenden Glaskuben fungieren als Oberlichter, die Tageslicht in den unterirdischen Ausstellungsraum einfallen lassen. Ihre Transparenz und strenge geometrische Form verändern im Eingangsbereich die Wahrnehmung des Außenraumes, indem sie unvermutet eine Atmosphäre erzeugen, die eine andere Sicht auf die Landschaft bewirkt. Gleichzeitig sind sie ein diskreter Hinweis auf die Präsenz des unterirdischen Ausstellungsraums." Die Nettofläche der Erweiterung beläuft sich auf 1280 m², während der Ausstellungsbereich selbst 750 m² umfasst. Mit Sicherheitsglas ausgestattete, schmiedeeiserne Ausstellungsvitrinen vermitteln einen Eindruck von Solidität, ein Gegensatz zur augenscheinlichen Fragilität der in der Bibliothek gezeigten Bücher und Dokumente. Es war die Absicht der Direktoren der Fondation, ihre Institution für eine breitere Öffentlichkeit reizvoll zu gestalten. Indem sie sich an Mario Botta wandten, gelang ihnen dies, ohne das Prestige ihrer Einrichtungen aufs Spiel zu setzen. Sein Erweiterungsbau vereint Zurückhaltung mit einem ausgeprägten Gefühl für architektonische Volumina.

C'est en 1998 que Mario Botta s'est vu confier la tâche délicate d'agrandir les prestigieuses installations de la Fondation Martin Bodmer à Cologny. Il a proposé un volume souterrain sur deux niveaux qui relie les deux villas de style éclectique abritant la Fondation. « La nature exceptionnelle des documents préservés ici suggérait une présentation enterrée, rien n'émergeant du sol, à l'exception de cinq parallélépipèdes en verre sur socle carré de 3,5 mètres de haut environ, alignés sur l'entrée et constituant un groupe d'écrans en perspective qui orientent l'œil du visiteur vers le lac. Ces volumes de verre s'élevant du sol sont en fait des lanterneaux qui orientent la lumière naturelle vers les zones d'exposition. Leur transparence et leur forme géométrique pure contribuent à modifier la perception de l'espace extérieur vue de l'entrée, en créant de façon inattendue une atmosphère qui pousse à une vision différente du paysage. Dans le même temps, elles révèlent discrètement la présence de l'espace d'exposition souterrain. » La surface de cette extension est de 1280 m², dont 750 m² consacrés à l'exposition. Des vitrines en fonte à verres blindés donnent une impression de puissance qui contraste avec la fragilité apparente des livres et des documents exposés. L'intention des responsables de la fondation est d'ouvrir davantage leur établissement au public. En faisant appel à Mario Botta, ils ont atteint leur objectif sans compromettre le prestige de leur institution. Cette extension combine discrétion et sens des volumes architecturaux.

On this page, an image, a section and a plan show how new exhibition space has been added between two older buildings. To the right, the underground galleries with a central opening permitting views from one floor to the other.

Ansicht, Schnitt und Grundriss zeigen, wie den beiden älteren Gebäuden neuer Ausstellungsraum angefügt wurde. Rechts die unterirdischen Galerien mit einer zentralen Öffnung, die Blicke von einem Geschoss zum anderen ermöglicht.

Sur cette page, image, coupe et plan montrant comment le nouvel espace d'exposition s'insère entre les deux bâtiments anciens. À droite, les galeries souterraines à vide central qui favorise les perspectives entre les niveaux.

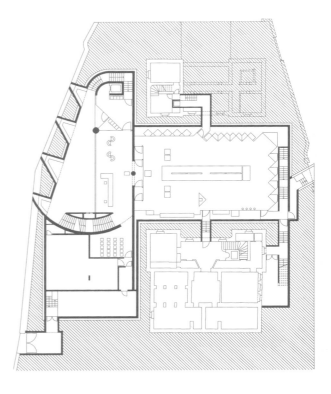

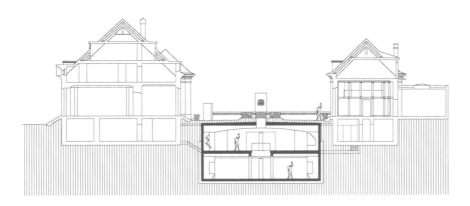

TOUR DE MORON
MALLERAY
1998 - 2004

SIZE: Diameter 6 meters, height 26 meters
CLIENT: Tour de Moron Foundation, Malleray
COST: not disclosed

This 26-meter-tall tower is located in the Bernese Jura area of Switzerland, in the town of Malleray. It was designed in 1998 and built in 2000–04. It is reached via a winding forest trail, and was intended to give importance to the work of local apprentice masons and stonecutters. The six-meter diameter of the tower is formed by an array of cantilevered solid stone steps fixed to the central load-bearing structure. A steel lookout platform at the top of the tower, reached by a narrow ladder, offers a 360° view of the countryside, which is at an attitude of 1300 meters. There is an intentional contrast with the natural setting here, as Botta says: "In these mountains above the sweeping plateau, the helical tower—like an arrow driven into the terrain—comes across as an unexpected and somehow disquieting sign. Tourists and wayfarers seeking idyllic landscapes are thus drawn into the reality of austere, authentic beauty that can be found only in a place where, alongside nature, the mark of humanity is also visible." Although it is in many ways atypical, this tower nonetheless bears the hallmarks of Botta's style—in particular his interest in the power of geometric forms and his desire to contrast architecture and its natural environment. Both in shape and in the slight intentional discomfort introduced by the ladder ascension to the actual viewing platform, Botta's design gives pause and does not necessarily create unanimous approval.

Der 26 m hohe Turm steht in Malleray im Berner Jura. Der Turm, den man über einen gewundenen Waldweg erreicht, wurde 1998 entworfen und 2000 bis 2004 errichtet. Das Projekt sollte die Arbeit von hier ansässigen Steinmetzauszubildenden fördern. Der Durchmesser des Turms von 6 m ergibt sich durch die massiven, vorkragenden Steinstufen der Wendeltreppe, die am zentralen Tragwerk verankert sind. Eine stählerne Aussichtsplattform an der Turmspitze, die über eine schmale Stiege zu erreichen ist, bietet einen Rundblick über die umliegende Landschaft, die 1300 m über dem Meeresspiegel liegt. Wie Botta bemerkt, gibt es hier einen bewussten Kontrast zur natürlichen Umgebung: „In diesen Bergen über der ausge-

dehnten Hochebene wirkt der gleich einem Pfeil in das Gelände getriebene, spiralförmige Turm wie ein unerwartetes und irgendwie beunruhigendes Zeichen. Touristen und Wanderer auf der Suche nach idyllischen Landschaften werden so mit der Realität strenger, authentischer Schönheit konfrontiert, die man nur an Orten findet, wo neben der Natur auch Spuren der Menschheit sichtbar sind." Obgleich in vieler Hinsicht untypisch, weist dieser Turm dennoch die Merkmale von Bottas Stil auf – insbesondere sein Interesse an der Kraft geometrischer Formen und sein Wunsch, Architektur der natürlichen Umgebung gegenüberzustellen. Sowohl in formaler Hinsicht als auch durch die bewusst eingeplante Mühe, die der Aufstieg zur eigentlichen Aussichtsplattform über eine Leiter verursacht, gibt Bottas Entwurf Anlass zum Nachdenken und löst nicht zwangsläufig einhelligen Beifall aus.

Cette tour de 26 mètres de haut et 6 de diamètre se dresse à Malleray, petite ville du Jura bernois à 1300 mètres d'altitude. Elle a été conçue en 1998 et construite en 2000–04 pour promouvoir le travail d'apprentis maçons et tailleurs de pierre locaux. Son habillage est en pierre massive fixée à une structure porteuse. Au sommet, une plate-forme d'observation en acier desservie par une étroite échelle offre une vue à 360° sur la campagne. Comme le précise Botta, le contraste avec le cadre naturel est intentionnel : « Dans ces montagnes dominant un vaste plateau, la tour hélicoïdale – telle une flèche plantée dans le sol – fonctionne comme un signal à la fois inattendu et un peu dérangeant. Les touristes et les randonneurs cherchant un paysage idyllique sont ainsi attirés vers la réalité d'une beauté austère et authentique qui ne se trouve que dans les lieux où la marque de l'homme est visible dans la nature. » Bien qu'elle soit à de nombreux égards atypique, cette tour n'en porte pas moins la marque du style de Botta, en particulier son intérêt pour la puissance des formes géométriques et sa recherche de contrastes entre l'architecture et la nature. Tant dans sa forme que dans le léger inconfort volontaire créé par l'ascension de l'échelle jusqu'à l'observatoire, ce projet assez discuté arrête l'attention.

SANTIAGO CALATRAVA

SANTIAGO CALATRAVA SA
Parkring 11
8002 Zurich

Tel: +41 12 04 50 00
Fax: +41 12 04 50 01
e-mail: admin.zurich@calatrava.com
Web: www.calatrava.com

Born in Valencia, Spain, in 1951, **SANTIAGO CALATRAVA** studied art and architecture at the Escuela Técnica Superior de Arquitectura in Valencia (1968–73) and engineering at the ETH in Zurich (doctorate in Technical Science, 1981). He opened his own architecture and civil-engineering office the same year. His built work includes Gallery and Heritage Square, BCE Place, Toronto (1987), the Bach de Roda Bridge, Barcelona (1985–87), the Torre de Montjuic, Barcelona (1989–92), the Kuwait Pavilion at Expo '92, Seville, and the Alamillo Bridge for the same exhibition, as well as the Lyon Satolas TGV Station (1989–94). He completed the Oriente Station in Lisbon in 1998. He was a finalist in the competition for the Reichstag in Berlin, and he recently completed the Valencia City of Science and Planetarium, Valencia, Spain (1996–2000); the Sondica Airport, Bilbao, Spain (1990–2000); and a bridge in Orléans (1996–2000). Other recent work includes: Blackhall Place Bridge, Dublin, Ireland (2003); Tenerife Auditorium, Santa Cruz, Canary Islands (2003); Petach Tikvah Bridge, Tel Aviv, Israel (2003); Milwaukee Art Museum, Milwaukee (2003); Turtle Bay Bridge, Redding, California (2004); the Athens Olympic Sports Complex (summer 2004); and the Valencia Opera House (2004), the last major building in his 'City of Arts and Sciences'. He is currently working on the Transportation Hub for the new World Trade Center site in New York and the 80 South Street Tower in the same city. Santiago Calatrava received the 2005 Gold Medal from the American Institute of Architects.

LAW FACULTY LIBRARY
ZURICH 1989-2004

FLOOR AREA: new building: 4800 m²;
total 25 500 m² (including old building)
CLIENT: Hochbauamt, Baudirektion Kanton Zurich
COST: CHF 50 million
(including reconstruction of old building)

The Faculty of Law of the University of Zurich had been divided into eight different buildings. The facilities for the faculty and the library, including the second largest rare book collection in Switzerland, were housed in a building designed in 1908 by Hermann Fiertz as a high school and laboratory. Santiago Calatrava was asked in 1989 to study extensions added to two wings of this structure in 1930 in order to modernize and enlarge them. Rather than filling in the existing courtyard with floor space as the University envisaged, Calatrava proposed to create an atrium in the place of the courtyard. In the final design, Calatrava created workspaces for the students, with direct access to the library and seminar spaces. A series of seven oval reading levels are hung within the atrium, "staggered on each level so that it is no longer the floor area that increases as they approach the roof but the space they circumscribe." This design allows natural light to penetrate deeper into the heart of the structure and its reading area. To support the cascade of galleries, eight attachment points have been created within or against the walls of the existing façade. As the architect describes the design, "The basic structure of each gallery is formed by a steel torsion tube, from which T-shaped, tapering steel beams cantilever in a regular rhythm. Each gallery is braced by balustrades, which have been designed as load-bearing trusses. By channeling the forces away from the center of the atrium, this design also leaves the basement areas free of obstruction." He goes on to say that "An important aspect of the design is the complete independence of old and new. The reading room, the two new stories, and the roof are treated as separate from the existing building, both architectonically and with regard to materials." Ever a master of spectacular shapes, Santiago Calatrava has created what is in good part a library that is at once practical for its users and architecturally inspiring.

Die Rechtswissenschaftliche Fakultät der Universität Zürich war auf acht Standorte verteilt. Die Einrichtungen für die Fakultät und die Bibliothek, darunter die zweitgrößte Sammlung seltener Bücher in der Schweiz, waren in einem 1908 von Hermann Fiertz als Schule und Labor entworfenen Gebäude untergebracht. Santiago Calatrava wurde 1989 aufgefordert, sich Gedanken über Anbauten an zwei 1930 ergänzte Flügel zu machen, mit dem Ziel, diese Gebäude zu modernisieren und zu vergrößern. Anstatt nun nach Vorstellung der Universität, den vorhandenen Hof zuzubauen, schlug Calatrava vor, ihn in ein Atrium umzuwandeln. Im endgültigen Entwurf plante Calatrava hier Arbeitsplätze für die Studenten mit direktem Zugang zur Bibliothek und den Seminarräumen. Innerhalb des Atriums wurde eine Folge von sieben ovalen Leseebenen aufgehängt und zwar so versetzt „dass nach oben hin nicht die Bodenfläche zunimmt, sondern der von ihnen umschriebene Raum." Diese Konzeption lässt das Tageslicht tief ins Zentrum des Gebäudes und in die Lesebereiche einfallen. Um die Kaskade von Galerien abzustützen, wurden innerhalb oder gegen die Wände der vorhandenen Fassade acht Befestigungspunkte geschaffen. Der Architekt über seinen Entwurf: „Die grundlegende Konstruktion jeder Galerie besteht aus einer Torsionsröhre aus Stahl, von der T-förmige, sich verjüngende Stahlträger in regelmäßigen Abständen vorkragen. Jede Galerie wird durch Balustraden versteift, die als tragende Konsolen konzipiert sind. Da die Kräfte vom Zentrum des Atriums weggelenkt werden, erlaubt diese Planung ein stützenfreies Untergeschoss." Er führt weiter aus: „Ein wichtiger Aspekt des Entwurfs ist die völlige Autonomie von Alt und Neu. Der Lesesaal, die beiden neuen Geschosse und das Dach werden sowohl in architektonischer Hinsicht als auch in Bezug auf die Materialien als gesondert vom bestehenden Gebäude behandelt." Stets ein Meister spektakulärer Formen, hat Santiago Calatrava eine Bibliothek geschaffen, die gleichermaßen zweckdienlich für ihre Benutzer wie architektonisch inspirierend ist.

La Faculté de droit de l'Université de Zurich est divisée en huit bâtiments. La Faculté et sa bibliothèque, qui abrite la seconde plus vaste collection de livres rares de Suisse, étaient logées dans un bâtiment de 1908 conçu par Hermann Fiertz pour être une école supérieure et un laboratoire. Santiago Calatrava se vit demander en 1989 d'étudier des extensions à deux ailes ajoutées en 1930, pour agrandir et moderniser ces installations. Plutôt que d'utiliser la cour existante pour y construire comme l'avait envisagé l'Université, Calatrava a proposé de la transformer en atrium. Dans le projet final, il a créé des espaces de travail pour étudiants qui ont un accès direct à la bibliothèque et aux salles de séminaire. Sept niveaux ovales pour lecteurs sont suspendus dans l'atrium et décalés de telle façon « que ce ne sont pas leur surface qui s'accroît en se rapprochant de la toiture, mais l'espace qu'ils circonscrivent ». Cette disposition permet également à la lumière naturelle de pénétrer plus profondément au cœur de l'ensemble et des zones de lecture. Pour soutenir cette cascade de galeries, huit points d'attache ont été créés dans ou contre les murs de la façade existante. Selon le descriptif de Calatrava : « La structure de base de chaque galerie est constituée par un tube d'acier en torsion, d'où partent selon un rythme régulier des poutres d'acier coniques en T en porte-à-faux. Chaque galerie est entourée de balustrades qui sont en fait des fermes porteuses. En canalisant les forces loin du centre de l'atrium, ce principe permet de dégager les zones en sous-sol de tout obstacle. Un important aspect de ce projet est l'indépendance totale des parties neuves et anciennes. La salle de lecture, les deux nouveaux étages et le toit sont traités comme des éléments séparés du bâtiment existant, aussi bien sur le plan architectonique que celui des matériaux. » Maître des formes spectaculaires, Santiago Calatrava a créé ici une bibliothèque qui est à la fois pratique pour ses utilisateurs et d'architecture stimulante.

One remarkable aspect of Calatrava's design is that students can enjoy a good deal of privacy, while sometimes being aware that they are in a fairly large, and indeed open, reading room. Anthropomorphic forms do not interfere with study; on the contrary, they underline the architectural originality of the structure.

Die besondere Eigenart von Calatravas Design gibt den Studenten eine gewisse Privatspäre und andererseits das Gefühl, sich dennoch in einem recht großen, offenen Lesesaal zu befinden. Anthropomorphe Formen beeinträchtigen das Lernen nicht, im Gegenteil, sie unterstreichen die architektonische Originalität des Bauwerks.

Un aspect remarquable du projet de Calatrava est que les étudiants bénéficient d'une réelle intimité, tout en restant conscients de se trouver dans une salle de lecture à la fois vaste et ouverte. Les formes anthropomorphiques n'interfèrent pas avec l'étude mais soulignent, au contraire, l'originalité architecturale de cette bibliothèque.

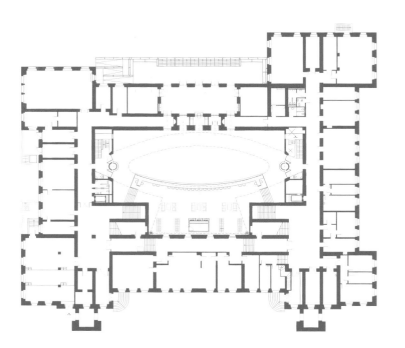

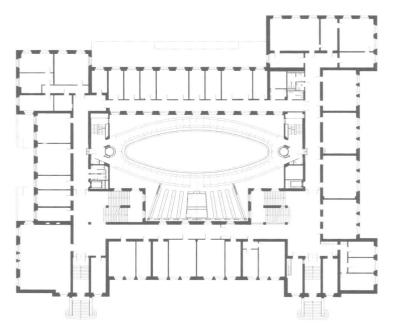

ALDO CELORIA

ALDO CELORIA ARCHITECT
Via delle Fornaci 8c
6828 Balerna

Tel: +41 91 6 82 43 88
Fax: +41 91 6 82 43 90
e-mail: a.celoria@ticino.com

ALDO CELORIA was born in 1969 in Mendrisio, Switzerland. In 1992, he was granted a diploma in industrial design at the Scuola Politecnica di Design in Milan. From 1993 to 1995, he worked in collaboration with several design offices in Ticino. In 1997–98, he lived in Buenos Aires, Argentina, where he worked in the office of Clorindo Testa. In 2002, he graduated in architecture from the Accademia di Architettura di Mendrisio, where he studied under Mario Botta, Peter Zumthor and Kenneth Frampton. In the same year, he opened his own office in Balerna, where he practices architecture and urban design and undertakes theoretical research. In 2004, he won two competitions—one for a Balerna school extension and another for the urban design of a square in Tenero near Locarno. He has just completed a second private house in Ticino on a site almost adjacent to the Travella House, both featured here.

TRAVELLA HOUSE
CASTEL SAN PIETRO
2002-04

FLOOR AREA: 350 m²
CLIENT: Paola and Rocco Travella
COST: CHF 800 000

The Travella House, located in Switzerland near the Italian border, is the first built work of Aldo Celoria, begun while he was still a student in Mendrisio. Clad in copper and glass, the 350 m² house is built around a thick concrete wall that forms its free-flowing interior spaces. Set on an old family property in a vineyard above the town, the structure emerges from a street-level garage with a sliding polycarbonate door. Concrete steps lead to the entry level, where a grassy incline gives way to a flat, black terrace. The 500 m² lot is intentionally minimalist: only grass and black concrete surround the house. The ground floor, containing the living room, dining room, and kitchen, is fully glazed, while the upper, bedroom level has an unusual exterior cladding made with a textured pattern of 20 x 25 cm custom-cut copper panels, applied in a vertical zigzag on all four sides of the house. The architect likes the contrast between the extreme transparency of the ground level, where he originally wanted no curtains, and the more "mysterious" top floor. He points out that it is almost impossible to guess what the windows cut into the copper façade correspond to—since large and small openings puncture the copper skin at irregular intervals. The nearly opaque weight of the upper floor appears to float on its glass base, essentially because of the inner structural design. A 30-cm-thick concrete wall running from the basement to the roof terrace supports the entire house. The architect compares its form to a folded piece of paper. The Travella House contains no doors in the traditional sense and the space flows around and through this concrete wall freely. Completed in February 2004 with a budget of about CHF 800 000, the Travella House shows a mastery of space and materials that is surprising for a young architect. His task was made easier by the fact that his sister gave him full freedom in the project, asking only that neutral colors be used for the interior.

Die nahe der italienischen Grenze auf Schweizer Gebiet gelegene Casa Travella ist der erste realisierte Bau von Aldo Celoria, den er noch während seiner Studienzeit in Mendrisio für seine Schwester entwarf. Das mit Kupfer und Glas verkleidete, 350 m² große Haus wurde um eine mächtige Betonmauer herum errichtet, die die Form des Innenraums bestimmt. Das auf altem Familienbesitz in einem Weinberg über der Stadt errichtete Haus erhebt sich über einer auf Straßenniveau gelegenen Garage mit einer Schiebetür aus Polycarbonat. Betonstufen führen zur Eingangsebene, wo ein grasbewachsener Abhang einer ebenen, schwarzen Terrasse Platz macht. Das 500 m² große Grundstück ist bewusst minimalistisch gestaltet: Nichts als Rasen und schwarzer Beton umgeben das Haus. Das Erdgeschoss mit Wohnraum, Esszimmer und Küche ist voll verglast, während der obere Stock mit den Schlafzimmern eine ungewöhnliche Verkleidung aufweist. Sie besteht aus 20 x 25 cm großen, eigens zugeschnittenen Kupferpaneelen, die auf allen vier Seiten des Hauses in einem vertikalen Zickzackmuster angebracht sind. Der Architekt schätzt den Kontrast zwischen der äußersten Transparenz der unteren Ebene, wo er ursprünglich keine Vorhänge vorsah, und dem „geheimnisvolleren" Obergeschoss. Celorias

Erläuterungen zufolge ist es kaum möglich, einen Zusammenhang zwischen den in die Kupferfassade eingeschnittenen Fenstern und der Gliederung im Innern zu erkennen, insbesondere, weil große und kleine Öffnungen die kupferne Außenhaut in unregelmäßigen Abständen durchlöchern. Das nahezu undurchsichtige Volumen des Obergeschosses scheint auf einem gläsernen Sockel zu schweben – war vor allem die konstruktive Gestaltung im Inneren zurückzuführen ist. Eine vom Keller bis zur Dachterrasse reichende, 30 cm starke Betonwand trägt das gesamte Haus. Der Architekt verglich ihre Form mit einem gefalteten Stück Papier. Die Casa Travella hat keine Türen im herkömmlichen Sinn, der Raum fließt frei um die Betonwand herum. Die im Februar 2004 für ein Budget von etwa 800 000 Schweizer Franken fertig gestellte Casa Travella lässt eine für einen jungen Architekten überraschende Beherrschung von Raum und Materialien erkennen. Seine Aufgabe wurde dadurch erleichtert, dass seine Schwester ihm bei diesem Projekt volle Freiheit ließ und einzig darum bat, im Inneren neutrale Farben zu verwenden.

Première réalisation d'Aldo Celoria, dont le projet a été lancé alors qu'il étudiait encore à Mendrisio, cette maison est située près de la frontière italienne. Élevée pour sa sœur sur une vieille propriété familiale dans une vigne au-dessus de la ville, la structure de 350 m² habillée de cuivre et de verre s'organise autour d'un épais mur de béton qui délimite des espaces intérieurs libres. Elle repose sur un garage à porte coulissante en polycarbonate situé au niveau de la rue. Des marches en béton conduisent au niveau d'entrée où un plan gazonné laisse place à une terrasse plate traitée en noir. Le terrain de 500 m² est aménagé dans un esprit minimaliste : seule de l'herbe verte et du béton noir entourent la maison. Le niveau du sol, contenant le séjour, la salle à manger et la cuisine est entièrement vitré, tandis que le niveau supérieur, celui des chambres, présente un curieux habillage extérieur texturé, fait de panneaux de cuivre de 20 x 25 cm appliqués en zigzag sur les quatre côtés de la maison. L'architecte apprécie le contraste entre la transparence extrême du niveau inférieur, où il ne voulait même pas de rideaux à l'origine, et le niveau supérieur plus « mystérieux ». Il fait remarquer qu'il est presque impossible de deviner à quoi correspondent les fenêtres tantôt grandes, tantôt petites, qui ponctuent la peau de cuivre à intervalles irréguliers. La partie supérieure opaque, pesante, semble flotter sur sa base en verre du fait de la conception structurelle interne. Un mur de béton de 30 cm d'épaisseur qui va du sous-sol à la terrasse en toiture soutient la totalité de la maison. L'architecte le compare à un morceau de papier replié. La maison Travella ne compte aucune porte au sens traditionnel du terme et l'espace se déploie librement autour et à travers ce mur. Achevée en février 2004 pour un budget d'environ 800 000 de francs suisses, cette maison témoigne d'une maîtrise de l'espace et des matériaux surprenante chez un jeune architecte. Sa tâche a été facilitée par le fait que sa sœur lui a laissé toute liberté, lui demandant seulement d'utiliser des couleurs neutres pour l'intérieur.

Set on a vineyard-covered hillside above the town, the house sits on a carefully cleared flat lot. The opaque volume containing bedrooms sits above the transparent "public" areas below.

Das auf einem mit Weinstöcken bedeckten Abhang liegende Haus steht auf einem sorgfältig gerodeten, ebenen Grundstück. Der opake Teil des Hauses mit den Schlafzimmern liegt über der transparenten „öffentlichen" Ebene unten.

Implantée sur une colline plantée de vigne dominant la ville, la maison occupe une parcelle plate soigneusement dégagée. Le volume opaque qui contient les chambres est posé sur la zone « de réception » transparente.

Simplified sections show the different levels of the house, including the garage, which projects toward the street below the house. The roof can be used as a terrace, although access is a little acrobatic.

Vereinfachte Schnitte zeigen die verschiedenen Ebenen des Hauses inklusive der Garage. Diese ragt zur unterhalb des Hauses verlaufenden Straße hin aus dem Volumen heraus. Das Dach kann als Terrasse benutzt werden, wenngleich der Zugang etwas beschwerlich ist.

Coupes simplifiées montrant les différents niveaux, dont le garage qui se projette vers la rue sous la maison. Le toit peut servir de terrasse, bien que son accès soit un peu acrobatique.

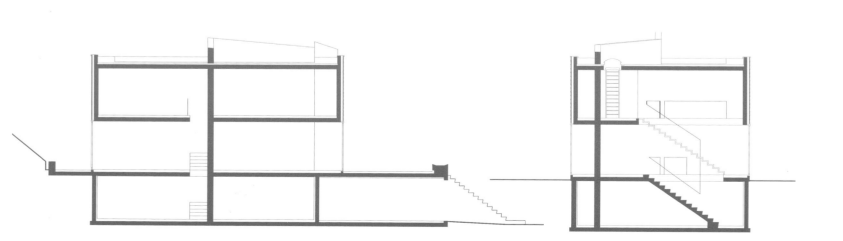

The internal concrete wall seen to the left supports the house, and offers a continuous band of space for the interior. In the living room at the front of the house (right), the entire corner of the floor to ceiling glazing opens onto the garden and the view of the town below.

Die links zu sehende Betonwand trägt das Haus und gestaltet das Interieur zu einem fortlaufenden Raumband. Im Wohnraum an der Vorderseite des Hauses (rechts) öffnet sich die deckenhoch verglaste Ecke zur Gänze zum Garten und gibt den Blick auf die tiefer liegende Stadt frei.

Le mur intérieur en béton, à gauche, qui semble soutenir la maison crée une bande intérieure d'espace continu. L'angle vitré toute hauteur du séjour situé à l'avant la maison (à droite) ouvre sur le jardin et la ville en contrebas.

TRAPANESE HOUSE
CASTEL SAN PIETRO
2004-05

FLOOR AREA: 318 m²
CLIENT: Giovanni and Barbara Trapanese
COST: not disclosed

Built at the opposite end of the same lot used for his Travella House in Castel San Pietro, the Trapanese House is Aldo Celoria's second completed project. With an overall floor area of 318 m² (106 m² per floor), it has certain similarities with the earlier residence. The garage is also located on the lower, street level and the floors above have the same height as those of the Travella House. As Celoria explains, "The plan and the section of the house were associated with the idea of a 'chromosome' intended as a double intersection: common spaces with private spaces. The stairs are in the center, creating a hinge of rotation from which all the different areas are organized on the different levels. This double height void associated with the stairway also connects the earth with the sky." Rather than the glass and copper used in his first project, Celoria opts here for cladding the house entirely with polycarbonate slabs. This surface permits a good deal of diffused natural light to penetrate the interior. As he did in the Travella House, where the snaking interior concrete wall supports the entire structure, Celoria used an unusual structural idea here. He explains, "The structural idea is that the perimeter of the upper floor works as a suspended Vierendeel beam. The forces run down to the ground through the four asymmetrically aligned walls. The beam is also displaced in section according to the different room levels. The windows pursue this structural idea. The voids mirror the structural function of the beam." A Vierendeel frame, invented by the Belgian engineer and writer Arthur Vierendeel (1852–1940), has rigid upper and lower elements connected by vertical beams.

Die Casa Trapanese, der zweite realisierte Bau von Aldo Celoria, ist am gegenüberliegenden Ende des Grundstücks gelegen, auf dem auch seine Casa Travella steht. Mit ihren 318 m² Fläche (106 m² pro Ebene) ähnelt die Casa Trapanese Celorias erstem Bau. Die Garage befindet sich ebenfalls auf der unteren Ebene auf Höhe der Straße, und Celoria wählte für die oberen Stockwerke die gleiche Geschosshöhe wie bei der Casa Travella. „Grundriss und Aufteilung des Hauses erinnern in ihrer Struktur an ein ‚Chromosom' mit einer doppelten Überschneidung von Gemeinschaftsbereichen und Rückzugsbereichen", erklärt Celoria. „Die Treppe befindet sich in der Mitte und bildet eine Drehachse, von der aus alle Bereiche auf den unterschiedlichen Ebenen erschlossen werden können. Der Hohlraum über zwei Ebenen, der sich an den Treppenaufgang schließt, ist zudem eine Verbindung zwischen Himmel und Erde." Während bei der Casa Travella Glas und Kupfer dominieren, hat Celoria hier eine vollständige Verkleidung des Hauses mit Platten aus Polycarbonat gewählt. Durch diese

Oberfläche kann reichlich diffuses natürliches Licht in den Innenraum dringen. Ähnlich wie bei seinem ersten Bau, in dem die geschlängelte Betonmauer die gesamte Gliederung bestimmt, entwickelte Celoria auch hier eine ungewöhnliche Idee für die Aufteilung. „Die Grundidee ist die, dass das gesamte Obergeschoss als hängender Vierendeel-Träger wirkt", erklärt er. „Der Schub wird durch die vier asymmetrisch ausgerichteten Wände in den Boden geleitet. Die Gurte und Riegel dieses Vierendeel-Rahmens sind entsprechend den unterschiedlichen Raumniveaus verschoben. Auch die Fenster unterstützen die Grundidee der Gliederung: Die Hohlräume spiegeln die Funktion des Vierendeel-Trägers." Ein Vierendeel-Rahmen, benannt nach dem belgischen Ingenieur und Schriftsteller Arthur Vierendeel (1852–1940), besteht aus steifen horizontalen Stäben oder Gurten, die durch vertikale Riegel oder Pfosten miteinander verbunden sind.

Située à l'extrémité opposée de la parcelle de la maison Travella qu'il avait construite à Castel San Pietra, la maison Trapanese est le second projet achevé par Aldo Celoria. D'une surface totale de 318 m² (106 m² par niveau), elle présente un certain nombre de similarités avec sa voisine. Le garage se trouve également au niveau de la rue et les niveaux présentent la même hauteur que la maison Travella. Comme l'explique l'architecte : « Le plan et la coupe de la maison sont associés à l'idée de › chromosome ‹ au sens de double intersection : espaces communs et espaces privés. Les escaliers occupent la partie centrale et créent une charnière à partir de laquelle toutes les zones s'organisent aux différents niveaux. Ce vide double-hauteur connecte également la terre au ciel. » Alors qu'il avait choisi le verre et le cuivre pour son premier projet, Celario a ici opté pour un bardage complet de la maison en dalles de polycarbonate. Il permet la pénétration d'une quantité importante de lumière à l'intérieur. Comme pour le mur de béton serpentin structurel de la maison Travella, Celoria a fait appel à ici une solution inhabituelle : « L'idée structurelle est que le périmètre du niveau supérieur fonctionne comme une poutre Vierendeel suspendue. Les forces sont dirigées vers le sol par les quatre murs asymétriques alignés. La poutre change également de section selon le niveau des pièces. Les fenêtres participent à cette solution. Le vide reflète la fonction structurelle de la poutre. » La poutre Vierendeel, inventée par l'ingénieur et auteur belge Arthur Vierendeel (1852–1940), se compose d'éléments hauts et bas connectés par des poutrelles verticales.

The polycarbonate cladding of the house is interrupted by clear glazing, but the overall effect is to allow light into the entire house, whether directly or in a diffused form. Built next to vineyards, the house looks down on Castel San Pietro.

Die Polycarbonat-Verkleidung wird durch eine Klarglas-Verglasung unterbrochen, der gewünschte Effekt ist, dass sowohl direktes als auch diffuses Licht in das gesamte Haus gelangen kann. Die Casa Trapanese wurde oberhalb von Castel San Pietro in einem Weinberg errichtet.

Le bardage en polycarbonate de la maison est interrompu par du verre clair, mais l'effet recherché est de laisser pénétrer la lumière dans la totalité de la maison, directement ou sous forme diffuse. Construite près de vignes, la maison donne sur Castel San Pietro en contrebas.

The floor area of each of the three levels is identical, but the lower, garage floor is not visible in these images. It sits beneath the concrete platform seen around the house and is entered from the street below the house. The apparently dislocated structure of the residence rises to the rear almost as a reaction to the steep hillside.

Der Bodenbereich ist bei allen drei Ebenen gleich, aber die unterste Ebene, auf der sich die Garage befindet, ist auf diesen Abbildungen nicht sichtbar. Sie liegt unterhalb der betonierten Fläche rings um das Haus und ist von der Straße aus zugänglich. Die verschobene, nach hinten ansteigende Struktur, die bei diesem Haus ins Auge fällt, erscheint wie eine Reaktion auf die steile Hanglage des Anwesens.

La surface au sol de chacun des trois niveaux est identique, mais le plus bas, celui du garage n'est pas visible sur ces images. Il se trouve sous la plateforme de béton qui entoure la maison et est accessible de la rue qui passe en dessous de la maison. La structure d'aspect disloqué s'élève à l'arrière, pratiquement en réaction au flanc abrupt de la colline.

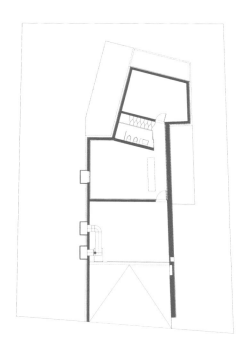
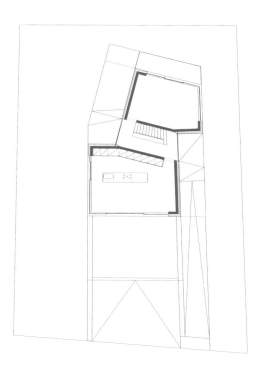
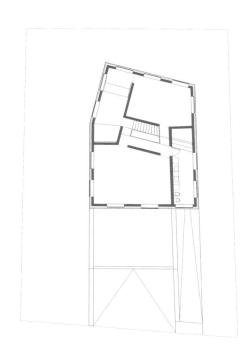

4

JÜRG CONZETT

CONZETT, BRONZINI,
GARTMANN AG
Bahnhofstrasse 3
7000 Chur

Tel. +41 81 2 58 30 00
Fax: +41 81 2 58 30 01
e-mail: cbg@cbg-ing.ch
Web: www.cbg-ing.ch

JÜRG CONZETT was born in 1956, in Schiers, Graubünden. He studied civil engineering at the EPFL in Lausanne and the ETH in Zurich, receiving his diploma in 1980. From 1981 until 1988 he worked in the office of Peter Zumthor at Haldenstein. After this architectural experience, he decided to start working as an independent structural engineer. Today, he heads an engineer's office of 21 persons with his partners Gianfranco Bronzini and Patrick Gartmann in Chur. Their main activities are designing structures for buildings together with architects as well as working on projects for bridges and bridge repairs. He also teaches the design of wooden structures for students of engineering and architecture at the University of Applied Sciences Chur. Conzett's most important works include: the extension of the school for timber engineering at Biel (with architects Marcel Meili and Markus Peter, Zurich); Landquartlöser Overpass and Glätti Overpass at San Bernardino National Highway; Traversina Footbridge and Pùnt da Suransuns in the Viamala Gorge near Thusis; the Swiss Pavilion at the EXPO 2000, Hanover (with Peter Zumthor); the Muota River Roadbridge at Ibach, Schwyz; and the Zurich Stadium (opening in 2006, with the architects Marcel Meili and Markus Peter)

SURANSUNS
FOOTBRIDGE
VIAMALA
1999

LENGTH: 40 meters
CLIENT: Verein KulturRaum Viamala, Sils i. D
COST: CHF 285 000

The "Pùnt da Suransuns" is a "stress-ribbon" bridge with a span of 40 meters crossing the Hinterrhein River in the Viamala Gorge. Part of the Veia Traversina, a path originally traced by the Romans, the pedestrian bridge has a thin deck made of local Andeer granite, which is pre-stressed over rectangular steel bars. In order to allow pedestrians to cross the Hinterrhein at a relatively convenient location, the bridge has a relatively long span and is angled to correspond to the riverbanks. A model at 1:20 scale was built to test the static properties of the unusual design. Although the bridge looks as though it might be unstable, the design allows less vertical oscillation than might be expected, giving pedestrians a feeling of unexpected solidity. Once the concrete abutments were built, the construction method required only stacking, tightening and screwing of the structural elements, which were brought to the site by helicopter. The cost of the bridge was CHF 285 000. Switzerland's mountain terrain has long made it an ideal testing ground for innovative bridge designs, such as those of Robert Maillart. Jürg Conzett's Suransuns footbridge demonstrates that modern methods and careful calculations can turn a modest project of this nature into a rewarding aesthetic experience that respects the natural environment.

Bei der „Pùnt da Suransuns" handelt es sich um eine Spannbandbrücke mit einer Spannweite von 40 m, die den Hinterrhein in der Viamala-Schlucht überquert. Die Fußgängerbrücke ist Teil der Veia Traversina, eines ursprünglich von den Römern angelegten Wegs. Sie ist mit dünnen Platten aus vor Ort vorkommendem Andeer-Granit belegt, die über rechteckigen Stahlstäben vorgespannt wurden. Die Brücke hat eine verhältnismäßig lange Spannweite und verläuft den Flussufern entsprechend schräg, um es Fußgängern zu ermöglichen, den Hinterrhein an einer relativ bequem zugänglichen Stelle zu überqueren. Mithilfe eines Modells im Maßstab 1:20 erprobte man die statischen Eigenschaften der ungewöhnlichen Konstruktion. Wenngleich die Brücke instabil wirkt, lässt die Konstruktion eine geringere vertikale Schwankung zu als man erwarten könnte und gibt so den Passanten ein Gefühl von Sicherheit. Sobald die Widerlager aus Beton errichtet waren, erforderte die Bauweise nur noch das Stapeln, Festziehen und Verschrauben der konstruktiven Elemente, die per Hubschrauber an Ort und Stelle gebracht wurden. Die Kosten der Brücke beliefen sich auf 285 000 Schweizer Franken. Ihr gebirgiges Terrain macht die Schweiz seit langem zu einem idealen Versuchsgelände für innovative Brückenentwürfe, wie schon die von Robert Maillart. Jürg Conzetts Suransuns Fußgängerbrücke beweist, dass moderne Verfahren und sorgfältige Kalkulation ein bescheidenes Projekt dieser Art in ein lohnendes ästhetisches Erlebnis verwandeln können, das die umgebende Natur respektiert.

Le « Pùnt da Suransuns » est un « ruban en tension » de 40 mètres de portée enjambant le Rhin postérieur dans la gorge de Viamala. Appartenant à la Veia Traversina, voie tracée à l'origine par les Romains, cette passerelle piétonnière possède un mince tablier en granite local de Andeer, précontraint sur des barres d'acier de section rectangulaire. Pour permettre la traversée du torrent à un endroit facilement accessible, la passerelle d'assez longue portée est implantée en biais en fonction de la configuration des rives. Une maquette au 1/20ᵉ a été fabriquée pour tester les propriétés statiques de ce projet original. Malgré son instabilité apparente, la structure limite les oscillations verticales et donne sous le pas une impression de solidité presque inattendue. Une fois les culées de béton en place, il a suffi d'empiler, de serrer et de visser les éléments structurels livrés sur place par hélicoptère. Le coût de ce chantier s'est élevé à 285 000 de francs suisses. La montagne suisse a longtemps été un banc d'essai idéal pour les ponts novateurs comme ceux de Robert Maillart. La passerelle Suransuns de Conzett montre que des méthodes modernes et des calculs précis peuvent transformer un projet modeste de cette nature en une réussite esthétique qui respecte l'environnement naturel.

Despite its sophistication, the bridge is narrow and does bring to mind the kind of rope and plank bridge, that might have existed in such a location in the past.

Diese Brücke besticht durch ihre Raffinesse; sie ist schmal und erinnert an die simplen Brückenkonstruktionen aus Seil und Brettern aus früheren Zeiten.

Bien que de conception très sophistiquée, ce pont étroit rappelle à sa façon les passerelles de planches et de corde qui existèrent sans doute dans le passé au même endroit.

Drawings show how the bridge is inserted into either side of the Viamala Gorge, as well as its inclination imposed by the natural setting. Despite being firmly anchored, the bridge appears to sit lightly on its concrete base (below).

Die Zeichnungen zeigen, wie die Brücke auf beiden Seiten der Viamala-Schlucht verankert ist; außerdem lässt sich die durch das unterschiedlich hohe Uferniveau vorgegebene Neigung gut erkennen. Die Brücke ist fest verankert und scheint doch leicht auf ihrem Betonfundament zu sitzen (unten).

Les dessins ci-dessous montrent l'insertion du pont sur les deux rives de la gorge de Viamala, ainsi que sa pente, imposée par les conditions naturelles. Solidement ancré, il semble cependant reposer délicatement sur ses culées.

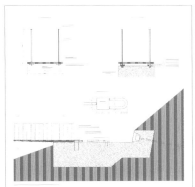
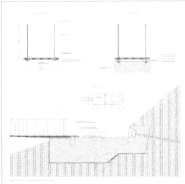
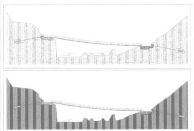

5

DEVANTHÉRY & LAMUNIÈRE

DEVANTHÉRY & LAMUNIÈRE
7, rue du Tunnel
1227 Carouge-Geneva

Tel: +41 22 3 07 01 30
Fax: +41 22 3 43 05 54
e-mail: mail@devanthery-
lamuniere.ch
Web: www.devanthery-lamuniere.ch

PATRICK DEVANTHÉRY and **INÈS LAMUNIÈRE** were born respectively in Sion and in Geneva in 1954. They both completed their studies at the École Polytechnique Fédérale de Lausanne (EPFL) in 1980. In 1983, they created their firm Devanthéry & Lamunière in Geneva and Lausanne, and an urban-design affiliate in Geneva in 2001 under the name Devanthéry, Lamunière & Marchand. They have taught at the Harvard Graduate School of Design (1996 and 1999), at the Université de Nancy (1994), and at the ETH in Zurich (1991–93 and 1994). Inès Lamunière is currently a professor of architectural theory at the EPFL in Lausanne. In 2001, she created the Laboratory of Architecture and Urban Mobility at the EPFL. Both architects have participated in the editorial committee of the magazine *Faces* (1989–2004). Their work includes numerous restoration projects as well as new buildings, such as a psychiatric clinic in Yverdon (1995–2003); an urban-housing district in the city of Neuchâtel completed in 2004; a 250-room hotel located on the Guisanplatz in Gerne (1999–2004); the primary school extension in Rolle featured here; Philip Morris International Headquarters in Lausanne (2002–06); as well as a number of private houses.

PRIMARY SCHOOL
ROLLE
2001 - 03

FLOOR AREA: 141 m²
CLIENT: DGEO, Etat de Vaud
COST: CHF 6,1 million

Winners of a 1999 competition, Devanthéry and Lamunière were given the task of enlarging a large 1930s school, adding six classrooms, a cafeteria and kitchen, a music room, and computer facilities. Built with panels of colored poured-in-place concrete, and blue-green reflecting glass varying between transparent and translucent, the structure appears less massive than it is in reality while giving a cheerful impression both inside and out. Seen from the exterior, the glass façade reflects neighboring trees and grass, adding to the impression of lightness, also emphasized by a thin, cantilevered roof. Openings toward a garden and more distant views featured in the design of the classrooms. The floor-to-ceiling glazing with bubble-shaped cut-outs in the classrooms, together with the bucolic setting, offer almost ideal conditions for children. A small second-floor library alternates a band of glazing near the floor with one near the ceiling. Built at a cost of CHF 6.1 million, the new building measures just 141 m². Notched into the inclined site, the addition is relatively discreet vis-à-vis the original building

Als Gewinner eines Wettbewerbs im Jahr 1999 übernahmen Devanthéry und Lamunière die Aufgabe der Erweiterung eines großen Schulkomplexes aus den 1930er Jahren um sechs Unterrichtsräume, eine Cafeteria mit Küche, ein Musik-zimmer und Computerräume. Der Bau, bestehend aus in situ gegossenen, farbigen Betonplatten und blaugrünem, reflektierendem Glas mit variierenden Transparenz-graden wirkt weniger massiv, als er in Wirklichkeit ist, und macht innen wie von außen einen freundlichen Eindruck. Von außen gesehen reflektiert die Glasfassade die umstehende Vegetation, was den Eindruck der Leichtigkeit verstärkt, der darüber hinaus von einem dünnen, vorkragenden Dach unterstrichen wird. Öffnungen zum Garten und Ausblicke in die Umgebung waren für den Entwurf der Klassenzimmer bestimmend. Die deckenhohe Verglasung mit blasenförmigen Ausbuchtungen schafft in den Klassenzimmern in Verbindung mit der idyllischen Lage nahezu ideale Bedingungen für Kinder. In der kleinen Bibliothek im zweiten Geschoss verlaufen die Fensterbänder alternierend unten am Fußboden und oben an der Decke. Das für 6,1 Millionen Schweizer Franken errichtete neue Gebäude umfasst eine Nutzfläche von nur 141 m². Gegenüber dem ursprünglichen Gebäude nimmt sich der in das abschüssige Gelände eingefügte Anbau entsprechend zurückhaltend aus.

C'est en 1999 que Devanthéry et Lamunière ont remporté le concours pour l'agrandissement d'une école datant des années 1930. Le projet consistait à créer six nouvelles classes, une cafétéria, une cuisine, une salle de musique et des instal-lations pour les ordinateurs. En panneaux de béton coloré coulé sur place et de verre réfléchissant bleu-vert allant du transparent au translucide, la construction paraît moins massive qu'elle n'est en réalité, tout en donnant une impression chaleureuse aussi bien à l'intérieur qu'à l'extérieur. La façade qui réfléchit les arbres et les pelouses renforce cette impression de légèreté mise en valeur par une mince toiture en porte-à-faux. Le plan des classes privilégie les ouvertures vers le jardin et des vues plus lointaines. Le vitrage du sol au plafond, les ouvertures découpées en forme de bulle dans les classes, ainsi que le cadre bucolique constituent des condi-tions d'enseignement quasi idéales pour les enfants. Dans la petite bibliothèque de l'étage, un bandeau de verre au sol répond à celui qui longe le plafond. Réalisée pour un budget de 6,1 millions de francs suisses, la nouvelle construction mesure 141 m² au sol. Venant s'imbriquer dans le terrain en pente, elle reste relativement discrète par rapport au bâtiment d'origine.

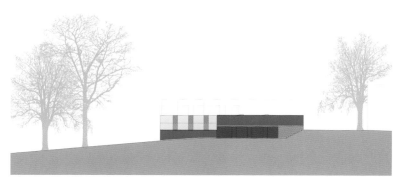

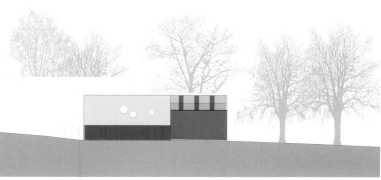

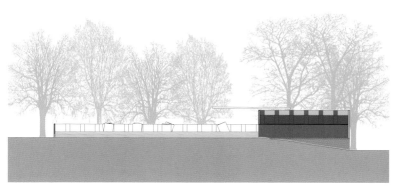

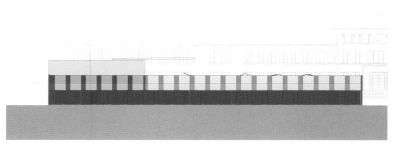

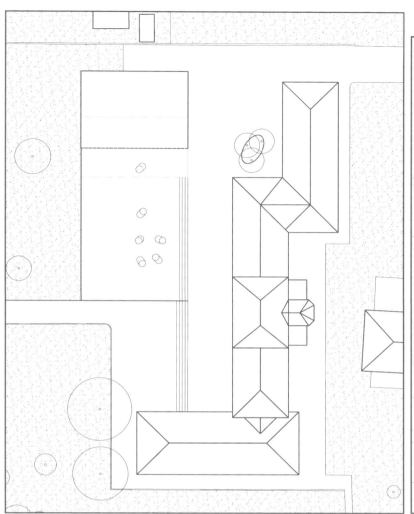

A view of the rooftops of the school (above, left) shows the relationship of the new rectangle to the roofs of the older building. The plan of the addition itself (above right) and photos and elevations show the geometric simplicity of the architects' work, heightened by a cheerful color scheme.

Ein Blick auf die Dächer der Schule (links oben) verdeutlicht die Beziehung des neuen rechteckigen Baukörpers zu den Dächern des älteren Gebäudes. Der Grundriss des eigentlichen Anbaus (rechts oben) sowie Fotos und Aufrisse zeigen die geometrische Schlichtheit des Entwurfs, unterstützt durch die farbenfrohe Gestaltung.

Le plan des toits de l'école (ci-dessus à gauche) montre la relation du bâtiment neuf avec les toits de l'ancien. Le plan de l'extension (ci-dessus à droite), les photos et les élévations illustrent la simplicité géométrique du travail de l'architecte, mis en valeur par une coloration joyeuse.

Interiors offer bright spaces, with numerous openings to the school's grounds, sometimes with floor-to-ceiling glazing.

Im Inneren gibt es helle Räume mit zahlreichen, zum Teil deckenhoch verglasten Öffnungen auf das Schulgelände.

Les intérieurs offrent des espaces lumineux et de nombreuses ouvertures sur les cours de l'école, parfois même à travers un plan vitré toute hauteur.

6

DIENER & DIENER

DIENER & DIENER ARCHITEKTEN
Henric Petri-Strasse 22
4010 Basel

Tel: +41 61 2 70 41 41
Fax: +41 61 2 70 41 00
e-mail: buero.basel@dienerdiener.ch
Web: www.dienerdiener.ch

ROGER DIENER was born in 1950 in Basel, and studied at the ETH in Zurich (1970–75). In 1976, he joined the firm that his father, MARCUS DIENER, had created in Basel in 1942. He became a partner in the firm, which was renamed Diener & Diener Architekten in 1980. He has taught at the EPFL (1985, 1987–89) and has been a Professor of Architecture and Design at the ETH in Zürich since 1999. He received the Gold Medal of the Académie d'Architecture in Paris in 2002 for the whole of his work. Based in Basel and Berlin, Diener & Diener employs about 40 persons. Their recent projects, aside from the Hotel Schweizerhof and Migros Shopping Center, Lucerne (1995–2000) featured here, are the renovation and extension of the Swiss Embassy in Berlin (1995–2000); housing for Java Island, Amsterdam (1995–2001); overall planning and new construction for the University of Malmö, Sweden, phase 1 (1997–2005); and the Forum 3 office building for the Novartis Campus in Basel (2002-05). Current work includes the Coop Bâleo Shopping Center, Basel (2004-); and the Spreedreieck office building in Berlin (2004-).

MIGROS SHOPPING CENTER & CLUB SCHOOL
LUCERNE
1995 - 2000

FLOOR AREA: Migros Shopping Center 7030 m²;
Migros Club School 2190 m²;
Töpferstrasse Building, Migros Club School
free-time activities 2800 m²
CLIENT: Genossenschaft Migros, Lucerne/
Hotel Schweizerhof AG, Lucerne
COST: CHF 36 million

This project caused some controversy at the outset because it required the replacement of the kitchen wing and coachhouses of the historic Hotel Schweizerhof. At a cost of the equivalent of CHF 36 million, the architects used the 7620 m² site to build two buildings. The Hertensteinstrasse building includes the 7030 m² Migros Shopping Center, a 2190 m² Migros Club School for languages and parking for 254 vehicles. The smaller building on Töpferstrasse (2800 m²) houses the "free-time activities" of the Migros Club School. As the architects have written, "The proximity to St Matthew's church [implies] that the new Migros building was obviously created in the tradition of the market halls, which have long been among the most important public edifices and architectonic inventories of towns everywhere. The tasks these buildings were designed for led to their special shapes and materials— and the same applies here. This explains its special attractiveness and the rather monumental approach decided on, although the Migros building is still rather modest in scale compared to the entire Hotel Schweizerhof ensemble. Its shape resembles a basilica, that basic form of all hall-type architecture." With its reinforced steel structure and glass and oxidized copper cladding, the Migros project unashamedly imposes its contemporary presence on what is otherwise a largely traditional city.

Dieses Projekt löste zu Anfang einige Diskussionen aus, da es den Abriss von Küchenflügel und Kutschenhäusern des historischen Hotels Schweizerhof erforderlich machte. Auf dem 7620 m² großen Gelände errichtete der Architekt zwei Gebäude für 36 Mio. Schweizer Franken. In dem Bau an der Hertensteinstrasse sind das 7030 m² große Migros-Einkaufszentrum, die 2190 m² umfassende Klubschule Migros für Sprachen sowie Parkmöglichkeiten für 254 Fahrzeuge untergebracht. Der kleinere, 2800 m² umfassende Bau an der Töpferstraße bietet Raum für die „Freizeitaktivitäten" der Migros Klubschule. Die Architekten lassen dazu verlauten: „Die Nähe zur St. Matthäuskirche impliziert, dass der neue Migros-Komplex die Tradition der Markthallen fortsetzt, die lange zu den wichtigsten öffentlichen Gebäuden und zum baulichen Bestand von Städten in aller Welt zählten. Die Aufgaben, für die diese Bauten konzipiert waren, führten zu speziellen Formen und Materialien; gleiches trifft auch hier zu. Dies erklärt den besonderen Reiz und die eher monumentale Herangehensweise, für die man sich hier entschied, wenngleich die Abmessungen des Migros-Gebäudes verglichen mit dem Gesamtkomplex des Hotel Schweizerhof bescheiden wirken. Die Form des Neubaus ähnelt der einer Basilika, der Urform aller Hallenarchitektur." Mit seiner Skelettkonstruktion aus Stahlbeton und der Verkleidung mit Glas und oxydierten Kupferplatten zwängt das Migros-Projekt der ansonsten weitgehend traditionellen Stadt ohne Skrupel seine zeitgenössische Präsenz auf.

Ce projet déclancha à l'origine une certaine polémique car il entraînait la destruction de l'aile de la cuisine et des écuries de l'Hôtel Schweizerhof, bâtiment historique. Les architectes ont utilisé le terrain de 7620 m² pour édifier deux constructions pour un budget de 36 millions de francs suisses. L'immeuble de la Hertensteinstrasse comprend un centre commercial Migros de 7030 m², une école-club Migros pour les langues de 2190 m² et un parking pour 254 véhicules. L'immeuble plus petit donnant sur la Töpferstrasse (2800 m²) abrite les « activités de temps libre » de l'école. Comme l'expliquent les architectes : « La proximité de l'église Saint-Mathieu [impliquait] que le nouvel immeuble Migros reprenne la tradition des halles de marché, qui ont pendant longtemps été les plus importants des édifices publics et ceux qui ont bénéficié des plus intéressantes inventions architectoniques urbaines partout dans le monde. Les tâches pour lesquelles ces immeubles devaient être conçus expliquent leur forme et leurs matériaux, ce qui se retrouve ici. Ceci explique leur attractivité particulière et leur approche assez monumentale, même si l'immeuble Migros est d'échelle relativement modeste par rapport à l'ensemble de l'Hôtel Schweizerhof. Son aspect évoque une basilique, forme de base de toute architecture de type halle. » Par sa structure en acier renforcé, son habillage en verre et en cuivre oxydé, le projet Migros impose franchement une présence contemporaine dans une ville restée par ailleurs essentiellement traditionnelle.

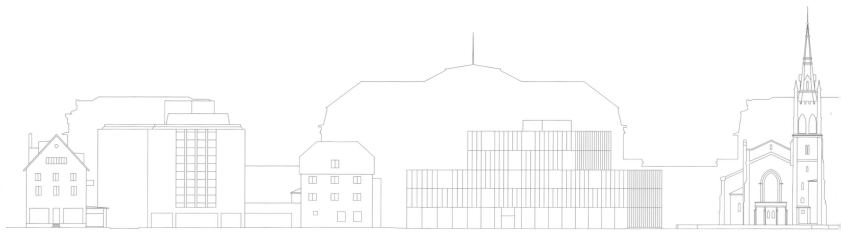

A plan, an elevation and images show how the architects have approached the delicate problem of inserting a contemporary structure into a traditional environment. The elevation above, in particular, shows how they have scaled their work to have a rapport with the existing architectural environment.

Grundriss, Aufriss und Abbildungen veranschaulichen, wie die Architekten die heikle Aufgabe bewältigten, einen zeitgenössischen Bau in ein sehr traditionelles Umfeld einzufügen.

Plan, élévation et images montrant la manière dont les architectes ont approché le délicat problème de l'insertion d'une structure contemporaine dans un environnement traditionnel. L'élévation ci-dessus, en particulier, illustre l'adaptation de l'échelle à l'environnement architectural.

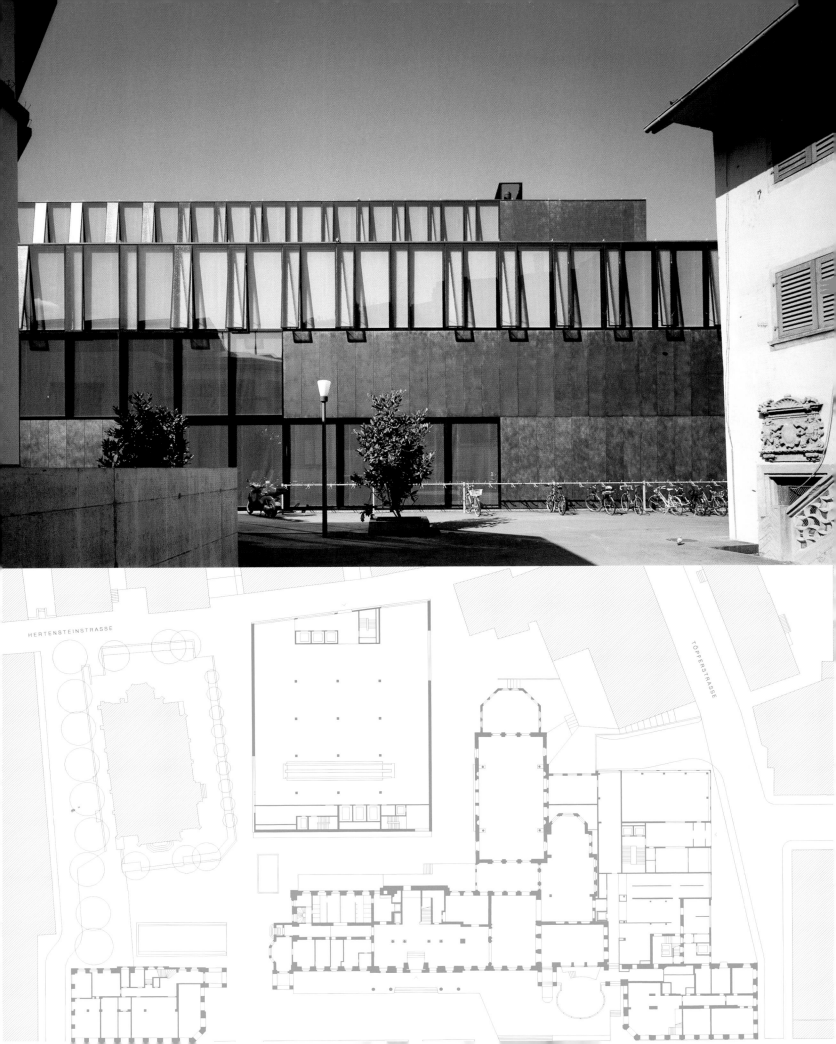

NOVARTIS PHARMA HEADQUARTERS BASEL 2003-05

FLOOR AREA: 8840 m²
CLIENT: Norvartis Pharma AG Basel CH
COST: not disclosed

The Novartis Campus of Knowledge is being developed in the St Johann area of Basel along the lines of a masterplan formulated in 2002 by Vittorio Magnano Lampugnani, a professor and director of the Institute of Urban Design at the ETH in Zurich. Novartis is a leading pharmaceutical company created when two Swiss firms, Ciba-Geigy and Sandoz, merged in 1996. One of the first completed structures of the Campus is Diener & Diener's Headquarters building, a project they won in a competition in which Bearth & Deplazes, Hans Kollhoff, Sejima & Nishizawa/SANAA, and Dominique Perrault also participated. The 83.5-meter-long, 22.5-meter-wide, 22-meter-high structure has a basement and five stories above ground. Its dimensions, but not its design, were dictated by the masterplan. From the exterior, one of the most striking features of the building is its unusual double-glass façade, whose outer layer is formed by an irregular arrangement of 25 different sizes of panes with 20 colors. Within, careful attention has been paid to the design of selected objects, such as the "Joyn" desk system ("joy" + "join") by Ronan and Erwan Bouroullec, Ingo Maurer lamps and Eames chairs. Diener & Diener also incorporated what they call microarchitecture in the interior, which is to say "elements of transition between space, design, and objects of daily use ... including panels and desktop covers." A total of 1400 plants populate the interiors, placed according to their natural habitats — bushes and trees on the ground level, creepers, epiphytes, and orchids above. At the western end of the building, the Plant Room is a ventilated four-story space including trees up to 12 meters high. Vogt Landscape Architects from Zurich worked on this strong natural presence within the building.

Der Campus des Wissens von Novartis entsteht in der Gegend von St. Johann in Basel nach den Richtlinien des 2002 von Vittorio Magnano Lampugnani entwickelten Gesamtplans. Lampugnani ist Professor und Direktor des Instituts für Stadtplanung an der ETH Zürich. Das führende pharmazeutische Unternehmen Novartis entstand, als 1996 die beiden Schweizer Firmen Ciba-Geigy und Sandoz fusionierten. Einer der ersten fertig gestellten Bauten des Campus ist das Gebäude der Hauptverwaltung von Diener & Diener, ein Auftrag, den sie in einem Wettbewerb gewannen, an dem sich auch Bearth & Depazes, Hans Kollhoff, Sejima & Nishizawa/SANAA und Dominique Perrault beteiligt hatten. Das 83,5 m lange, 22,5 m breite und 22 m hohe Gebäude verfügt über ein Kellergeschoss und fünf Stockwerke. Seine Dimensionen, nicht jedoch seine Gestaltung wurden vom Gesamtplan vorgegeben. Eines der auffälligsten Merkmale des Gebäudes von außen ist seine ungewöhnliche Doppelglasfassade, deren äußere Schicht sich aus unregelmäßig angeordneten Scheiben in 20 Farbtönen und 25 verschiedenen Größen zusammensetzt. Im Inneren finden mit großer Sorgfalt ausgewählte Objekte Verwendung,

wie das „Joyn"-Schreibtischsystem („joy" [Freude] + „join" [verbinden]) von Ronan und Erwan Bouroullec, Lampen von Ingo Maurer oder Stühle von Charles Eames. Darüber hinaus bezogen Diener & Diener die von ihnen so genannte „Mikroarchitektur" in die Ausstattung des Interieurs ein, das heißt „Elemente des Übergangs zwischen Raum, Design und Objekten des täglichen Gebrauchs ..., darunter Panele und Schreibtisch-Abdeckungen." Das Innere wird von 1400 Pflanzen belebt, die ihrem natürlichen Habitat entsprechend platziert wurden – Büsche und Bäume im Erdgeschoss, darüber Kletterpflanzen, Epiphyten und Orchideen. Bei dem am westlichen Ende des Gebäudes gelegenen Pflanzenraum handelt es sich um einen belüfteten, viergeschossigen Raum mit bis zu 12 m hohen Bäumen. Für die starke Präsenz der Natur im Gebäude zeichnet die in Zürich ansässige Firma Vogt Landschaftsarchitekten verantwortlich.

Le « Campus de la connaissance » de Novartis est en cours de réalisation dans le quartier Sankt-Johann de Bâle sur les bases du plan directeur mis au point en 2002 par Vittorio Magnano Lampugnani, professeur et directeur de l'Institut d'urbanisme de l'Institut fédéral suisse de technologie (ETH) de Zurich. Novartis est né de la fusion des laboratoires Ciba-Geigy et Sandoz en 1996. L'une des premiers bâtiments achevés est le siège social de Novartis Pharma par Diener & Diener, projet remporté à l'issue d'un concours auquel avaient également participé Bearth & Deplazes, Hans Kollhoff, Sejima et Nishizawa/SANAA et Dominique Perrault. De 83,5 m de long, 22,5 m de large et 22 m de haut, l'immeuble compte six niveaux, dont un en sous-sol. Ses dimensions, mais non sa conception, ont été dictées par le plan directeur. De l'extérieur, la caractéristique la plus frappante est l'étonnante façade à double vitrage dont le plan extérieur est une composition irrégulière de panneaux de 25 tailles et 20 couleurs différentes. Les aménagements intérieurs ont bénéficié d'une sélection rigoureuse comme le système de bureaux « Joyn » de Roman et Erwan Bouroullec, des lampes d'Ingo Maurer et des sièges de Eames. Diener & Diener ont également appliqué leur principe de microarchitecture intérieure, c'est-à-dire « d'éléments de transition entre l'espace, le design et les objets d'usage quotidiens ... y compris des panneaux muraux et des couvre-bureaux ». 1400 plantes ont été introduites et disposées en fonction de leurs habitats « naturels » : buissons et arbres au niveau du sol, épiphytes, plantes grimpantes et orchidées ailleurs. À l'extrémité ouest de l'immeuble, la Salle des plantes est un volume sur quatre niveaux de haut où poussent des arbres de 12 m. Vogt Landscape Architects, une agence de Zurich, est responsable de cette forte présence végétale.

orum 3

The building presents a long rectangular façade to the white granite Forum square. The glass was selected from existing productions, hues, strengths, and sizes. The pattern alternates between colored glass on white (carrier glass), white on white, or colored on colored.

Das Gebäude bietet seine lang gestreckte, rechtwinklige Fassade zum Forumsplatz aus weißem Granit dar. Das Glas wurde aus handelsüblichen Farbtönen, Stärken und Größen ausgewählt. Die Musterung variiert zwischen Farbglas auf weißem Trägerglas, weiß auf weiß oder Farbglas auf farbigem Untergrund.

Le bâtiment déploie sa longue façade rectangulaire sur la place du Forum en granit blanc. Les panneaux de verre ont été sélectionnés sur catalogue de produits existants. La composition joue de la superposition de verre coloré sur verre blanc, blanc sur blanc ou coloré sur coloré.

One of the most surprising features of the interior is the Plant Room at the western end of the building (right). Galleries on the upper three floors allow a view of the trees and plants from various heights.

Eines der überraschendsten Elemente im Inneren ist der Pflanzenraum am westlichen Ende des Gebäudes. Galerien in den oberen drei Geschossen ermöglichen Blicke auf die Bäume und Pflanzen aus unterschiedlicher Höhe.

L'un des éléments les plus surprenants de l'aménagement intérieur est la Salle des plantes à l'extrémité ouest de l'immeuble (à droite). Les galeries des trois niveaux supérieurs donnent sur les plantes et arbres de hauteurs variées.

The interior design concept was created in collaboration with the London based interior architect Sevil Peach, of Peach Gence Associates. Careful attention has been paid throughout to the selection of furniture and more architectural elements, such as the wooden stairway to the left.

Die Innenraumgestaltung entstand in Zusammenarbeit mit der in London ansässigen Innenarchitektin Sevil Peach von Peach Gence Associates. Insgesamt wurde viel Wert auf die Auswahl von Möbeln und die Gestaltung architektonischer Elemente wie der links zu sehenden Holztreppe gelegt.

Le concept de l'aménagement intérieur a été mis au point en collaboration avec Sevil Peach de l'agence d'architecture intérieure londonienne Peach Gence Associates. Une attention particulière a été portée à la sélection du mobilier et à certains éléments plus architecturaux comme l'escalier de bois à gauche.

Although in many respects the building seems to be quite straightforward, or even rectilinear in spirit as well as form, it contains many surprises as these images indicate.

Das Gebäude erscheint in vielerlei Hinsicht geradlinig, in seiner Philosophie ebenso wie in seiner Form, und doch birgt es im Inneren viele Überraschungen.

Bien qu'à de nombreux égards ce bâtiment puisse sembler raide et même un peu simple dans son esprit comme dans sa forme, il dissimule de nombreuses surprises, comme le montrent ces images.

7

E2A

E 2 A
eckert eckert architekten ag
Hardstrasse 219
8005 Zurich

Tel: +41 44 2 78 78 11
Fax: +41 44 2 78 78 15
e-mail: info@e2a.ch
Web: www.e2a.ch

PIET ECKERT was born in 1968 in Mumbai (Bombay), India. He studied architecture at the ETH in Zurich, where he received his diploma in 1994. He went on to the Columbia University Graduate School of Architecture in New York. From 1995 to 1997, he worked in the office of Rem Koolhaas (OMA) in Rotterdam. He has been an independent architect in Zurich since that time. In 2001, he founded e2A Eckert Eckert Architects with his brother. **WIM ECKERT** was born in 1969 in Zurich. He also studied architecture at the ETH, graduating in 1995. In 1996 and 1997, he also worked at OMA. They have completed a housing complex at Katzenbach, Zurich (2005), and terrace housing in Meilen (2002–05). Their current work includes a school center, Lättenwiesen, Opfikon (2005–07), and the Juchhof Football Training Center, Zurich (2005–06). An interesting design proposal formulated by e2a concerns the former military air base of Valkenburg north of The Hague (The Netherlands). The architects propose a test plan integrating 25 000 housing units developed over a period of 15 years in an Arcadian landscape with high-rise housing between 35 and 95 meters in height. They are also working on the Cantonal School for Deaf Pupils, Zurich Wollishofen (2005–07).

BROËLBERG HOUSING COMPLEX ZURICH 2002-03

FLOOR AREA: 7500 m²
CLIENT: Baukonsortium Broëlberg
COST: CHF 25 million including park

The unusual site of this housing complex is one of the last untouched park areas in Zurich. Two areas within the 35 000 m² park space were designated for housing projects. The architects e2a won a 2001 competition for these buildings. A sunken base contains the required infrastructure for the structures whose gross floor area is 7500 m². A free-span living space on the ground floor, a group of individual rooms on the upper floor, and an open summer house on the roof shape the CHF 25 million structures. The design, which places an emphasis on cast-in-place pigmented concrete, includes 15 apartments and parking for 45 cars. As the architects say, "The project is based on a horizontal striation formulating three antithetic architectures with four conceptual horizons." The "democratic" intention of the project is to provide equal access to the park view. In the words of the architects, "Horizons act like sight and site filters, selective methods, eliminating what is not desired, scanning the topographic progression of a place. Systematic stacking makes it possible to contrast boundaries and freedom—a juxtaposition of different models in one totality. It is well known that most people do not share the same horizon. This project at least offers everyone the possibility of obtaining the same one. The Broëlberg housing complex was programmatically formulated to suit a total of 1% of the overall rental market. The client's program defined an explicit type, with equality among the users as a requirement—a high-end housing for foreigners and expatriates unable to find residential conditions to match their expectations."

Bei dem ungewöhnlichen Standort für diese Wohnanlage handelt es sich um eines der letzten unangetasteten Parkgelände Zürichs. Zwei Bereiche in dem 35 000 m² großen Parkgebiet wurden für Wohnbebauung vorgesehen. Das Architekturbüro e2a gewann im Jahr 2001 den für diese Gebäude ausgeschriebenen Wettbewerb. Ein abgesenktes Sockelgeschoss enthält die notwendige Infrastruktur für die Gebäude, deren Bruttogeschossfläche 7500 m² umfasst. Ein stützenfreier Wohnraum im Erdgeschoss, eine Reihe von Einzelräumen im Obergeschoss und ein offenes Sommerhaus auf dem Dach bilden die beiden 25 Millionen Schweizer Franken teuren Gebäude. Der Entwurf umfasst 15 Apartments sowie Stellplätze für 45 Autos. Den Architekten zufolge „basiert das Projekt auf einer horizontalen Schichtung aus drei antithetischen Architekturen mit vier konzeptuellen Zonen." Die „demokratische" Absicht des Projekts ist es, allen Wohnungen gleiche Sicht auf den Park zu bieten. In den Worten der Architekten „fungieren Horizontlinien wie Sicht- und Lagefilter, selektive Verfahren, die Unerwünschtes ausklammern und die topografische Lage eines Ortes überprüfen. Systematische Schichtung ermöglicht es, Grenzen und Freizügigkeit gegenüberzustellen – das Nebeneinander unterschiedlicher Modelle in einer Gesamtheit. Es ist bekannt, dass die wenigsten Leute den gleichen Horizont haben. Dieses Projekt bietet zumindest jedem die Möglichkeit, sich den gleichen zu verschaffen. Die Wohnanlage Broëlberg wurde speziell so konzipiert, dass sie den Bedürfnissen von insgesamt einem Prozent des gesamten Marktes für Mietobjekte entspricht. Die Ausschreibung des Auftraggebers legte einen bestimmten Typus fest, wobei u. a. die Gleichheit für die Nutzer vorgeschrieben war – Luxuswohnungen für Ausländer und im Ausland Lebende, denen es nicht gelingt, ihren Erwartungen entsprechende Wohnbedingungen zu finden."

Le site de cet ensemble de logements est l'une des dernières zones vertes intactes de Zurich. Deux parcelles ont été affectées à la construction de logements dans un parc de 35 000 m². Le concours organisé fut remporté en 2001 par e2a. Un socle souterrain contient les infrastructures nécessaires aux 7500 m² de construction. L'immeuble dont le budget s'est élevé à 25 millions de francs suisses comprend quinze appartements et un parking pour quarante-cinq voitures. Pour les architectes : « Le projet repose sur une striation horizontale formulant trois architectures antithétiques dans quatre horizons conceptuels. » Son intention « démocratique » est d'offrir à tous des vues équivalentes sur le parc. « Les horizons agissent comme des filtres de la vue et du site, comme des méthodes sélectives éliminant ce qui n'est pas désiré, analysant la progression topographique du lieu. La systématisation de l'empilement rend possible l'organisation de contrastes entre les limites et la liberté, la juxtaposition en un tout de différents modèles. On sait que la plupart des gens ne partagent pas le même horizon. Ce projet offre au moins à chacun la possibilité d'obtenir le même. La programmation de l'ensemble de Broëlberg correspond à 1% du marché locatif. Le projet du client définissait un type explicite, requérant l'égalité parmi les usagers, un type de logement de haut de gamme pour étrangers et expatriés qui ne peuvent pas trouver ailleurs des conditions résidentielles correspondant à leurs attentes. »

The relative "coldness" of the architecture contrasts with the greenery of the surrounding park, but is also attenuated by the use of colored walls or stones, as in the image to the right.

Die relative Kühle der Architektur kontrastiert mit der Vegetation des umgebenden Parkgeländes. Darüber hinaus wird die Strenge durch farbige Wände und Steine (rechts) gemildert.

La « froideur » relative de l'architecture contraste avec la verdure du parc qui l'entoure, mais est également atténuée par le recours à des murs de pierre ou de couleur, comme ici à droite.

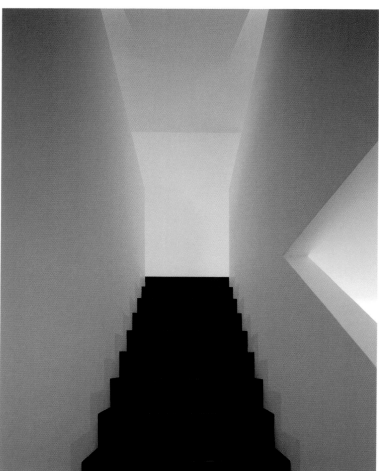

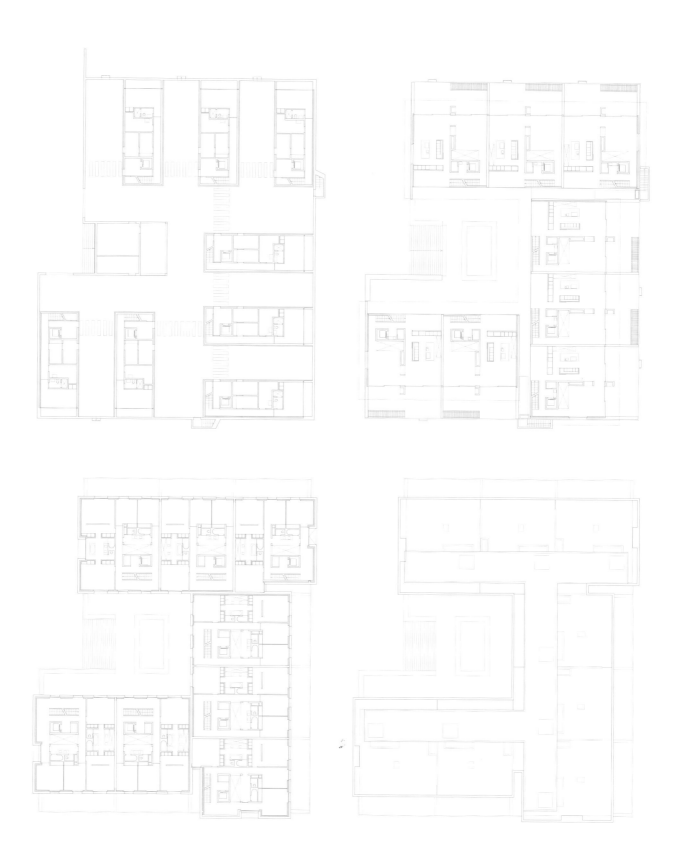

As the architects describe the apparently quite austere design of the building, "The vertical stacking expresses a menu, with superimposed living models, one on top of the other; a sunken infrastructure, an open-plan, a chamber work of individual rooms and a summerhouse on the roof. "

Zur recht nüchternen Gestaltung des Projektes äußersten die Architekten: „Die vertikale Schichtung nimmt sich aus wie eine Speisenfolge mit sich überlagernden Modellen, eines über dem anderen; eine versunkene Infrastruktur, ein offen angelegtes Konglomerat von Einzelräumen sowie ein Sommerhaus auf dem Dach."

Décrivant la conception assez austère de leur projet, les architectes écrivent : « L'empilement vertical exprime un menu de modèles animés et superposés : une infrastructure souterraine, un plan ouvert, un espace de travail composé pièces et une maison d'été sur le toit. »

8

NORMAN FOSTER

FOSTER AND PARTNERS
Riverside Three
22 Hester Road
SW11 4AN London

Tel: +44 20 77 38 04 55
Fax: +44 20 77 38 11 07
e-mail:
enquiries@fosterandpartners.com
Web: www.fosterandpartners.com

Born in Manchester in 1935, **NORMAN FOSTER** studied Architecture and City Planning at Manchester University (1961). He was awarded a Henry Fellowship to Yale University, where he received his Masters of Architecture degree, and met Richard Rogers, with whom he created Team 4. He received the Royal Gold Medal for Architecture (1983), and was knighted in 1990. The American Institute of Architects granted him their Gold Medal for Architecture in 1994. Lord Norman Foster has notably built: the IBM Pilot Head Office, Cosham (1970–71); the Sainsbury Centre for Visual Arts and Crescent Wing, University of East Anglia, Norwich (1976–77; 1989–91); the Hong Kong and Shanghai Banking Corporation Headquarters, Hong Kong (1981–86); London's Third Airport, Stansted (1987–91); the University of Cambridge Faculty of Law, Cambridge (1993–95); and the Commerzbank Headquarters, Frankfurt (1994–97). Recent projects include: the Airport at Chek Lap Kok, Hong Kong (1995–98); the new German Parliament, Reichstag, Berlin (1995–99); and the British Museum Redevelopment, London (1997–2000). More recently the office completed the Greater London Authority (1998–2002); the Millennium Bridge, London (1996–2002) and the much larger Millau Viaduct in France (1993–2005); and 126 Philip Street, Sydney (1997–2005). Wembley Stadium, London (1996–2006), and Florence Station (2003–08) are underway.

CHESA FUTURA
ST MORITZ
2000 - 02

FLOOR AREA: 4650 m²
CLIENT: SISA Immobilien AG
COST: not disclosed

This three-story, 4650 m² apartment building is intended to combine local tradition and the most recent computer-assisted design. Wooden shingles are often used as roofing in the Swiss mountains, but here the architect has covered the entire, rather unusually shaped structure with larch shingles. As always, Norman Foster emphasizes the environmental aspects of his work, insisting for example that "timber is a renewable resource; the trees absorb carbon dioxide as they grow; felling older trees reinforces the foresting practice of harvesting to encourage regeneration; and by using locally cut timber, little energy is consumed in its transportation." The bubble-like form allows for panoramic views on the southern side of St Moritz and the lake, as well as exposure to the sun, which is sought after in the cold winter months in this location. The northern façade of the building is more closed. In another bow to local building traditions, the building is lifted off the ground on eight pilotis, although there is an underground level for car parking, storage and heating facilities. The idea of lifting farm buildings off the ground in Switzerland was devised to keep pests out of storage buildings, but also to preserve the wood from prolonged exposure to moisture. Foster's "house of the future" did not need to relate to such ancient preoccupations, but clearly he wanted to make reference to the past of Swiss architecture, while pointing in new directions. As the office statement has it, "Taken overall, Chesa Futura might be regarded as a mini manifesto for architecture, not just here but in other parts of the world. Contrary to the pattern of sprawl that disfigures the edges of so many expanding communities, it shows how new buildings can be inserted into the existing grain at increased densities, while sustaining indigenous building techniques and preserving the natural environment."

Bei diesem dreigeschossigen, 4650 m² umfassenden Apartmenthaus sollten heimische Traditionen mit den neuesten, computergestützten Entwurfsverfahren kombiniert werden. Während man in den Schweizer Bergen die Dächer häufig mit Holzschindeln deckt, verkleidete der Architekt hier den gesamten, eher ungewöhnlich geformten Bau mit Schindeln aus Lärchenholz. Wie stets unterstreicht Norman Foster die umweltrelevanten Aspekte seiner Arbeit, indem er darauf verweist, dass „Nutzholz ein erneuerbarer Rohstoff ist. Bäume nehmen während ihres Wachstums Kohlenstoff auf. Durch das Fällen älterer Bäume wird gemäß der forstwirtschaftlichen Praxis die Regeneration unterstützt; durch die Verwendung von vor Ort gefälltem Holz reduziert sich der Aufwand an Energie für den Transport." Die Blasenform des Hauses gestattet auf der Südseite Rundblicke über St. Moritz und zum See hin ebenso wie größtmögliche Sonneneinstrahlung, ein an diesem Ort in den kalten Wintermonaten wünschenswerter Aspekt. Die Nordfassade des Hauses wirkt geschlossener. Auch der Umstand, dass der Bau durch acht Stützen über den Boden angehoben ist, verweist auf lokale Bautraditionen. Darüber hinaus gibt es

ein Untergeschoss mit Parkplätzen, in dem auch Lagerräume und die Heizanlage untergebracht sind. Traditioneller Weise werden Bauernhöfe in der Schweiz nicht direkt auf dem Erdboden errichtet, um Ungeziefer von gelagerten Vorräten fernzuhalten und auch, um das Holz vor der im Boden enthaltenen Feuchtigkeit zu schützen. Fosters „Haus der Zukunft" resultierte nicht aus solchen uralten Notwendigkeiten, sondern soll einen Bezug zur Vergangenheit herstellen, während es neue Richtungen aufzeigt. Wie es im Exposé des Büros heißt, könnte Chesa Futura „insgesamt als Architekturmanifest en miniature betrachtet werden, und zwar nicht nur für die Schweiz, sondern auch für andere Teile der Welt. Im Gegensatz zu den baulichen Wucherungen, die die Ränder so vieler wachsender Städte verschandeln, zeigt es einen Weg, wie neue Bauten zur Verdichtung in bestehende Strukturen eingefügt, gleichzeitig heimische Bauverfahren erhalten und die umgebende Natur geschont werden können."

Cet immeuble de logements de 4650 m² associe des traditions locales et les logiciels de CAO les plus récents. Si les bardeaux sont souvent utilisés en toiture dans les montagnes suisses, l'architecte en a recouvert ici la totalité de la forme assez inhabituelle de son immeuble. Comme toujours, Norman Foster insiste sur les aspects environnementaux de son travail, par exemple sur le fait que « le bois est une ressource renouvelable ; les arbres absorbent le dioxyde de carbone au cours de leur pousse. Exploiter les arbres à maturité fait partie des bonnes pratiques sylvicoles en encourageant la régénération des forêts. En utilisant des bois locaux, la quantité d'énergie nécessaire à leur transport est réduite ». La forme en bulle permet d'obtenir des vues panoramiques sur la partie sud de Saint-Moritz et le lac ainsi qu'une généreuse exposition au soleil, toujours recherchée dans cette station de montagne. La façade nord est plus fermée. Autre clin d'œil aux traditions locales de construction, l'immeuble est surélevé sur huit pilotis, bien que le parking, des pièces de rangement et les équipements de chauffage se trouvent en sous-sol. Cette surélévation se justifiait historiquement pour protéger les greniers des animaux nuisibles, mais également pour protéger le bois d'une exposition prolongée à l'humidité du sol. La « maison du futur » de Foster ne répond bien évidemment pas à ce genre de préoccupation, mais l'architecte a voulu cette référence au passé, tout en indiquant de nouvelles orientations. Chesa Futura, comme l'explique la présentation de l'agence, peut être considérée comme un mini-manifeste d'architecture, non seulement pour la Suisse mais pour d'autres parties du monde. Contrairement au mouvement d'extension urbanistique qui défigure les abords de tant de villes et de villages, elle montre que de nouvelles constructions plus denses peuvent être insérées dans le tissu urbain, tout en conservant des techniques de constructions locales et en préservant l'environnement.

9

FUHRIMANN & HÄCHLER

ANDREAS FUHRIMANN/GABRIELLE
HÄCHLER ARCHITEKTEN
Hardturmstrasse 66
8005 Zurich

Tel: +41 44 271 0480
Fax +41 43 204 0609
e-mail: mail@afgh.ch
Web: www.afgh.ch

ANDREAS FUHRIMANN was born 1956 in Zürich. He studied physics and architecture at the ETH Zürich. He obtained his degree in architecture there in 1985. He worked for one year in the architectural office of Marbach + Rüegg. As of 1987 he worked in cooperation with Christian Karrer. In 1988, he was a lecturer at the School of Design and Crafts in "interior architecture". As of 1995 he has worked with Gabrielle Hächler. Gabrielle Hächler was born in 1958 in Lenzburg. She studied art history studies at Zürich University, and architecture at the ETH Zürich, where she obtained her degree in 1988. As of 1988, she had her own architectural office and held an assistant lecturer's position in the Department of Construction at the ETH. Aside from the Üetliberg residence published here, they have built a Pavilion at Riesbach harbor in Zürich (2001-04); a room for art in Zumikon (1999-2000); a holiday house on the Rigi, Scheidegg (2002-03); and participated in the competition for the A-Park in Albisrieden (2003).

RESIDENCE UETLIBERG ZURICH 2003·04

FLOOR AREA: 1035 m²
CLIENT: Andreas Fuhrimann,
Gabrielle Hächler, Pipilotti Rist
COST: CHF 2,6 million

A view of the city to the north, a garden area to the south, and the need to create four different, reasonably priced apartments were the programmatic challenges faced by the architects in designing this small building, intended for the architects themselves and a well-known artist. The apartments are all accessible via a double-height entrance hall. The concrete, wood, and galvanized steel chosen by the architects are intentionally "commonplace and unrefined." The galvanized sheet steel façade has varied window openings on the north and south sides. The architects describe the appearance of the whole building as "crystalline and compact." Inside, the ceiling elements are secured to the concrete core and the wall elements of the external façade. The interior cladding consists of plywood on the walls and bonded boarding on the ceilings. The east double-story apartment measures 240 m², while the west double-story apartment is a 150 m² residence. A basement studio of 70 m² and the west roof apartment (80 m²) round out the interior space. The basement, stairwells and partitioning walls between the apartment units are made of cast-in-place concrete. As the architects explain, "The concrete core constitutes the 'skeleton' of the actual wooden structure, the organic softness of which heightens the rawness of the concrete." Ventilation slats of larch "make external reference to the internal timber construction."

Der Blick auf die Stadt im Norden, ein Garten im Süden und vier unterschiedliche Wohnungen, deren Kosten sich in einem vernünftigen Rahmen halten sollten, waren die programmatischen Herausforderungen, die es beim Entwurf dieses kleinen Gebäudes zu berücksichtigen galt. Die Wohnungen waren für die Architekten selbst und für eine bekannte Künstlerin gedacht. Sämtliche Wohnungen sind über eine Eingangshalle in doppelter Höhe erreichbar. Die von den Architekten gewählten Materialien – Beton, Holz und verzinkter Stahl – sind bewusst „alltäglich und unveredelt". Die mit verzinktem Stahl verkleidete Fassade weist auf der Nord- und Südseite verschiedenartige Fensteröffnungen auf. Die Architekten beschreiben die Erscheinung des ganzen Gebäudes als „kristallin und kompakt". Die Deckenelemente im Inneren sind direkt im Betonkern und an den Wandelementen der Außenfassade verankert. Die Wände sind innen mit Sperrholz, die Decken mit verleimten Brettern verkleidet. Das nach Osten gelegene, zweistöckige Appartement umfasst 240 m², während die westliche, ebenfalls doppelgeschossige Wohnung 150 m² groß ist. Ein Kellerstudio von 70 m² und die nach Westen orientierte Dachwohnung von 80 m² komplettieren das Innere. Keller, Treppenhäuser sowie die Trennwände zwischen den Wohnungen bestehen aus in situ gegossenen Betonelementen. Die Architekten erläutern dazu: „Der Betonkern bildet das ‚Skelett' des eigentlichen Holzhauses, das mit seiner organischen Weichheit das Rohe des Betons übertönt." Lüftungsklappen aus Lärchenholz „stellen den Bezug zur inneren Holzkonstruktion her".

Une vue de la ville au nord, un jardin au sud et la création de quatre appartements à un prix raisonnable, tels étaient les enjeux du programme auquel étaient confrontés les architectes de ce petit immeuble conçu pour eux-mêmes et une artiste célèbre. Les appartements sont tous accessibles par un hall d'entrée double hauteur. Le béton, le bois et l'acier galvanisé choisis par les architectes sont volontairement « de type courant et sans raffinement ». La façade en tôle d'acier galvanisé présente des fenêtres de dimensions variées au nord et au sud. Les architectes décrivent l'aspect de l'ensemble comme « cristallin et compact ». À l'intérieur, les plafonds sont directement accrochés au béton et aux murs extérieurs. L'habillage interne consiste en contreplaqué sur les murs et planches collées sur les plafonds. L'appartement est, sur deux niveaux, mesure 240 m², celui de l'ouest, également sur deux niveaux, 150 m². Un atelier en sous-sol de 70 m² et un attique de 80 m² à l'ouest complètent le volume intérieur. Le sous-sol, la cage d'escalier et les murs de séparation entre les appartements sont en béton coulé sur place. Comme l'expliquent les architectes : « Le cœur en béton constitue le ‹ squelette › de la structure qui est en fait en bois dont la douceur organique met en valeur le côté brut du béton. » Des lamelles de ventilation en bouleau « sont une référence externe à la construction en bois de l'intérieur ».

In its green setting, the building appears, almost like the model drawings to the right, to be like a metallic sculpture set down in the natural environment. Its relatively cold grayness contrasts with the park space sharply.

In seiner grünen Umgebung erscheint das Gebäude – ähnlich wie die Modell-Zeichnungen rechts – wie eine Skulptur aus Metall, die in die Landschaft gesetzt wurde. Das relativ kalte Grau steht im scharfen Kontrast zur parkartigen Umgebung.

Dans son cadre de verdure, le bâtiment – très proche des dessins de la maquette à droite – semble une sculpture en métal posée dans un environnement naturel. Sa grisaille assez froide contraste avec le parc qui l'entoure.

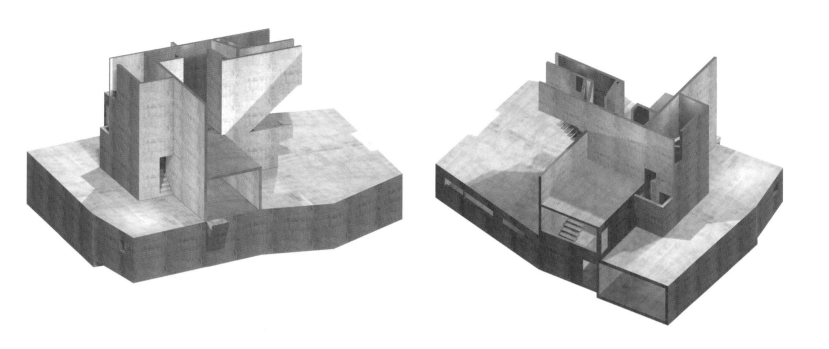

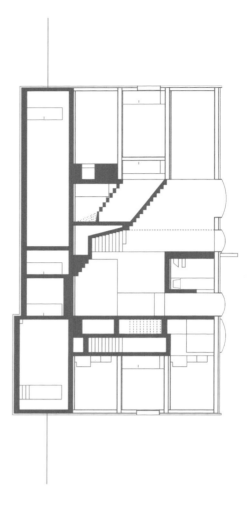

Flat, rather hard concrete surfaces are livened by the presence of a few colorful objects (right), while ample views of the surrounding area are offered through a broad glazed band in a living room space (right page).

Flache und harte Oberflächen aus Beton werden durch wenige farbige Objekte belebt (rechts), während sich durch ein breites Fensterband im Wohnzimmerbereich der Blick auf die Umgebung öffnet (rechte Seite).

Les surfaces planes assez agressives sont animées par la présence de quelques objets colorés (à droite). D'amples perspectives sur l'environnement s'ouvrent à travers l'important bandeau vitré de ce séjour (page de droite).

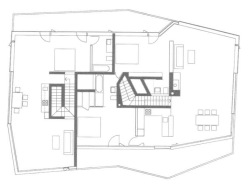
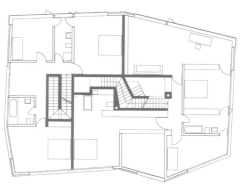

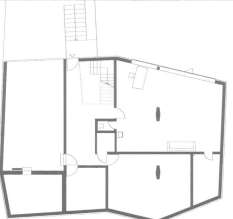

An open kitchen space and a fireplace might well bring a bit more warmth to the interior space when they are being used. Here, concrete is the main surface and structural material.

Eine offene Küche und ein Kamin werden im Alltag etwas Wärme in den Innenraum bringen. Beton ist hier das dominierende Oberflächenmaterial und strukturgebendes Element.

Lorsqu'elles sont utilisées, la cuisine ouverte et la cheminée apportent un peu de chaleur au volume intérieur. Le béton est ici le principal matériau structurel et de parement.

Obviously rather hard in its appearance, the concrete is handled with a formal deftness that leaves the residents the task of bringing life to these spaces.

Das nüchterne und mit formalem Geschick behandelte Erscheinungsbild des Betons wird es den Bewohnern überlassen, diesen Ort mit Leben zu füllen.

D'apparence assez sèche, le béton est traité avec une dextérité formelle qui laisse aux résidents la charge d'animer ces volumes.

10

PATRICK GARTMANN

**CONZETT, BRONZINI,
GARTMANN AG**
Bahnhofstrasse 3
7000 Chur

Tel: +41 81 2 58 30 00
Fax: +41 81 2 58 30 01
e-mail: cbg@cbg-ing.ch
Web: www.cbg-ing.ch

PATRICK GARTMANN was born in 1968 in Chur. He obtained his degree as an engineer in 1994 and as an architect in 1998. In 1998, he also worked as an assistant to Valerio Olgiati at the EHT in Zurich. In 1998, he created the joint venture Conzett, Bronzini and Gartmann with the engineers Jürg Conzett and Gianfranco Bronzini. In 1995, he worked with Gigon/Guyer on the Grandstand Sports Center, Davos; in 1997 on the Frommelt House in Triesen with Bearth & Déplazes; in 1999 with Peter Zumthor on the Swiss Pavilion at the EXPO 2000, Hanover; and on the Yellow House in Flims with Valerio Olgiati, also in 1999. In 2004, Gartmann acted as a consulting engineer with Smarch on a pedestrian walkway for the train station in Berne.

GARTMANN HOUSE
CHUR
2004

FLOOR AREA: 306 m²
CLIENT: Patrick Gartmann
COST: CHF 1 million

Patrick Gartmann designed his own house, oriented toward the west, with a view of the city of Chur. On the 828 m² site, he built the three-story residence (each floor measuring 102 m²) with single-layer, solid, thermally insulated concrete. He will also oversee future construction on the entire 5000 m² site, ensuring that "solid construction, bright looks, and flat roofs" are employed. Particularly interested in the technical aspects of the construction, Gartmann collaborated with the Olten firm Liapor to create concrete in which gravel and sand were replaced by clay and glass. As he says, "This yields a cement-bonded, crystalline mixture of clay and glass which can be processed as a homogeneous, lightweight, and porous material and can be dyed arbitrarily while making good use of the thermal properties of expanded concrete and its load-bearing ... virtues." Appearing to be a single-story structure from the street entrance, the house reveals its three stories only once visitors are inside. Patrick Gartmann insists on the house affording views of the "Bündner Oberland" and the Rhine Valley. The ground or entrance floor includes bedrooms and bathrooms, as well as the living room. The lower level features a large space devoted to the kitchen and dining area.

Patrick Gartmann entwarf sein eigenes Haus mit Ausrichtung nach Westen und Blick auf die Stadt Chur. Auf dem 828 m² großen Grundstück errichtete er das dreistöckige Haus (jedes Geschoss umfasst 102 m²) aus einlagigem, massivem, wärmegedämmtem Beton. Außerdem wird er die Bauaufsicht für die künftige Bebauung des gesamten 5000 m² großen umliegenden Areals übernehmen und damit gewährleisten, dass „Massivbauweise, helle Fassaden und Flachdächer" zur Anwendung kommen. Der besonders an den technischen Aspekten des Gebäudes interessierte Gartmann arbeitete mit der Firma Liapor aus Olten zusammen, um bei der Herstellung des Betons Kies und Sand durch Ton und Glas zu ersetzen. „So entsteht", wie er sagt, „eine kristalline Mischung aus Ton und Glas auf Zementbasis, die als

homogenes, leichtes, poröses Material verarbeitet und nach Belieben pigmentiert werden kann, während es sich die wärmedämmenden und tragenden Eigenschaften von geblähtem Beton zunutze macht." Von der Straße aus wirkt das Haus wie ein eingeschossiger Bau; seine drei Stockwerke erschließen sich dem Besucher erst, nachdem er das Haus betreten hat. Patrick Gartmann bestand darauf, dass von hier sowohl das Bündner Oberland als auch das Rheintal zu überschauen sind. Das Erd- bzw. Eingangsgeschoss umfasst Schlafzimmer, Bäder und den Wohnbereich. In dem großen Raum in der unteren Ebene sind Küche und Speisezimmer untergebracht.

Il s'agit de la propre maison de l'ingénieur-architecte, orientée à l'ouest et donnant sur la ville de Coire. Édifiée sur un terrain de 828 m², elle se compose de trois niveaux de 102 m² chacun. P. Gartmann s'est également chargé de la supervision de l'aménagement de ce site de 5000 m² pour assurer « des constructions solides, un bon aspect et des toits plats ». Ingénieur lui-même, il s'intéresse tout naturellement aux aspects techniques de la construction. Ici, il a utilisé un béton monocouche massif servant d'isolant thermique dans lequel le gravier et le sable ont été remplacés par de l'argile et du verre, formule mise au point en collaboration avec Liapor, la firme d'Olten. Selon Gartmann : « Ceci permet d'obtenir une mélange cristallin lié au ciment d'argile et de verre qui peut se traiter comme un matériau homogène, léger et poreux qui se teint à volonté, tout en bénéficiant des propriétés thermiques du béton expansé et de ses capacités porteuses. » Vue de l'extérieur, la maison semble ne compter qu'un seul niveau, les deux autres ne se révélant qu'en y pénétrant. Le niveau de l'entrée comprend les chambres, les salles de bains et le séjour, le niveau inférieur la cuisine et la zone des repas. Patrick Gartmann ne se lasse pas du panorama sur le Bündner Oberland et la vallée du Rhin.

The powerful, even hard lines of the house actually frame the view of the natural setting in an exceptional way, leading to it and concentrating the viewer's attention. Floor-to-ceiling glazing accentuates the strong rapport between interior and exterior.

Die kantigen, geradezu harten Umrisse des Hauses rahmen in außergewöhnlicher Weise natürliche Umgebung und lenken so die Aufmerksamkeit des Betrachters auf die Aussicht. Die deckenhohe Verglasung unterstreicht die starke Bindung zwischen Innen- und Außenraum.

Puissantes, presque agressives, les lignes de la maison cadrent la vue sur la nature d'une manière spectaculaire qui concentre l'attention du spectateur. Le vitrage toute hauteur accentue ce rapport vigoureux entre l'intérieur et l'extérieur.

11

GIGON/ GUYER

GIGON/GUYER ARCHITEKTEN
Carmenstrasse 28
8023 Zurich

Tel: +41 44 2 57 11 11
Fax: +41 44 2 57 11 10
e-mail: info@gigon-guyer.ch
Web: www.gigon-guyer.ch

Born in 1959, **ANNETTE GIGON** received her diploma from the ETH in Zurich in 1984. She worked in the office of Herzog & de Meuron in Basel (1985–88) before setting up her own practice (1987–89) and creating her present firm with Mike Guyer in 1989. Born in 1958, **MIKE GUYER** also graduated from the ETH in Zurich in 1984, and worked with Rem Koolhaas (OMA, 1984–87), and taught with Hans Kollhoff at the ETH (1987–88). Their built work includes the Kirchner Museum, Davos (1990–92); the Vinikus Restaurant, Davos (1990–92); and the renovation of the Oskar Reinhart Collection, Römerholz, Winterthur (1997–98). Gigon/Guyer has participated in numerous international competitions, such as those for the Nelson-Atkins Museum extension, Kansas (1999), or the Santiago de Compostela "City of Culture" project (1999). Recent work includes the extension of the Aviation/Space Museum in Lucerne (2000–03); the Museum for the Albers/Honegger Collection, Mouans-Sartoux, France (2004); and a housing project in Rüschlikon, Switzerland. The office employs a total of 18 architects.

KUNST-DEPOT HENZE & KETTERER WICHTRACH 2002-04

FLOOR AREA: 920 m²
CLIENT: Gallery Henze & Ketterer, Wichtrach
COST: CHF 2 460 142

Located near Bern, this building was intended for both the display and the storage of art. A hollow, load-bearing wall in the middle of the building carries the utilities, while particular attention was paid to the insulation and climate control in order to protect the art. Concrete and insulation 20 cm thick ensure that the indoor temperature will not vary greatly, while a "free-floating layer of perforated sheet metal helps reduce the amount of sunlight that falls on the windows and façade." Tetra metal sheeting, frequently used in warehouses, was employed by the architects and, as they point out, the smooth sheets echo the irregular parallelogram form of the floor plan. The local building codes required the roof form used with respect to local farm architecture, while the unusual floor plan evolved from the shape of the site and the need to park cars nearby. At once modern and industrial in appearance, the Kunst-Depot demonstrates the ability of Gigon and Guyer to solve a very particular set of problems with a coherent and intelligent building.

Das in Wichtrach bei Bern gelegene Gebäude ist gleichermaßen dafür gedacht, Kunstwerke auszustellen wie sie sachgerecht zu lagern. In einer hohlen, tragenden Wand in der Mitte des Gebäudes sind sämtliche nötigen Installationen untergebracht. Zum Schutz der Kunstwerke wurde besonderer Wert auf die Isolierung und Klimatisierung der Räume gelegt. Beton und eine 20 cm starke Isolierung gewährleisten, dass die Innentemperatur kaum schwankt, während eine „frei bewegliche Lage Lochblech dazu beiträgt, das auf Fenster und Fassade fallende Sonnenlicht zu minimieren". Von den Architekten wurden dafür die häufig in Lagerhäusern verwendeten Tetrafeinbleche verwendet, da diese die Form des Grundrisses, ein unregelmäßiges Parallelogramm, aufnehmen. Die lokalen Baugesetze schrieben mit Rücksicht auf die heimische Bauernhausarchitektur die Dachform vor, während sich der ungewöhnliche Grundriss aus der Beschaffenheit des Geländes und dem Bedarf an Parkplätzen in unmittelbarer Nähe des Gebäudes ergab. Das modern und industriell wirkende Kunst-Depot demonstriert die Fähigkeit von Gigon und Guyer, eine sehr spezifische Problemstellung mit einem kohärenten und intelligenten Gebäude zu lösen.

Situé près de Berne, ce bâtiment a pour fonction la présentation et la conservation d'œuvres d'art. Le mur creux porteur central a reçu l'ensemble des gaines techniques et une attention particulière a été portée à l'isolation thermique et au contrôle de la température pour la protection des œuvres. Le recours au béton et une couche d'isolation thermique de 20 cm d'épaisseur assurent une température intérieure régulière tandis qu'une « strate flottante en tôle de métal perforé contrôle la quantité de lumière solaire tombant sur les ouvertures et la façade ». La tôle de tetra-metal souvent utilisée dans la construction d'entrepôts a été employée. Son aspect lisse répond bien à la forme de parallélogramme irrégulier du plan au sol. Ce plan lui-même est issu de la forme du terrain et de la nécessité de prévoir un parking à proximité immédiate, tandis que celle du toit vient du règlement local de construction qui oblige à respecter les formes de l'architecture des bâtiments agricoles locaux. D'aspect à la fois moderne et industriel, ce Kunst-Depot illustre la capacité de Gigon et Guyer à résoudre un ensemble de problèmes très spécifiques dans un bâtiment cohérent et intelligent.

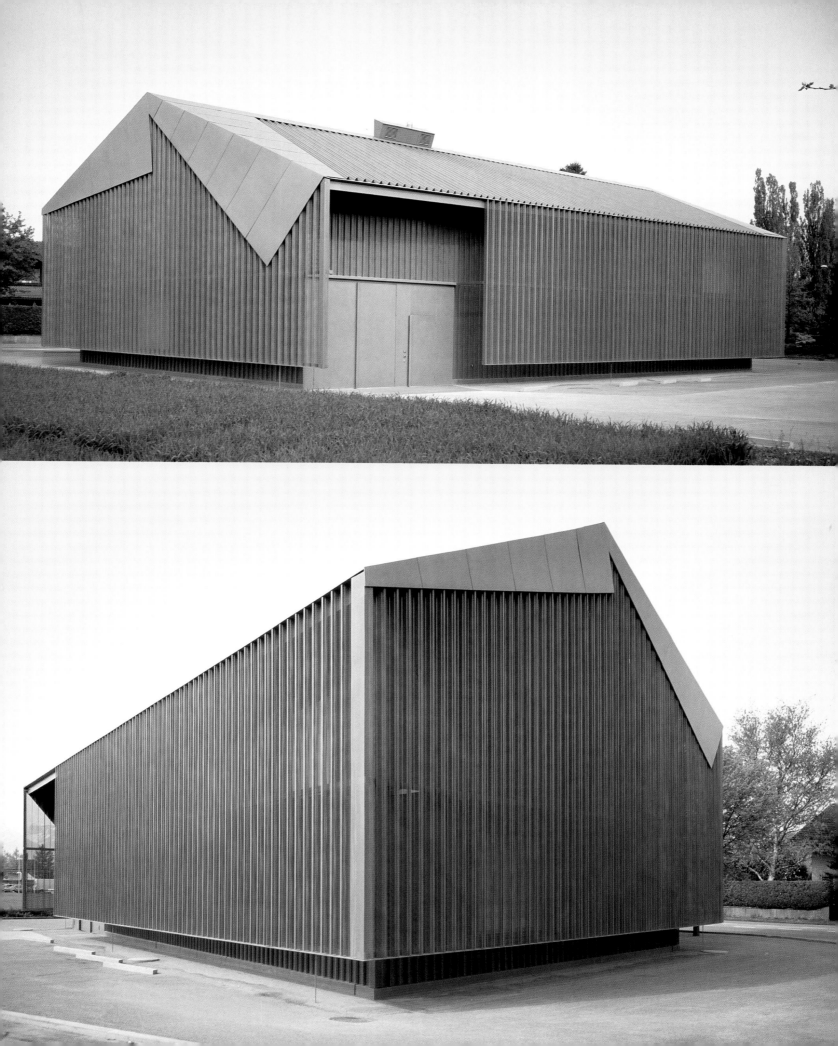

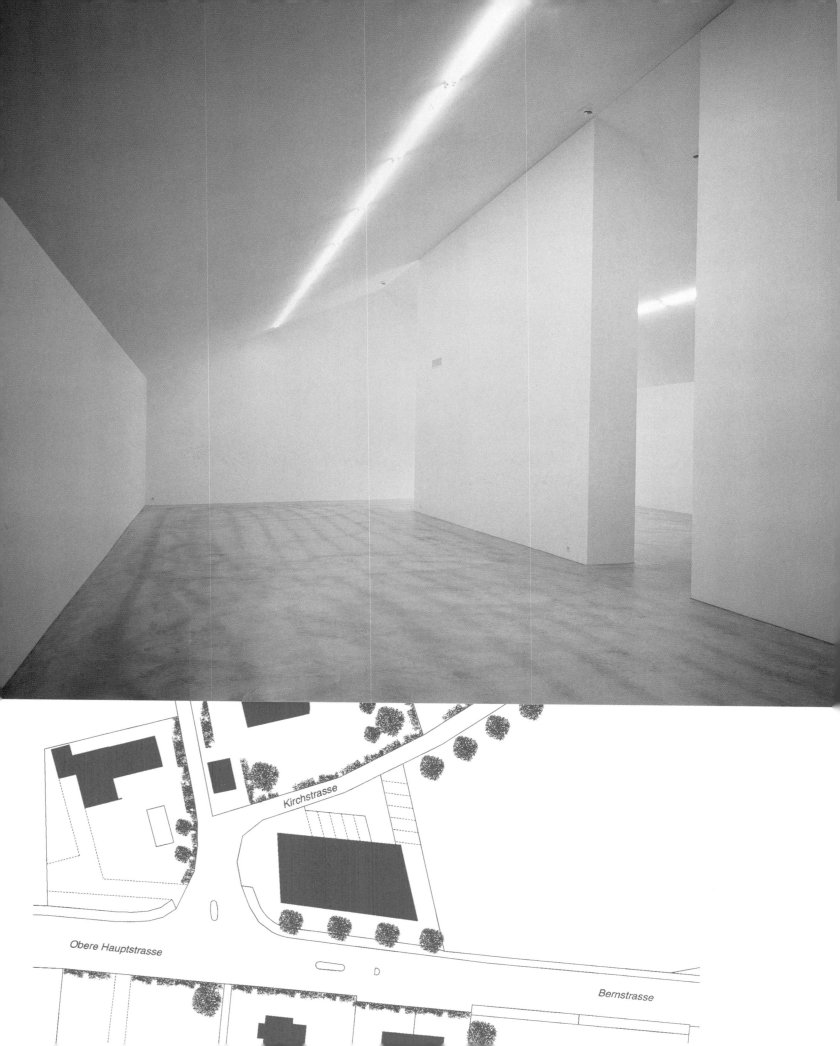

Kirchstrasse

Obere Hauptstrasse

Bernstrasse

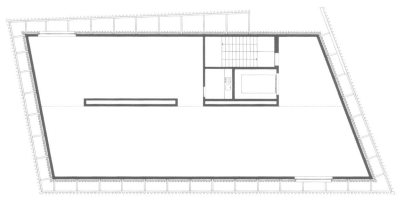
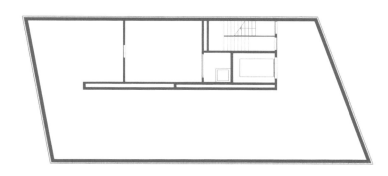

The simple quadrilateral layout of the building is intended both in plan and in section to create a variety and movement that the building would otherwise have lacked. An exterior layer of perforated sheet metal controls sunlight but also enriches the appearance of the façades.

Die einfach, vierseitige Anlage des Gebäudes weist sowohl im Grundriss wie auch im Schnitt eine Schräge auf, die Vielfalt und Bewegung erzeugt, die dem Bauwerk sonst gefehlt hätten. Eine äußere Schicht aus perforiertem Blech regelt die Lichteinstrahlung und sorgt für optisch interessante Fassaden.

Le plan en quadrilatère est déformé, en plan comme en coupe, pour créer un sentiment de variété et de mouvement dont cet entrepôt aurait autrement manqué. Une couverture extérieure en acier perforé permet de contrôler l'éclairage naturel, tout en enrichissant l'aspect des façades.

VILLA ANNAMARIA
KASTANIENBAUM
2003 - 04

FLOOR AREA: Living space: 958 m² ; Terrace: 307 m²
CLIENT: Alfred Richterich, Laufen
COST: CHF 2,98 million structural alteration villa;
CHF 540 000 extension

This project involved the remodeling and extension of an 1860 Italianate summer residence located in a park overlooking Lake Lucerne. The house had been substantially modified in 1927. The work included the removal of the later alterations, but the owner and the architects opted not to attempt to return the house entirely to its original state. One small room in the tower of the house was found to have interesting drawings under the wallpaper made by workers and it was decided to leave these pencil sketches intact. A new brass chimney and fireplace were added, as was a chrome-plated steel stove in the kitchen. The former kitchen annex of the house was demolished in order to create a concrete, trellis-covered garage. The trellises continue above the actual level of the garage to give the extension proportions more directly related to the original house than the concrete parking facility alone would have allowed. Olive-green was chosen as the color of the trellises, and the concrete of the garage was also colored to echo the vegetation of the park, and the greenish tinge of the villa's sandstone. Modernizing this type of house is not an easy task for contemporary architects. This type of renovation requires a very good understanding of the original building as well as respect for the client and a sense of how modernity can improve the existing design.

Bei diesem Projekt ging es um die Umgestaltung und Erweiterung eines 1860 erbauten Sommerhauses im italienisierenden Stil, das in einem Park mit Blick auf den Vierwaldstättersee steht. Das Haus war 1927 erheblich verändert worden. Der Bauauftrag umfasste die Entfernung der damaligen Veränderungen, wenngleich Eigentümer und Architekten sich dagegen entschieden, das Haus gänzlich in seinen ursprünglichen Zustand zurückzuversetzen. In einem kleinen Raum im Turm des Hauses entdeckte man aufschlussreiche Zeichnungen, die die Arbeiter unter der Tapete hinterlassen hatten, und entschied sich dafür, diese Bleistiftskizzen zu erhalten. Es wurden ein neuer kupferner Rauchabzug und ein Kamin ergänzt, ebenso ein mit Chrom beschichteter Stahlherd in der Küche. Der frühere Küchenanbau wurde zugunsten einer Garage aus Beton abgerissen, die mit einem Pflanzgitter bedeckt wurde. Die Spaliere setzen sich über der eigentlichen Höhe der Garage fort, um deren Proportionen jenen des ehemaligen Hauses anzupassen. Als Farbe für die Spaliere wählte man ein Olivgrün, und auch der Beton der Garage erhielt in Anlehnung an die Vegetation des Parks und den grünlichen Sandstein der Villa eine grünliche Färbung. Ein solches Haus zu renovieren, ist für heutige Architekten keine leichte Aufgabe. Die Renovierung setzt nicht nur ein eingehendes Verständnis des ursprünglichen Gebäudes voraus sondern auch ein respektvolles Verhältnis zum Auftraggeber und ein Gespür dafür, wie eine Modernisierung die vorhandene Gestaltung verbessern kann.

Ce projet consistait en la rénovation et l'extension d'une résidence d'été de style italianisant datant de 1860 dans un parc dominant le lac des Quatre-Cantons. La maison avait déjà été substantiellement modifiée en 1927. Ces transformations ont été supprimées, mais ni le propriétaire ni les architectes ne souhaitaient revenir entièrement à l'état original. Par exemple, on a retrouvé sous les papiers peints d'une petite pièce de la tour d'intéressants dessins au crayon réalisés jadis par les ouvriers. Une cheminée en cuivre a été ajoutée ainsi qu'une cuisinière en acier chromé dans la cuisine. L'ancienne annexe consacrée à la cuisine a été démolie pour créer un garage en béton recouvert d'un treillis qui s'élève au-dessus de la construction, pour retrouver des proportions plus proches de celles de la maison que celles d'un simple abri à voitures. Le treillis vert olive et le béton teinté font écho à la végétation environnante et à la nuance verte du grès dont est construite la villa. Moderniser une maison de ce type n'est pas une tâche indifférente pour un architecte contemporain. C'est un chantier qui requiert une compréhension approfondie du bâtiment d'origine, le respect du client et la perception de ce que peut apporter la modernité à une architecture existante.

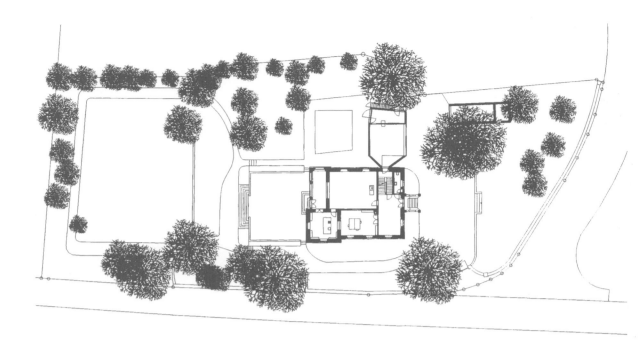

A trellis-like structure clads the new concrete garage or rather encloses it, giving an impression of lightness and also matching the proportions of the older structure.

Eine Art Pflanzgitter umgibt die neue, aus Beton errichtete Garage und verhilft ihr damit zu optischer Leichtigkeit; außerdem wurde sie auf diese Weise an die Proportionen des alten Gebäudes angepasst.

Une structure en treillis habille adaptée aux proportions bâtiment ancien habille le nouveau garage en béton ou plutôt l'enveloppe, lui conférant une apparence de légèreté.

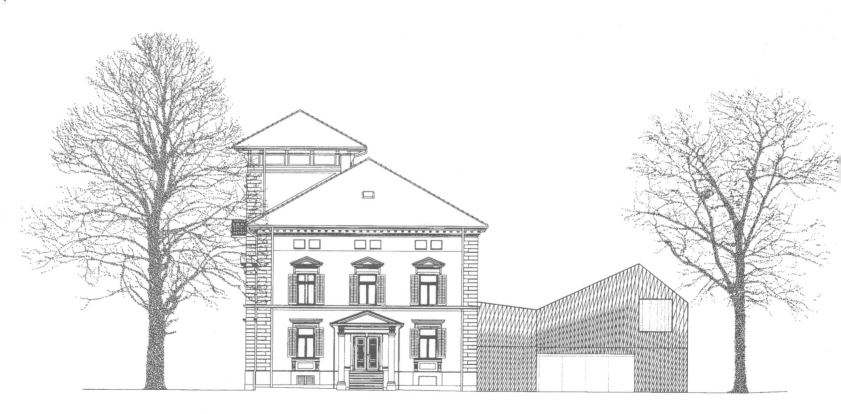

Interventions in the existing house are discreet and well designed in relation to the older architecture. A brass chimney (above) plays on the proportions of the room, while bringing a strong touch of modernity into the house.

Eingriffe in das vorhandene Gebäude sind zurückhaltend und gut an die ältere Architektur angepasst. Ein kupferner Rauchabzug (oben) nimmt Bezug auf die Proportionen des Raumes und bringt gleichzeitig ein dezidiert modernes Element in das Haus ein.

Les interventions sur la maison existante sont discrètes et habilement dessinées par rapport à l'architecture ancienne. Une cheminée de cuivre (ci-dessus) joue sur les proportions de la pièce tout en apportant une note marquée de modernité.

12

HERZOG &
DE MEURON

HERZOG & DE MEURON
Rheinschanze 6
4056 Basel

Tel: +41 61 3 85 57 57
Fax: +41 61 3 85 57 58
e-mail: info@herzogdemeuron.com

JACQUES HERZOG and PIERRE DE MEURON were both born in Basel in 1950. They received degrees in architecture at the ETH in Zurich in 1975, after studying with Aldo Rossi, and founded their firm Herzog & de Meuron Architecture Studio in Basel in 1978. Harry Gugger and Christine Binswanger joined the firm in 1991, while Robert Hösl and Ascan Mergenthaler became partners in 2004. Their built work includes the Antipodes I Student Housing at the Université de Bourgogne, Dijon (1991–92); the Ricola Europe Factory and Storage Building in Mulhouse (1993); and a gallery for a private collection of contemporary art in Munich (1991–92). Most notably, they were chosen early in 1995 to design the new Tate Modern extension for contemporary art, situated in the Bankside Power Station, on the Thames, opposite St Paul's Cathedral that opened in May 2000. They were also shortlisted in the competition for the new design of the Museum of Modern Art in New York (1997). More recently, they built the Forum 2004 Building and Plaza, Barcelona (2002–04) the Prada Aoyama Epicenter in Tokyo (2003), the Allianz Arena in Munich (2002–05), the De Young Museum in San Francisco (2002–05). They plan to design the Caixa Forum-Madrid and the National Stadium, main stadium for the 2008 Olympic Games in Beijing.

SCHAULAGER
MÜNCHENSTEIN
2000 - 03

FLOOR AREA: 20 000 m²
CLIENT: Laurenz Stiftung, Basel
COST: not disclosed

The Schaulager is an unusual facility located at the periphery of the city of Basel. It is intended for the storage of the Emanuel Hoffmann Foundation collection. Today the Emanuel Hoffmann Foundation contains works by over 150 artists. The early acquisitions of the collection, dating from the 1930's on—by Arp, Dalí, Delaunay, Klee, Ernst, or the Belgian Expressionists—long ago became classics of modern art, and have their established place in art history. Today, the Foundation "aims to buy works of art looking to the future, and not yet generally understood in the present." The works of art are stored in optimal conditions, with occasional visitors or scholars allowed to view specific works on request. The architects chose to create a "heavy" building as opposed to the lightweight structures that have become more popular for such use in other locations. The thick walls and floors of the building give it a large amount of thermal "inertia," meaning that it retains heat in winter and does not warm quickly in summer. 28 meters high, the Schaulager has two exhibition floors, used once a year for such artists as Jeff Wall (2005), and 3 storage floors. The exhibition area of the facility is 4300 m², the storage space 7244 m² with the basic storage units measuring 32 m² each. Some rooms however are up to six times larger, 771 m² of art handling space and 800 m² of administrative offices are also part of the project. Two large (44 m²) LED screens are the only exterior indication of the function of the structure. They show images related to art and the once-yearly public exhibitions held in the Schaulager. The smooth white walls and bare concrete floors of the interior contrast with the rough exterior cladding containing pebbles from the construction site. This is by no means a "warm" building in the sense that it is spare and sparsely decorated, but it makes a strong statement for a new relationship between architecture and the conservation of contemporary art.

Das Schaulager, das in einem Vorort von Basel liegt, ist eine ungewöhnliche Einrichtung. Hier werden die Werke der Sammlung der Emanuel Hoffmann-Stiftung aufbewahrt, die heute Werke von mehr als 150 Künstlern umfasst. Die frühen Erwerbungen datieren aus den 1930er Jahren - Werke von Arp, Dalí, Delaunay, Klee, Ernst und den belgischen Expressionisten - und sind längst zu Klassikern der modernen Kunst geworden, die ihren festen Platz in der Kunstgeschichte einnehmen. Heute ist es Ziel der Stiftung, „Kunstwerke zu erwerben, die in die Zukunft weisen und in der Gegenwart noch kein breites Verständnis finden". Die Kunstwerke werden unter optimalen räumlichen und klimatischen Bedingungen gelagert, und Besucher, Studenten und Wissenschaftler können auf Anfrage einzelne Werke sehen. Die Architekten entschieden sich für ein „schweres" Gebäude im Gegensatz zu den leichtgewichtigen Bauten, die andernorts für eine solche Nutzung bevorzugt werden. Die massiven Wände und Böden des Gebäudes führen zu einer ausgeprägten thermischen Trägheit, das heißt, im Winter wird die Wärme zurückgehalten und im Sommer erwärmt sich das Gebäude nur langsam. Das 28 m hohe Schaulager verfügt über zwei Ausstellungsebenen, die einmal im Jahr für Ausstellungen – so 2005 für Jeff Wall - genutzt werden, und drei Lagerebenen. Die Ausstellungsfläche des Gebäudes bemisst sich auf 4300 m², die Lagerebenen auf 7244 m², wobei die einzelnen Lagereinheiten jeweils 32 m² umfassen. Einige Räume sind allerdings bis zu sechsmal so groß. 771 m² Fläche, auf denen Kunstwerke restauriert, konserviert und für den Transport vorbereitet werden können und 800 m² Verwaltungsbüros sind ebenfalls Teil des Projekts. Zwei großformatige LED-Schirme mit 44 m² sind die einzigen äußeren Indikatoren auf die Funktion des Gebäudes. Sie zeigen Bilder, die in Bezug zur Kunst und den jährlich stattfindenden, öffentlichen Ausstellungen stehen. Die glatten, weißen Wände und nackten Betonfußböden des Inneren stehen im Gegensatz zur rauen, mit Kieseln von der Baustelle angereicherten Verkleidung der Außenwände. Es handelt sich hier keineswegs um ein „warmes" Gebäude, das lediglich einfach und sparsam ausgestattet ist, sondern es setzt ein Zeichen für eine neue Beziehung zwischen Architektur und dem Umgang mit zeitgenössischer Kunst.

La Fondation Schaulager, en banlieue de Bâle, est un équipement de type nouveau consacré à la conservation d'œuvres d'art la Fondation Emanuel Hoffmann qui possède des œuvres de plus de 150 artistes. Ses premières acquisitions remontent aux années 1930 avec des œuvres d'Arp, Dalí, Delaunay, Klee, Ernst ou des expressionnistes belges, devenues depuis des classiques de l'art moderne. Aujourd'hui, la Fondation « a pour objectif d'acheter des œuvres d'art regardant vers le futur, même si elles ne sont pas encore comprises. » Les œuvres sont conservées dans des conditions optimales, les visiteurs ou chercheurs pouvant les voir sur demande. Les architectes ont choisi de créer un bâtiment « lourd » par opposition aux structures « légères » qui les ont rendues particulièrement célèbres. L'épaisseur des murs et des plateaux présente une très importante inertie thermique puisqu'ils retiennent la chaleur en hiver et ne se réchauffent que lentement en été. De 28 m de haut, la Fondation possède deux niveaux d'exposition (4300 m²), utilisés une fois par an pour des artistes comme Jeff Wall en 2005, et trois niveaux de réserves (7244 m²), chaque unité de stockage mesurant 32 m², mais certaines salles étant six fois plus vastes. 771 m² sont consacrés à des ateliers techniques et 800 m² aux bureaux administratifs. Deux importants écrans LED de 44 m² qui diffusent des images d'art contemporain constituent la seule indication extérieure de la fonction du bâtiment. Ils présentent des images sur l'art et l'exposition publique annuelle organisée dans les lieux. Les murs blancs lisses et les sols en béton brut de l'intérieur contrastent avec l'habillage brut de l'extérieur qui intègre des galets trouvés sur le chantier. Aménagé dans un esprit d'économie épurée, ce bâtiment n'est certainement pas convivial au sens courant du terme, mais instaure une relation nouvelle entre l'architecture et la conservation de l'art contemporain.

The external walls of the Schaulager were made from layers of concrete with pebbles extracted from the building's site during excavation. These layers of material also play an essential role in regulating the climate of the interior. In the plans to the right, the basement level is on the left, the ground floor in the middle and the first upper floor on the right.

Die Außenmauern des Schaulagers wurden aus Betonschichten errichtet, deren Oberfläche mit Kieseln aus der Baugrube angereichert wurde. Diese Materialschichten spielen auch eine wichtige Rolle für die Regulierung der Innentemperatur. Die Pläne zeigen das Untergeschoss (links) das Erdgeschoss (Mitte) und den ersten Stock (rechts).

Les murs extérieurs du Schaulager sont réalisés en couches de béton dans lequel ont été incorporés des cailloux extraits des fouilles de fondation. Ces couches de matériaux jouent un rôle essentiel dans la régulation thermique des volumes intérieurs. Sur les plans de droite, le niveau du sous-sol est à gauche, le rez-dechaussée au milieu et le premier étage à droite.

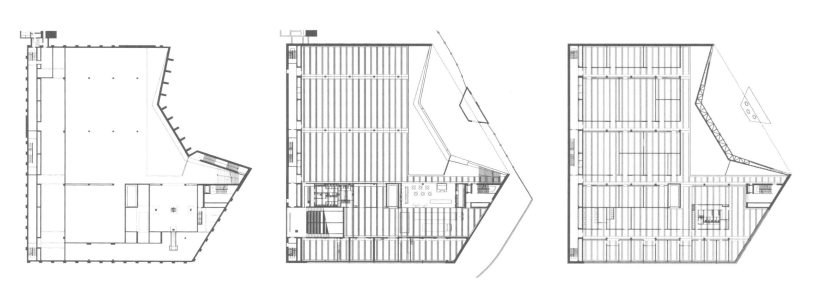

A void or full-height atrium located in the front part of the building permits visitors on the ground floor to see the lower-level exhibition area, as well as the storage floors above (right). On this page, the café and the upper storage level with its concrete floors and strict fluorescent lighting scheme.

Ein Hohlraum oder Atrium über die gesamte Höhe des Gebäudes ermöglicht Besuchern vom Erdgeschoss aus den Blick sowohl in die Ausstellungsbereiche im Untergeschoss als auch auf die Lagerebenen im oberen Bereich (rechts). Auf dieser Seite erkennt man das Café und die obere Lagerebene mit ihren Betonböden und dem strengen fluorseszierenden Beleuchtungsschema.

Le vide de l'atrium toute hauteur situé dans la partie avant du bâtiment permet aux visiteurs du rez-de-chaussée d'apercevoir l'espace d'exposition en sous-sol ainsi que les niveaux des réserves en haut (à droite). Sur cette page, le café et le niveau supérieur des réserves à sols de béton et rigoureux système d'éclairage fluorescent.

13

DAVIDE MACULLO

DAVIDE MACULLO, ARCHITETTO
Via Monte Boglia 7
6904 Lugano

Tel: +41 91 9 71 82 34
e-mail: davidemacullo@macullo.com
Web: www.macullo.com

DAVIDE MACULLO was born in Giornico, Ticino, in 1965. He studied at the Technical University in Lucerne and graduated in 1989 from the University of Applied Arts in Lugano. He has been a member of The Swiss Register of Architects and Engineers (REG A) since 1998. He worked in the office of Mario Botta in Lugano beginning in 1990, where he was assigned to the foreign projects of the architect. He has worked on numerous residential and reconversion projects in Switzerland and other countries, most recently: houses in Cadro, Ticino (2004); an apartment building in Davesco, Ticino (2004); lofts in an old factory in Carate, Italy (2004); an apartment building in Vimercate, Italy (2004); conference spaces for the Hotel Galaxy in Heraklion, Crete, Greece (2005); Elounda BB Spa in Crete, Greece (2005); a house in Lugano, Ticino (2005); an Alzheimer clinic in Como, Italy (2005); a house in Comano, Ticino (2005); and an apartment building in Carí, Ticino (2005).

HOUSE
GORDUNO
2002 - 03

FLOOR AREA: 150 m² internal space, 45 m² loggias
CLIENT: Alessandro and Paola Darold
COST: CHF 700 000

The site of this house is located at the edge of the old village of Gorduno. To the north and west, it faces the 1970s urban extension of the town, while the garden of a primary school is located to the south. To the west stands an older house owned by the client, and to the northwest is the urban extension of the village. As the architect says, "The peculiarity of the site and the wish of the client to have as much privacy as possible for the members of the family define the choice for this project: a large wall is placed to the north with an opening that frames an almost untouched view of nature, the dilatation of the interior spaces facing the new court-yard and the vertical shifting of the floors." Large balconies offer added living space. An excavated volume, partially covered with translucent elements, "generates a particular micro-climate," according to the architect. As he says, "Taking advantage of the seasonal position of the sun, its heat is collected through dark flooring in winter while it is protected in summer, offering a shadow covered in-between space."

Das Grundstück dieses Hauses liegt am Rand des alten Dorfes Gorduno. Nach Norden und Westen hin liegt es einer Stadterweiterung aus den 1970er Jahren gegenüber, während sich im Süden der Garten einer Grundschule befindet. Im Westen grenzt es an ein älteres Haus, das dem Auftraggeber gehört. Dem Architekten zufolge „waren für die Gestaltung dieses Projekts die Besonderheiten des Ortes und der Wunsch des Bauherren ausschlaggebend, die Privatsphäre seiner Familie weitestgehend zu schützen: Im Norden entstand eine hohe Mauer mit einer Öffnung, die einen Ausblick auf die nahezu unberührte Natur rahmt. Die Erweiterung der Innenräume führt zum neuen Innenhof und den vertikal verschobenen Geschossen." Großflächige Balkone bieten zusätzlichen Wohnraum. Ein z. T. mit lichtdurchlässigen Elementen verkleideter, ausgeschnittener Kubus erzeugt dem Architekten zufolge „ein ganz bestimmtes Mikroklima und nutzt je nach Jahreszeit die Sonneneinstrahlung. Im Winter wird hier die Wärme durch einen dunklen Fußbodenbelag gesammelt, während der Bereich im Sommer geschützt ist und eine schattige Zwischenzone bietet."

Le terrain sur lequel s'élève cette maison est situé en bordure du village ancien de Gorduno. Au nord et à l'ouest, il donne sur l'extension urbaine des années 1970 et à l'ouest touche à une maison ancienne également propriété du client. Le jardin d'une école primaire fait face au sud. Pour Macullo : « La particularité du site et le souhait du client d'assurer le maximum d'intimité aux membres de sa famille a déterminé les choix de ce projet : le grand mur implanté au nord dans lequel une ouverture cadre la vue sur une nature presque intacte, la dilatation des espaces intérieurs face à la nouvelle cour et le décalage vertical des niveaux. » Les grands balcons élargissent l'espace habitable. Un volume excavé, en partie recouvert d'éléments transparents « génère un microclimat particulier ... il bénéficie du mouvement du soleil en fonction des saisons. La chaleur est collectée par les sols sombres en hiver mais il en est protégé en été, pour offrir un espace entre-deux ombragé ».

Strong massing and an alternation of opaque and more open surfaces characterize the house, almost rendering its structure incomprehensible from the exterior. A sketch by the architect brings to mind the style of Mario Botta.

Eine prägnante Gliederung und der Wechsel zwischen opaken und durchlässigeren Oberflächen kennzeichnen das Haus, dessen Aufbau sich von außen nicht erschließt. Eine Skizze des Architekten lässt an den Stil Mario Bottas denken.

Une puissante répartition des masses et l'alternance de surfaces opaques ou plus ouvertes caractérisent cette maison, dont la structure est presque incompréhensible, vue de l'extérieur. Le croquis de l'architecte évoque le style de Mario Botta.

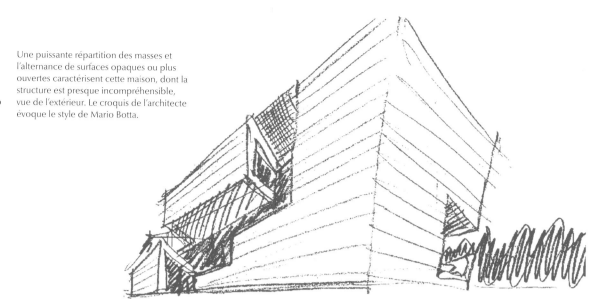

The orchestration of volumes and the degrees of opacity seen on the exterior of the house are continued within, where light plays a significant role.

Die außen sichtbare Anordnung der Volumina und der wechselnde Grad der Lichtdurchlässigkeit setzen sich im Inneren fort, wo Licht eine entscheidende Rolle spielt.

L'orchestration des volumes et des degrés d'opacité de la façade de la maison se retrouve à l'intérieur où la lumière joue un rôle significatif.

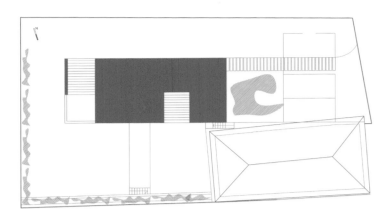

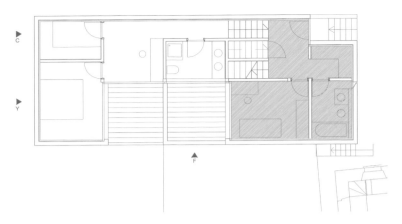

The architect uses metal window frames, stairs, lighting, and internal walls to create a symphonic effect of geometric variations, while working within the confines of a regular, rectangular plan containing notched openings.

Der Architekt verwendet Fensterrahmen, Treppen, Beleuchtung und Innenwände aus Metall, um eine Sinfonie aus geometrischen Varianten zu erzeugen, und arbeitet gleichzeitig innerhalb des regelmäßigen, rechtwinkligen Grundrisses mit eingekerbten Öffnungen.

Les architectes ont fait appel à des huisseries, escaliers, cloisonnements et systèmes d'éclairage en métal pour créer une symphonie d'effets de variations géométriques dans les limites d'un plan rectangulaire régulier à ouvertures découpées.

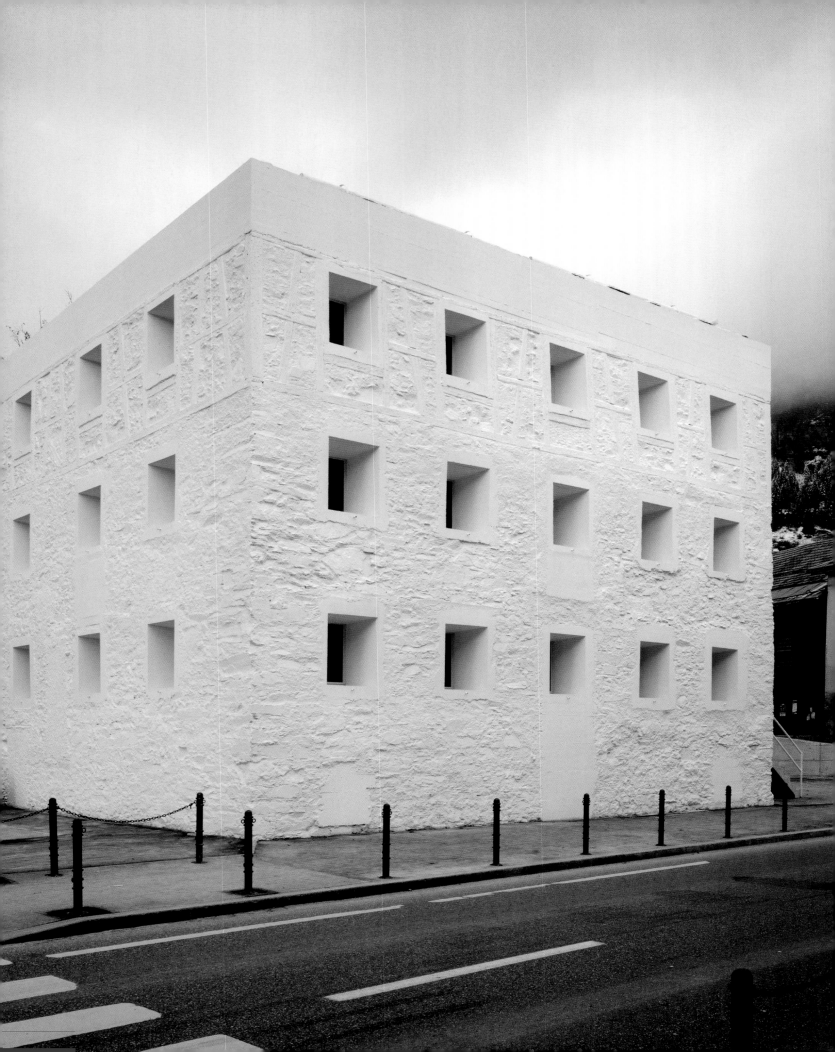

14

VALERIO OLGIATI

VALERIO OLGIATI
Hafnerstrasse 60
8005 Zurich

Tel: +41 14 40 51 61
Fax: +41 14 40 51 62
e-mail: mail@olgiati.net
Web: www.oligati.net

VALERIO OLGIATI was born in Chur in 1958. He studied architecture at the ETH in Zurich. In 1986 he created his own architectural office in Zurich. From 1993 to 1995, he collaborated with Frank Escher in Los Angeles. Escher is a specialist in the work of John Lautner. In 1994, he was visiting professor at the University of Applied Sciences in Stuttgart, and since 1998 he has taught at the ETH Zurich and served as guest lecturer at the Architectural Association (AA) in London. Since 2001, he has been a full professor at the Accademia di architettura at the Università della Svizzera Italiana in Mendrisio. He has built a number of private homes and participated in competitions, such as that for the National Palace Museum, Taiwan (2004, finalist), or the Learning Center of the EPFL in Lausanne. Two of the projects featured here, the Peak Gornergrat and the University of Lucerne, were winning 2003 competition entries.

YELLOW HOUSE
FLIMS
1999

FLOOR AREA: 400 m²
CLIENT: Community of Flims
COST: CHF 1 500 000

Valerio Olgiati's father, Rudolph (1910–95), made an agreement with the Parish of Flims in the Graubunden region to renovate a house that had been unoccupied for 20 years. Because it had been painted yellow, it took on the name of "Yellow House," which it has retained despite its change of color. The purpose of the renovation was to display a large collection of cultural artifacts donated by the elder Olgiatis, and he stipulated that the house should be painted white and that the roof should be finished with stone slabs. As Valerio Olgiati writes, "After my father's death the Parish decided to turn it into an exhibition space. Since the intricate internal structure of the dwelling house was not suitable for the new purpose, we had to take rigorous action. The building was completely gutted; the interior was rebuilt in solid wood, the old external plasterwork was removed to reveal the natural stone walls, the roof was removed and replaced with randomly shaped stone slabs. Windows and openings that were no longer needed were filled in; others were fitted with new concrete reveals cast in situ. Finally the new interior wood structure, the existing external stone walls and the new slab-stone roof were all painted white." Continuing his own description in somewhat more poetic terms, Valerio Olgiati concludes, "The final coat of white, the finest of lime-washes, forms the outermost skin of the building. It conceals anything left unfinished. At the same time it points to a certain contradiction. The white lime-wash seems to turn the childlike archaism and animal substance of this structure into an abstract thought—which for its part gives the house itself the appearance of a 'vision.'"

Valerio Olgiatis Vater Rudolph (1910–95) traf mit der Gemeinde Flims im Kanton Graubünden die Vereinbarung, ein seit 20 Jahren unbewohntes Haus zu renovieren. Wegen seines gelben Anstrichs wurde es „Gelbes Haus" genannt, ein Name, den es ungeachtet des Farbwechsels beibehielt. Zweck der Renovierung war es, hier eine Kulturgüter-Sammlung auszustellen, die Olgiatis Vater der Gemeinde vermacht hatte. Er machte zur Bedingung, dass das Haus weiß verputzt und das Dach mit Steinplatten gedeckt werden sollte. Valerio Olgiati schreibt dazu: „Nach dem Tod meines Vaters beschloss die Gemeinde, das Haus zu einem Ausstellungsgebäude umzugestalten. Da die diffizile innere Aufteilung des Wohnhauses für den neuen Zweck nicht geeignet war, mussten wir konsequent vorgehen. Das Gebäude wurde komplett entkernt, das Innere mit Massivholz wieder aufgebaut und der alte Außenputz entfernt, wodurch die ursprünglichen Steinmauern zum Vorschein kamen. Auch das Dach wurde entfernt und durch unregelmäßig geformte Steinplatten ersetzt. Nicht mehr benutzte Fenster und Öffnungen wurden ausgefacht, andere mit in situ gegossenen, neuen Betonlaibungen versehen. Schließlich wurden der neue Innenausbau aus Holz, die bestehenden, steinernen Außenmauern sowie das neue Steinplattendach weiß gestrichen." Valerio Olgiati setzt seine Beschreibung in etwas poetischerer Sprache fort und schließt: „Der abschließende weiße Anstrich aus feinster Tünche bildet die Außenhaut des Gebäudes. Sie verbirgt alles Unfertige. Gleichzeitig verweist sie auf einen bestimmten Widerspruch. Die weiße Tünche scheint den kindlichen Archaismus und die animalische Substanz dieses Gebäudes in einen abstrakten Gedanken zu verwandeln – der wiederum das Haus selbst wie eine ‚Vision' erscheinen lässt."

Le père de Valerio Olgiati, Rudolph (1910–95), avait signé un accord avec la paroisse de Flims dans le canton des Grisons pour rénover une maison inoccupée pendant vingt ans et en faire un lieu de présentation de sa vaste collection d'artefacts culturels offerte à la ville. Surnommée « la Maison jaune » pour la couleur de sa façade, elle a conservé ce nom en dépit de son changement de teinte. Il était stipulé qu'elle devait être peinte en blanc, et la charpente recouverte de lauzes. Comme l'explique Valerio Olgiati : « Après la mort de mon père, la paroisse décida de transformer le bâtiment en espace d'exposition. Comme la structure interne complexe de cette maison d'habitation n'était pas adaptée à sa nouvelle fonction, des décisions drastiques étaient à prendre. L'ensemble fut entièrement évidé, l'intérieur reconstruit en bois massif, l'habillage de plâtre des façades supprimé pour mettre au jour la pierre des murs. La couverture fut démontée et remplacée par des lauzes de forme irrégulière. Les fenêtres et ouvertures inutiles furent bouchées, d'autres renforcées de béton coulé sur place. Finalement, la nouvelle structure intérieure en bois, les murs de pierre existants et le nouveau toit de lauzes furent peints en blanc. » Poursuivant sa description en termes un peu moins concrets, Olgiati conclut : « La couche finale de blanc, ce badigeon de chaux d'une très grande finesse, constitue la peau extérieure du bâtiment. Il cache tout ce qui a été laissé non achevé. En même temps, il met le doigt sur une certaine contradiction. Il semble transformer l'archaïsme enfantin et la substance animale de cette construction en un concept abstrait qui donne à la maison elle-même l'apparence d'une « vision ».

Working with the existing architecture, but stripping it to its bare essentials, the architect succeeded in giving an unexpected feeling of modernity to the old building, at the same time revealing its structure and the texture of its walls.

Dem Architekten gelang es, dem vorhandenen, völlig entkernten Gebäude eine überraschend moderne Anmutung zu verleihen und dabei seinen Aufbau und das Mauerwerk freizulegen.

Travaillant sur l'architecture existante, mais en la réduisant à l'essentiel, l'architecte a réussi à conférer un sentiment inattendu de modernité au bâtiment ancien, tout en révélant sa structure et la texture de ses murs.

PEAK GORNERGRAT ZERMATT 2003-

FLOOR AREA: 420 m²
CLIENT: GGB (Gornergrat-Monte-Rosa-Bahnen),
MGH (Matterhorn Group)
COST: CHF 8,2 million

This unusual 420 m² concrete structure will be built opposite the Matterhorn at an altitude of 3100 meters. Its purpose will be to show images of the mountain throughout the year on a circular screen, 20 meters in diameter. Located on the main, upper level of the structure, the projection room will be reached by a ramp. Neither heated nor insulated, the Peak Gornergrat will have a round hole in the roof of the projection room, allowing "virtual reality to mingle with the real situation," as the architect says. Box-like forms are relatively common in contemporary Swiss architecture, but the nature and location of this design make it exceptional. Olgiati writes: "Ornamented with a characteristic, scale-less, large structure, the new building will elucidate the dimensions of this extraordinary landscape."

Dieser außergewöhnliche, 420 m² umfassende Betonbau soll in einer Höhe von 3100 m gegenüber dem Matterhorn errichtet werden. In seinem Inneren ist geplant, auf einer runden Leinwand mit einem Durchmesser von 20 m Bilder des Berges vorzuführen. Der auf der oberen Hauptebene des Gebäudes gelegene Projektionsraum wird über eine Rampe erreichbar sein. Ohne Heizung oder Isolierung wird das Dach des Projektionsraums eine runde Öffnung aufweisen, die es, dem Architekten zufolge, zulässt, „dass sich virtuelle Realität und reale Situation vermischen". Während Kastenformen in der zeitgenössischen schweizerischen Architektur relativ häufig vorkommen, machen Charakter und Standort dieses Projekt zu einer Ausnahme. Olgiati schreibt dazu: „Dank seiner prägnanten, maß-stabslosen, großen Struktur wird das neue Gebäude die Dimensionen dieser außerordentlichen Landschaft verdeutlichen."

Cette étrange construction en béton de 420 m² sera édifiée face au Matterhorn à 3100 mètres d'altitude. Son objectif est de présenter tout au long de l'année des images de la célèbre montagne sur un écran circulaire de 20 m de diamètre. Située à l'étage principal – le plus élevé –, la salle de projection sera accessible par une rampe. Ni chauffée, ni même isolée du froid, elle présentera une ouverture circulaire en toiture permettant « à la réalité virtuelle de se fondre avec la situation réelle », comme l'explique l'architecte. Si la forme de boîte est assez courante dans l'architecture suisse contemporaine, la nature et la situation de ce projet en font une exception. Pour Olgiati : « Pourvu d'une structure hors d'échelle originale, le nouveau bâtiment élucidera les dimensions de cet extraordinaire paysage. »

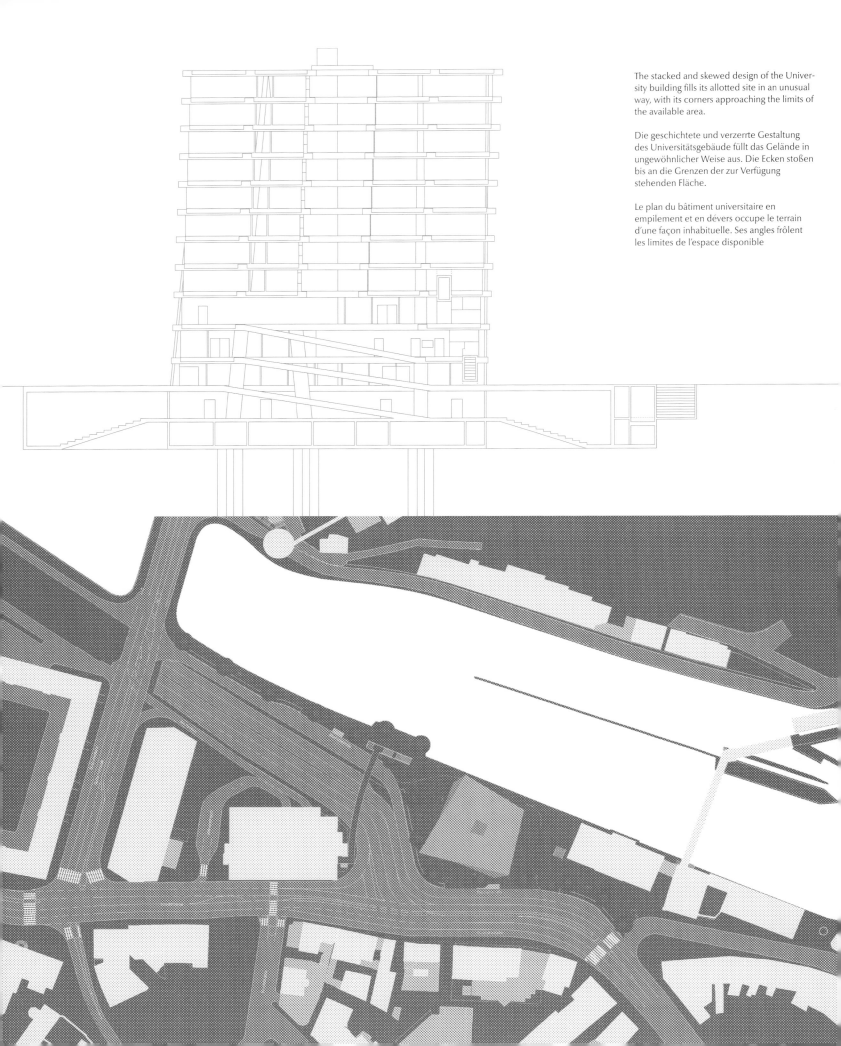

The stacked and skewed design of the University building fills its allotted site in an unusual way, with its corners approaching the limits of the available area.

Die geschichtete und verzerrte Gestaltung des Universitätsgebäude füllt das Gelände in ungewöhnlicher Weise aus. Die Ecken stoßen bis an die Grenzen der zur Verfügung stehenden Fläche.

Le plan du bâtiment universitaire en empilement et en dévers occupe le terrain d'une façon inhabituelle. Ses angles frôlent les limites de l'espace disponible

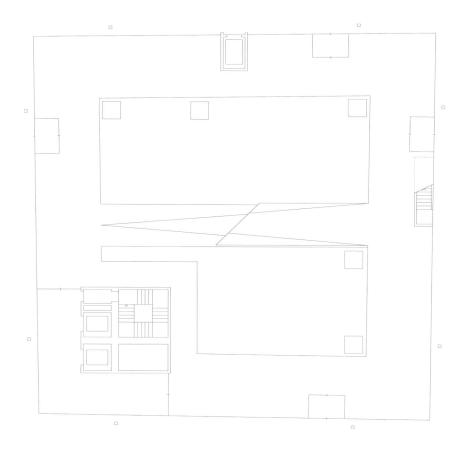

Plans of the ground floor (above) and the ninth floor (below) show the irregularity of the structure, as though a relatively straightforward, square design had been twisted and deformed by the architect.

Die Pläne des Erdgeschosses (oben) und des neunten Stockwerks (unten) zeigen die Unregelmäßigkeit der Aufteilung unter dem Eindruck, als ob ein ursprünglich gradliniger und rechteckiger Entwurf von dem Architekten gedreht und verformt worden sei.

Plans du rez-de-chaussée (en haut) et du neuvième niveau (en bas), montrant l'irrégularité obtenue par l'architecte par la déformation et la torsion d'un quasi-carré.

15

RENZO
PIANO

**RENZO PIANO
BUILDING WORKSHOP**
34, rue des Archives
75004 Paris

Tel: +33 1 44 61 49 00
Fax: +33 1 42 78 01 98
e-mail: info@rpbw.com
Web: www.rpbw.com

RENZO PIANO was born in 1937 in Genoa, Italy. He studied at the University of Florence, and at the Polytechnic Institute, Milan (1964). He formed his own practice (Studio Piano) in 1965, then associated with Richard Rogers (Piano & Rogers, 1971–78). Piano completed the Center Pompidou in Paris in 1977. From 1978 to 1980, he worked with Peter Rice (Piano & Rice Associates). Piano received the RIBA Gold Medal in 1989. He created the Renzo Piano Building Workshop in 1981 in Genoa and Paris. His built work includes: the Menil Collection Museum, Houston, Texas (1981–86); the San Nicola Stadium, Bari, Italy (1987–90); 1989 extension for the IRCAM, Paris; the renovation of Lingotto complex, Turin; Mercedes-Benz Center, Stuttgart (1992–96); Kansai International Airport Terminal, Osaka, Japan (1988–94). Recent work includes: Cité Internationale de Lyon, Lyon, France (1985–96); Jean-Marie Tjibaou Cultural Center, New Caledonia (1994–98); the Padre Pio Pilgrimage Church, San Giovanni Rotondo, Foggia, Italy (1995–2004); Reconstruction of a section of Potsdamer Platz, Berlin (1996–2000); Beyeler Foundation Museum, Riehen, Basel (1994–97); Parma Auditorium, Parma, Italy (1997–2001); Maison Hermès, Tokyo, Japan (1998–2001); and the Rome Auditorium, Rome, Italy (1994–2002). Current projects include: New York Times Tower, New York; Morgan Library, New York; Whitney Museum of American Art, New York; Woodruff Arts Center Expansion, Atlanta, Georgia; London Bridge Tower, London; California Academy of Sciences, San Francisco; and Chicago Art Institute Expansion, Chicago.

PAUL KLEE CENTER
BERN
1999 - 2005

FLOOR AREA: Klee Exhibition 1650 m² ;
temporary exhibitions 800 m² ; gross total area 16 000 m² ;
landscaped area 60 000 m²
CLIENT: Maurice E. and Martha Müller Foundation, Berne
COST: CHF 71 million (building)

The site of the new Paul Klee Center is outside Bern in a landscape of gently rolling hills, with the Alps in the distance and close to the artist's tomb. It was this topography that inspired the design of the museum itself, although the site has been considerably altered due to nearby roads. Intended to house 40 % of the 10 000 known works of the German artist, who spent much of his life in Switzerland, the structure is integrated into three artificial hills. The first of these hills contains a 300-seat auditorium and a museum for children. The middle hill contains the main exhibition space with space for temporary shows below ground. The final volume contains works not on public display and a center for the study of Klee's work. Due to the sensitivity to light of many of the artist's works, overhead natural light is not really part of this scheme, and part of the roof area will be covered with vegetation, emphasizing its symbiosis with the landscape. That said, Piano has pierced the roof at various points to bring in daylight, where the conservation of the works permits. The arches forming the volumes of the complex are clearly inspired by naval construction. As Piano says, the shape of a boat is not dictated by any real concerns of geometry, but rather by the rules of movement through water.

Das Gelände des neuen Zentrum Paul Klee liegt außerhalb von Bern; nahe dem Schlosshaldenfriedhof mit dem Grab des Künstlers. Die sanfte Hügellandschaft mit den Alpen in der Ferne lieferte die Anregung zur architektonischen Gestaltung des Museums, wenngleich das Gelände wegen nahe gelegener Straßen beträchtlich verändert wurde. Die Einrichtung, in der 40 % der etwa 10 000 bekannten Werke des Schweizer Künstlers untergebracht werden, ist in drei aufgeschüttete Hügel eingebettet. In dem ersten dieser Hügel finden ein Auditorium mit 300 Sitzplätzen sowie ein Kindermuseum Platz. Der mittlere Hügel enthält die Hauptausstellungsfläche mit Raum für Wechselausstellungen im Souterrain. Im dritten Baukörper sind nicht öffentlich zugängliche Werke und ein Zentrum für die wissenschaftliche Forschung über Paul Klee untergebracht. Wegen der hohen Lich-

tempfindlichkeit vieler Werke des Künstlers spielte von oben einfallendes Tageslicht in der Planung kaum eine Rolle. Ein Teil des Daches wird begrünt, um die Symbiose mit der Landschaft zu unterstreichen. Dennoch durchbrach Piano an verschiedenen Punkten die Dachfläche, um, wo es die konservatorischen Rücksichten auf das Werk gestatten, Tageslicht einzulassen. Die Wellenformen der Anlage sind offensichtlich vom Schiffsbau inspiriert. Wie Piano es ausdrückt, „wird die Form eines Bootes nicht wirklich von geometrischen Überlegungen bestimmt, sondern von den Gesetzen der Bewegung im Wasser."

Le site du nouveau Centre Paul Klee est un terrain voisin de la tombe de l'artiste non loin de Berne, au milieu d'un paysage de petites collines dominé par les Alpes dans le lointain. Cette topographie a inspiré la conception du musée, bien que le site ait été considérablement altéré par la présence de routes. Conçue pour abriter 40 % des 10 000 œuvres répertoriées de l'artiste allemand qui passa la plus grande partie de sa vie en Suisse, cette construction se compose de trois collines artificielles. La première contient un auditorium de 300 places et un musée pour les enfants. L'élément central abrite le principal espace d'exposition, dont des salles d'expositions temporaires en sous-sol. Le dernier volume est destiné aux œuvres qui ne sont pas présentées et à un centre pour l'étude de l'œuvre de l'artiste. Les travaux de celui-ci étant particulièrement sensibles à la lumière, l'éclairage zénithal n'était pas souhaité et une partie de la toiture sera végétalisée, renforçant du même coup la symbiose avec le paysage. Ceci étant, Piano a cependant percé cette couverture en différents points pour amener la lumière du jour là où la conservation des œuvres le permet. Les arches constituant ces « collines » s'inspirent à l'évidence de la construction navale. Comme le dit l'architecte, la forme d'un bateau n'est pas dictée par un quelconque souci de géométrie, mais par les règles du déplacement dans l'eau.

The undulating structure of the museum allows for a dynamic variation of ceiling heights and views of the exterior. Wood alternates with metal and glass, while a sense of lightness pervades the entire building.

Der geschwungene Grundriss des Museums erlaubt eine dynamische Variation der Deckenhöhen und Ausblicke nach draußen. Holz wird im Wechsel mit Metall und Glas verwendet, und der gesamte Bau ist von einem Gefühl der Leichtigkeit durchdrungen.

La forte ondulation du bâtiment permet des variations dynamiques des hauteurs de plafonds et des perspectives vers l'extérieur. Le bois alterne avec le verre et le métal dans des volumes placés sous le signe de la légèreté.

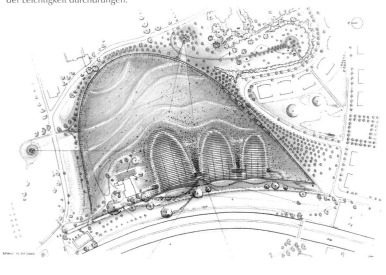

Exhibition galleries provide ample space to the mostly small works, while lighting must be carefully controlled in order to conserve the works on paper, for example.

Die Ausstellungsgalerien bieten den zumeist kleinformatigen Werken reichlich Raum. Der Lichteinfall wird sorgfältig gesteuert, um beispielsweise die Arbeiten auf Papier zu schützen.

Les galeries d'exposition assurent aux œuvres, pour la plupart de petites dimensions, un ample espace. L'éclairage doit être soigneusement contrôlé, en particulier pour la conservation des œuvres sur papier.

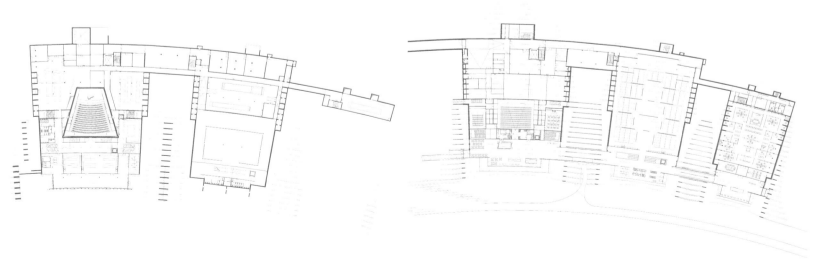

16

PHILIPPE RAHM

PHILIPPE RAHM ARCHITECTES
12, rue Chabanais
75002 Paris

Tel: +33 14 9 26 91 55
e-mail: contact@low-architecture.com
Web: www.philipperahm.com

PHILIPPE RAHM was born in 1967 and studied architecture at the EPFL in Lausanne and the ETH in Zurich. He created the firm Décosterd & Rahm associés with Gilles Décosterd in 1995 in Lausanne. They won a number of competitions in Switzerland and participated in numerous exhibitions in Europe and the United States and later in Japan. Amongst these were the 2003 Biennal de Valencia, Spain, and Archilab, Orléans, France, 2000. Décosterd & Rahm represented Switzerland in the 2002 Venice Architecture Biennale, and received the Swiss Federal Art Prize in 2003. They worked on an atelier-residence for the artist Fabrice Hybert in the Vendée region of France, and on a project for a park in San Sebastián, Spain, with the landscape architects Gilles Clément and Joseph Andeuza. Rahm and Déscosterd ceased direct collaboration in 2005 and Philippe Rahm created his own firm in Paris.

HORMONORIUM SWISS PAVILION VENICE 2002

CLIENT: Swiss Confederation
COST: not disclosed

As official representatives of Switzerland at the 2002 Venice Architecture Biennale, Philippe Rahm and his partner Gilles Décosterd surprised a number of visitors by proposing a pavilion that had as much to do with physiology as it did with architecture in the more traditional sense. As they explained, "The Hormonorium is a proposal for the design of a new public space. It is based on the disappearance of the physical boundaries between space and the organism, as revealed by biology and the neurosciences. Going beyond visual and metric mediation, establishing a continuity between the living and the non-living, the Hormonorium opens up to the invisible, to electromagnetic and biological determinations." And yet the Hormonorium was quite typical of the work of this young Swiss firm. Rather than a "normal" floor, the architects created "a dazzling, luminous false floor made of Plexiglas to allow the passage of UV light. It is made up of 528 florescent tubes, which emit a white light that reproduces the solar spectrum, with UV-A and UV-B. ... This very bright light of between 5000 and 10 000 lux stimulates the retina, which transmits information to the pineal gland that causes a decrease in melatonin secretion. By so lowering the level of this hormone in the body, this environment allows us to experience a decrease in fatigue, a probable increase in sexual desire, and regulation of our mood." They also lowered the oxygen level in the pavilion from the normal 21% to 14.5%, or that found at an altitude of about 3000 meters in the Swiss mountains. As they explained, "This oxygen-rarefied space causes slight hypoxia, which may initially be manifested by clinical states such as confusion, disorientation or bizarre behavior, but also a slight euphoria due to endorphin production. ... Decreasing the oxygen level will therefore have a stimulating effect that may improve the body's physical capabilities by up to 10 %."

Als offizielle Vertreter der Schweiz bei der Architekturbiennale 2002 in Venedig verblüfften Philippe Rahm und Gilles Décosterd die Besucher mit einem Pavillon, der ebensoviel mit Physiologie wie mit Architektur im herkömmlichen Sinn zu tun hatte. Sie beschrieben ihr Projekt so: „Das Hormonorium ist ein Vorschlag für die Gestaltung einer neuen Art von öffentlichem Raum. Es basiert auf dem Verschwinden der physischen Grenzen zwischen Raum und Organismus sowie auf Erkenntnissen aus Biologie und Neurowissenschaften. Das Hormonorium geht über visuelle und metrische Vermittlung hinaus und stellt eine Kontinuität zwischen Belebtem und Nichtbelebtem her. Es öffnet sich dem Unsichtbaren, den elektromagnetischen und biologischen Determinanten." Und doch war das Hormonorium recht bezeichnend für die Arbeit dieser jungen Schweizer Architekten. Anstelle eines „normalen" Fußbodens schufen sie „einen gleißend hellen, falschen Boden aus Plexiglas, der UV Strahlen durchdringen lässt. Er besteht aus 528 Leuchtstoffröhren, die ein weißes Licht abgeben, das mit UV-A- und UV-B-Strahlen dem Spektrum der Sonne entspricht. ... Dieses äußerst helle Licht von 5000 bis 10 000 Lux stimuliert die Netzhaut, die Informationen an die Zirbeldrüse übermittelt, die ihrerseits die Absonderung von Melatonin vermindert. Indem so der Pegel dieses Hormons im Körper gesenkt wird, erleben wir in dieser Umgebung verminderte Müdigkeit, vermutlich gesteigerte sexuelle Lust sowie die Regulierung unserer Stimmungen." Darüber hinaus senkten sie im Pavillon den normalen Sauerstoffgehalt der Luft von 21 auf 14,5 % und damit auf den in 3000 m Höhe in den Schweizer Bergen existierenden Wert ab. Dazu heißt es: „Die in diesem Raum vorhandene, dünne Luft verursacht einen leichten Sauerstoffmangel im Blut, der sich anfangs durch klinische Zustände wie Verwirrung, Desorientierung oder absonderliches Verhalten äußern kann, aufgrund der Endorphinausschüttung aber auch durch leichte Euphorie. ... Das Senken des Sauerstoffgehalts hat demzufolge eine belebende Wirkung, die die physischen Fähigkeiten des Körpers um bis zu 10 % steigern kann."

Représentants officiels de la Suisse lors de la Biennale d'architecture de Venise en 2002, Philip Rahm et son associé Gilles Décosterd ont surpris un certain nombre de visiteurs en proposant un pavillon qui traitait autant de physiologie que d'architecture au sens traditionnel. Ils expliquent : « L'Hormonorium est une proposition de concept de nouvel espace public. Il repose sur la disparition des frontières physiques entre l'espace et l'organisme comme l'enseignent la biologie et les neurosciences. Allant au-delà des médiations visuelles et métriques, établissant une continuité entre le vivant et le non-vivant, il s'ouvre à l'invisible et aux déterminants biologiques et électromagnétiques. » Cette réalisation est assez caractéristique du travail de cette jeune agence suisse. Plutôt qu'un sol « normal », les architectes ont créé un « sol étincelant, un faux sol lumineux fait de plexiglas qui permet le passage des ultraviolets et composé de 528 tubes fluorescents qui émettent une lumière reproduisant le spectre solaire. ... Ce flux lumineux puissant – entre 5000 et 10 000 lux – stimule la rétine qui transmet l'information à la glande pinéale provoquant une diminution de la sécrétion de mélatonine. En réduisant le niveau de cette hormone dans le corps, l'environnement nous permet d'expérimenter une diminution de la fatigue, une augmentation probable du désir sexuel, et une régulation de notre humeur. Ils ont également diminué le niveau d'oxygène dans le pavillon, de 21 à 14,5 %, état que l'on trouve habituellement à 3000 mètres d'altitude dans les montagnes suisses. » Cet espace à oxygène raréfié provoque une légère hypoxie, qui peut au départ se manifester par des états cliniques comme la confusion, la désorientation ou un comportement bizarre, mais également une légère euphorie due à la production d'endorphine. Après dix minutes environ, on constate une augmentation mesurable ‹ naturelle › des niveaux d'érythropoïétine (EPO) et d'hématocrite, ainsi que le renforcement des systèmes cardiovasculaires et respiratoires. L'érythropoïétine est produite par les reins. Cette hormone protéine atteint la moelle des os où elle stimule la production de cellules rouges sanguines accroissant ainsi la fourniture d'oxygène aux muscles. En baissant le niveau d'oxygène, on obtient ainsi un effet stimulant qui peut améliorer les capacités physiques du corps de jusqu'à 10 %. »

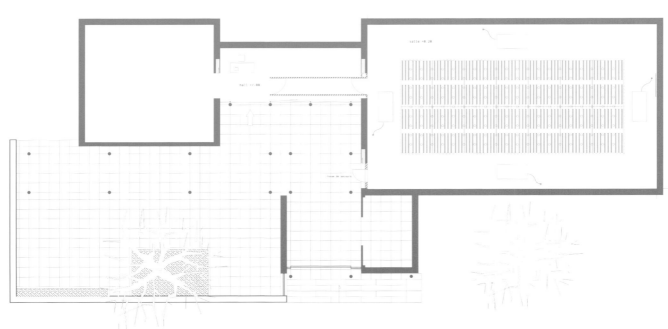

Using the main room of the Swiss Pavilion in the Giardini in Venice, the architect created a rectangular floor of light in the middle of the room. As Rahm wrote, "After about ten minutes, there is a measurable 'natural' increase in erythropoietin (EPO) and hematocrit levels, as well as a strengthening of the cardiovascular and respiratory systems."

Die Architekten nutzten den Hauptraum des Schweizer Pavillons in den venezianischen Giardini, um in dessen Zentrum eine rechteckige Lichtfläche zu schaffen. Rahm schrieb dazu: „Nach etwa zehn Minuten tritt eine messbare, natürliche Erhöhung der Pegel von Erythropoietin (EPO) und Haematokrit auf, die eine Stärkung des Herz-Kreislaufsystems und der Atmung zur Folge hat."

Au centre de la salle principale du pavillon suisse des Giardini à Venise, Rahm a créé un sol rectangulaire lumineux. Comme il l'explique : « Après dix minutes environ, on constate une augmentation mesurable ‹ naturelle › des taux d'érythropoïétine (EPO) et d'hématocrites ainsi qu'une action sur les systèmes respiratoires et cardio-vasculaires. »

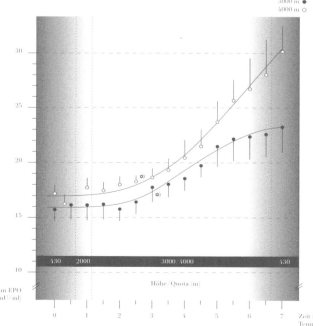

17

PETER ZUMTHOR

PETER ZUMTHOR
Süsswinkel 20
7023 Haldenstein

Tel: +41 81 3 54 92 92
Fax: +41 81 3 54 92 93
e-mail: arch@zumthor.ch

PETER ZUMTHOR was born in 1943 in Basel. In 1958, he worked as an apprentice carpenter. He graduated from the Basel School of Design in 1963 and then attended the Pratt Institute in New York, studying architecture and design. From 1968 to 1977, he worked as an architect for the preservation of historic monuments in the Graubünden region of Switzerland. He served as tutor at the University of Zurich in 1978 and created his own firm in the town of Haldenstein, also in Graubünden, in 1979. He has taught at SciArc in Santa Monica, the Technical University of Munich, Tulane University in New Orleans, and at the Academy of Architecture in Mendrisio, beginning in 1996. His major buildings include the Thermal Baths in Vals, Switzerland (1996); the Kunsthalle in Bregenz, Austria (1997), and the Swiss Pavilion at the EXPO 2000, Hanover.

THERMAL BATHS
VALS
1990 - 96

FLOOR AREA: 1300 m²
CLIENT: Hotel & Thermalbad AG (Hoteba),
Community of Vals
COST: not disclosed

Located in the Graubünden region of Switzerland, Vals is rather difficult to get to, located in a narrow valley at an altitude of 1200 meters above sea level. The existence of a hot spring there with water at a temperature of 30° centigrade was the reason for the creation of a bathing facility, beginning in 1990. Zumthor describes his building as "a geometric cave system" and revels in the fact that it appears to be much older than the neighboring modernist hotel. Entirely clad in Vals gneiss, quarried a kilometer further up the valley, the structure appears to be monolithic in an almost geological sense, and its openings and baths are clearly designed to take advantage of the spectacular natural setting, with framed views of the Alps. In particular in the large outdoor pool. There is something about the Vals baths that harkens back to the earliest times, perhaps those of Swiss mountain tradition, or perhaps something even older. As Zumthor wrote, "Mountain, stone, water, building in stone, building with stone, building into the mountain, building out of the mountain—our attempts to give this chain of words an architectural interpretation, to translate into architecture its meanings and sensuousness, guided our design for the building and step by step gave it form."

Das im Kanton Graubünden in einem engen Tal in 1200 m Höhe gelegene Vals ist nicht eben leicht erreichbar. Da es dort eine heiße Quelle mit einer Temperatur von 30° Celsius gibt, entschloss man sich 1990 zum Bau einer Therme. Zumthor beschreibt seinen Bau als „ein geometrisches System von Höhlen" und hat seine Freude an dem Umstand, dass er viel älter erscheint als das benachbarte modernistische Hotel. Zur Gänze mit heimischem Gneis verkleidet, der einen Kilometer talaufwärts abgebaut wird, erscheint der Bau im geologischen Sinn fast monolithisch. Die Öffnungen und Bäder sind offenkundig im Hinblick auf die spektakuläre natürliche Umgebung gestaltet und gestatten, insbesondere vom großen Außenbe-

cken, Ausblicke auf die Alpen. Etwas an der Felsentherme in Vals gemahnt an früheste Zeiten, vielleicht an Schweizer Bergtraditionen oder vielleicht an etwas, das noch viel weiter in der Vergangenheit liegt. Zumthor schrieb dazu: „Berg, Stein, Wasser – Bauen im Stein, Bauen mit Stein, in den Berg hineinbauen, aus dem Berg herausbauen, im Berg drinnen sein –, wie lassen sich die Bedeutungen und die Sinnlichkeit, die in der Verbindung dieser Wörter stecken, in Architektur umsetzen? Entlang dieser Fragestellungen haben wir das Bauwerk entworfen, hat es Schritt für Schritt Gestalt angenommen."

Vals est une station thermale des Grisons située à 1200 mètres d'altitude dans une vallée étroite d'accès assez difficile. C'est la présence d'une source d'eau chaude à 30° qui explique la construction de ces thermes à partir de 1990. Zumthor décrit son projet comme « un système géométrique de grottes » et aime faire remarquer que son œuvre semble bien moins récente que l'hôtel moderniste voisin. Entièrement habillée de gneiss de Vals provenant d'une carrière distante d'un kilomètre, la construction semble monolithique dans un sens quasi géologique, ses ouvertures et ses bains sont orientés pour bénéficier au maximum du spectaculaire environnement naturel à travers des vues cadrées sur les Alpes, en particulier à partir du vaste bassin extérieur. Quelque chose semble rappeler ici des temps très anciens, peut-être ceux de traditions montagnardes suisses, voire plus anciennes encore. Pour Zumthor : « Montagne, pierre, eau, construction en pierre, construction dans les montagnes, construction à partir des montagnes, nous avons tenté de donner à cette chaîne de mots une interprétation architecturale, de traduire en architecture son sens et sa sensualité, ce qui a guidé notre conception et lui a donné pas à pas sa forme. »

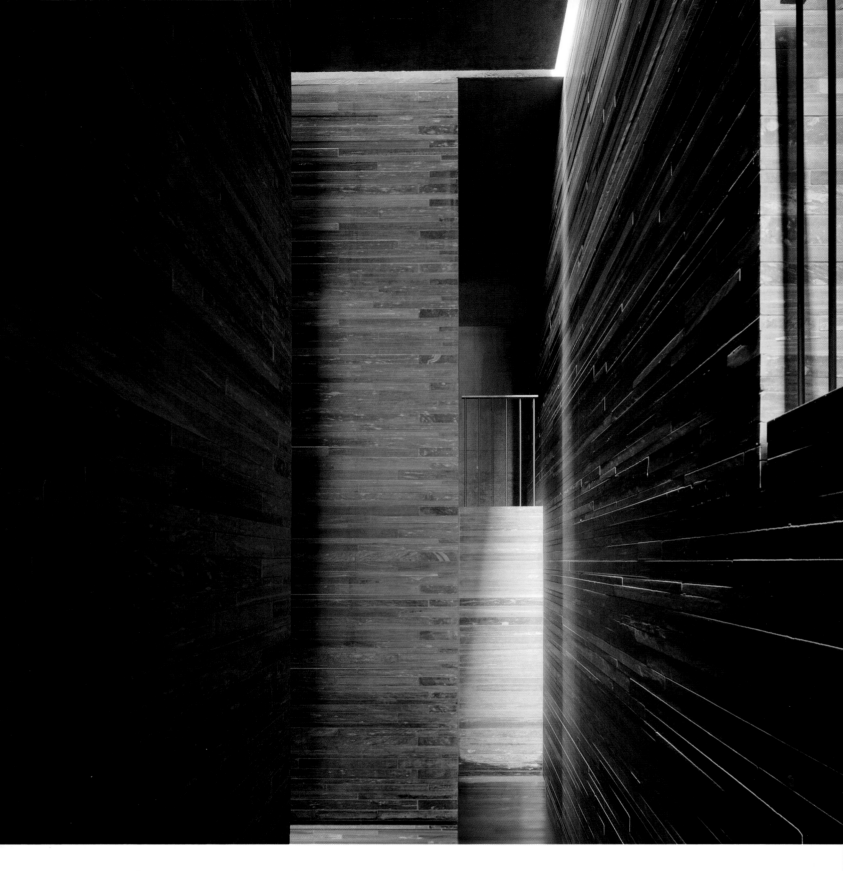

The striated bands of stone used by the architect inside of the baths accentuate the impression that the structure is actually part of the mountain that it is placed on.

Die gestreiften Steinbänder, die in den Bädern einsetzt sind, unterstreichen den Eindruck, dass die Struktur Teil des Berges sei, auf dem das Gebäude steht.

Les bandeaux de pierre utilisés pour l'intérieur accentuent l'impression que ces thermes font partie de la montagne sur laquelle ilsreposent.

The building opens generously out onto the mountain scenery of Vals, but it is actually closer to other buildings than the image to the right might suggest.

Das Gebäude öffnet sich großzügig zu der Bergkulisse von Vals; dabei steht es näher an benachbarten Gebäuden, als die Abbildung rechts vermuten lässt.

Le bâtiment s'ouvre généreusement vers le panorama spectaculaire des montagnes de Vals, mais se trouve en fait plus près d'autres constructions que l'image de droite ne le laisse supposer.

KLANGKÖRPER [SOUND BOX] SWISS PAVILLON HANOVER 2000

SIZE: 52 x 56 m
CLIENT: Swiss Confederation
COST: CHF 18 million

Designed like stacked wood, the Swiss Pavilion at the Hanover Expo 2000 was nonetheless quite impressive because of its dimensions—it measured 52 by 56 meters and was made of twelve stacks of spruce—in all 40 000 wooden beams piled nine meters high. Just as he encouraged certain forms of contemporary music in Vals, Zumthor worked here with the composer Daniel Ott to create sounds that blended with his concept of a kind of modernity that finds its roots in the past. A total of 350 musicians wandering through the space created sounds that were sometimes carefully planned and others more improvisational. With 50 entrances and exits, and by stacking the wood with numerous openings to the sky, the pavilion presented the appearance of a massive modern sculpture or, perhaps more appropriately, of an ambiguous, indeterminate architectural space that took on the sounds of music and the color of the weather.

Der als Holzstapel gestaltete Pavillon der Schweiz auf der Expo 2000 in Hannover war schon aufgrund seiner Dimensionen eindrucksvoll: Auf einer Grundfläche von 52 x 56 m waren 40 000 Fichtenholzbretter zu zwölf jeweils 9 m hohen Stapeln aufgeschichtet. Ebenso wie er für die Therme in Vals bestimmte Formen zeitgenössischer Musik empfahl, arbeitete Zumthor hier mit dem Komponisten Daniel Ott zusammen, um Klänge zu schaffen, die zu seinem Konzept einer in der Vergangenheit verwurzelten Moderne passten. Insgesamt 350 durch den Raum wandelnde Musiker erzeugten Klänge, die bisweilen sorgfältig geplant, manchmal aber auch eher improvisiert waren. Mit 50 Ein- und Ausgängen und zahlreichen Öffnungen zum Himmel glich der Pavillon einer gigantischen modernen Skulptur oder, vielleicht angemessener, einem mehrdeutigen, unbestimmten architektonischen Raum, erfüllt von Klängen und den Farben der jeweiligen Witterung.

Conçu comme un empilement de bois, le pavillon suisse de l'Expo 2000 à Hanovre n'en était pas moins impressionnant de par ses dimensions : 52 x 56 m et douze piles d'épicéa (en tout 40 000 poutres de bois empilées sur 9 m de haut). De même qu'il a encouragé à Vals l'utilisation de certaines formes de musique contemporaine, Zumthor a travaillé ici avec le compositeur Daniel Ott pour créer un son fusionnant avec ce concept d'une forme de modernité qui trouve ses racines dans le passé. Trois cent cinquante musiciens, déambulant dans l'espace ont créé des sons qui étaient parfois soigneusement préparés, parfois laissés à l'improvisation. Avec ses cinquante entrées et sorties et sa masse de bois dégageant de nombreuses ouvertures vers le ciel libre, le pavillon avait l'aspect d'une sculpture contemporaine massive, ou mieux, d'un espace architectural ambigu animé par les sons de la musique et la couleur du temps.

Daniel Ott's Klangkörperklang (2000) was a partly composed and partly improvised piece prepared for the "Sound Box" in Hanover. The music was intended to be "linked to the larch and pine architecture."

Bei Daniel Otts Klangkörperklang (2000) handelt es sich um ein teils komponiertes, teils improvisiertes Stück, das für die „Sound Box" in Hannover geschaffen wurde. Die Musik sollte „mit der Architektur aus Lärchen- und Kiefernholz verbunden sein".

Le Klangkörperklang de Daniel Ott (2000) était une pièce en partie composée et en partie improvisée, préparée pour la « Sound Box » de Hanovre. La musique était « liée à la construction en mélèze et en pin ».

By stacking and aligning wood, the architect created a geometrically simple design that defies normal "modern" classifications, linking the past and present of his own country in this international setting.

Indem er Hölzer stapelt und ausrichtet, lässt der Architekt eine geometrisch schlichte Konstruktion entstehen, die sich normalen „modernen" Klassifizierungen entzieht. In diesem interationalen Kontext verknüpft er Vergangenheit und Gegenwart seines Heimatlandes.

Par l'empilement et l'alignement du bois, l'architecte a créé un motif d'une grande simplicité géométrique qui défie les classifications « modernes » classiques et relie le passé au présent de son pays dans le cadre d'une exposition internationale.

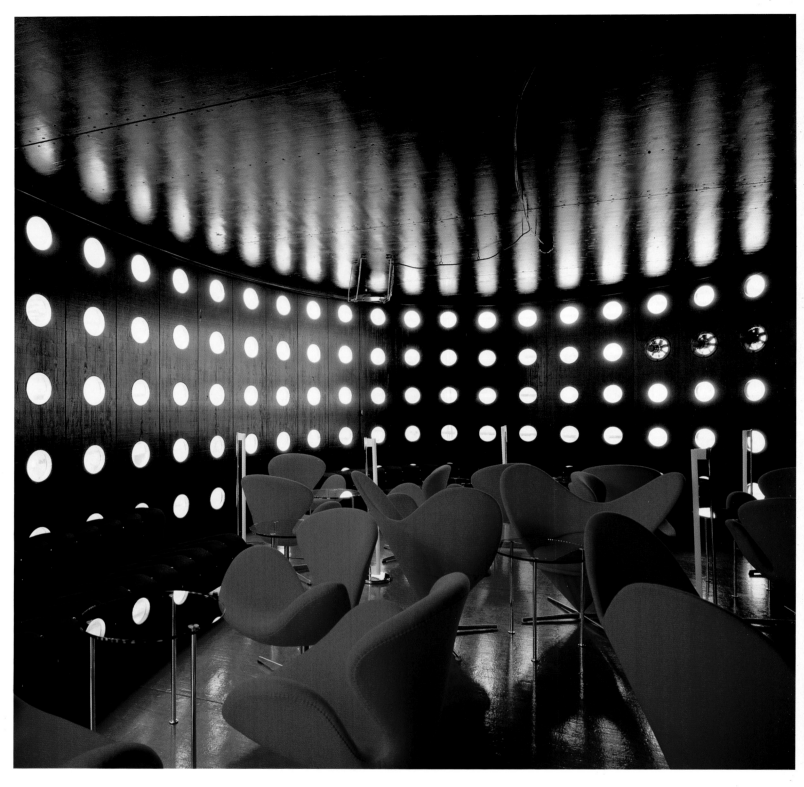

Zumthor's architecture controls light and climate as well as the spatial impressions generated by the stacking of wood. Not in any sense industrial, despite its repetitive massing, the building is difficult to place in any existing category of architecture.

Zumthors Architektur steuert Licht und Klima ebenso wie die von seinen Holzschichtungen geschaffenen räumlichen Impressionen. Das trotz seiner sich wiederholenden Massen in keiner Weise industriell wirkende Gebäude ist kaum in eine bestehende Architekturgattung einzuordnen.

L'architecture de Zumthor contrôle la lumière et le climat mais aussi les impressions spatiales générées par cet amoncellement de bois. En rien industriel, malgré sa répétition de masses, le bâtiment est difficile à classer dans une catégorie d'architecture existante.

SINGLE-FAMILY HOUSE
GRAUBÜNDEN
1997-2003

FLOOR AREA: not disclosed
CLIENT: Liliane and Valentin Luzi
COST: not disclosed

Just as he emphasized on the idea of the typical wooden construction of his country in Hanover, so, too, Zumthor was interested in the idea of creating a single-family timber house in the Graubünden region. A simple, cruciform plan for a slanted, overhanging roof, the house again bridges tradition and modernity, creating an unadorned design where light and the color and form of wood are the only elements that define space. With its views of the countryside and its bow to local vernacular, albeit in the most strictly modern sense, this single-family house is a testimony to what makes Zumthor quite different from other contemporary architects, even in Switzerland. Based in a rural mountain valley, he accepted this commission from a local family, whereas others of his level of fame might well have said they were too busy for such a "minor" project. His point seems to be that architecture is not only a public expression and one meant to contribute to the designer's reputation, but one that is practiced in a patient and modest way. Zumthor's modesty has not kept him from defining new paradigms within an apparently narrow set of precepts, although he is fully capable of working with glass and concrete as well as wood or locally quarried stone.

Ebenso wie Zumthor in Hanover die typische schweizerische Holzbauweise zelebrierte, faszinierte ihn die Vorstellung, im Kanton Graubünden ein Einfamilienhaus aus Holz zu errichten. Mit seinem schlichten, kreuzförmigen Grundriss und einem geneigten, überhängenden Dach stellt auch dieses Haus eine Verbindung zwischen Tradition und Moderne her. Bei seiner schmucklosen Gestaltung stellen Licht sowie Farbton und Form des Holzes die einzigen, den Raum bestimmenden Elemente dar. Dieses Einfamilienhaus mit seinen Ausblicken in die Landschaft und seiner Reverenz an die heimische Architektur, wenn auch im streng modernen Sinn, zeugt von dem, was Zumthor selbst innerhalb der Schweiz von anderen zeitgenössischen Architekten unterscheidet. Zumthor, der in einem ländlichen

Alpental wohnt, akzeptierte diesen Auftrag von einer ebenfalls dort ansässigen Familie, obwohl die meisten ähnlich bekannten Architekten ein so kleines Projekt wahrscheinlich eher abgelehnt hätten. Seiner Auffassung nach scheint Architektur nicht nur eine öffentliche Äußerung zu sein, die zur Mehrung des Ruhms ihres Erzeugers dient, sondern sollte auf geduldige und bescheidene Weise betrieben werden. Zumthors Bescheidenheit hält ihn nicht davon ab, innerhalb eines scheinbar engen Regelwerks neue Paradigmen festzulegen, zumal er ebenso fähig ist, mit Glas und Beton zu arbeiten wie mit Holz oder vor Ort gebrochenem Stein.

Après avoir mis l'accent sur l'idée de la construction en bois typique de son pays à Hanovre, Zumthor s'est également intéressé à la création d'une maison monofamiliale en bois dans le canton des Grisons. De simple plan cruciforme à toit pentu à large surplomb, la maison est un pont entre tradition et modernité dans lequel la lumière, la couleur et la forme du bois sont les seuls éléments qui définissent l'espace. Donnant sur la campagne, elle est un salut au style vernaculaire local, mais dans le sens le plus strictement moderne. Elle est un témoignage de ce qui différencie Zumthor des autres architectes contemporains, même suisses. Sans doute parce qu'il s'est installé dans une vallée rurale, il a accepté cette commande d'une famille locale là où d'autres praticiens de son niveau auraient répondu être trop occupés pour un projet aussi « mineur ». Pour lui, l'architecture n'est pas seulement une expression publique qui doit contribuer à la célébrité du créateur mais quelque chose qui se pratique de façon patiente et modeste. Sa modestie ne l'a pas empêché de définir de nouveaux paradigmes dans un cadre de principes apparemment stricts, bien qu'il soit parfaitement capable, comme il l'a montré à Bregenz, de travailler aussi bien avec le verre et le béton qu'avec le bois et la pierre locale.

Again using the wooden architecture and careful joinery that is typical of the Swiss Alps, Zumthor succeeds in allying past and present, giving a decidedly contemporary feeling to the interior and exterior of the house.

Zumthor, der auch in diesem Fall die für die Schweizer Alpen typische Holzarchitektur mit sorgfältiger Tischlerarbeit verbindet, gelang es, Vergangenheit und Gegenwart zu vereinen und dem Haus eine entschieden moderne Anmutung zu verleihen.

Utilisant là aussi l'architecture en bois soignée typique des Alpes suisses, Zumthor réussi à allier le passé et le présent tout en donnant un caractère résolument contemporain à l'intérieur et à l'extérieur de la maison.

PHOTO CREDITS IMPRINT

CREDITS: PHOTOS/PLANS/DRAWINGS/CAD DOCUMENTS

18–22 top, 23 © Pino Musi – Italy / 22 bottom, 26 bottom © Mario Botta / 25, 27 © Thomas Jantscher / 28–35 top © architekturphoto / 35 bottom © Santiago Calatrava SA / 36–41 top, 42–48, 49 bottom © Milo Keller / 41 bottom, 49 top © Aldo Celoria Architect / 50–54, 55 bottom © Christian Richters / 55 top © Jürg Conzett / 56–60 top, 61 bottom, 62–63 © Fausto Pluchinotta / 60 bottom, 61 top © Devanthéry & Lamunière / 64–67, 68 bottom, 69 top, 71–77 © Christian Richters / 68 top, 69 bottom © Diener & Diener Architekten / 78, 81 bottom, 82 top left and right, 83 © Andreas Rubin / 81 top, 82 bottom 84 top left and right © Michael Freisager, Zurich / 84 bottom Tobias Mendörin / 85 © e2a / 86–89, 91–93 © Nigel Young/Foster and Partners / 90 © Foster and Partners / 94–98, 99 bottom, 100 top left and bottom, 101, 102 and 103 top, 104–106 © Valentin Jeck / 99 top, 100 top right, 102 and 103 bottom © Fuhrimann & Hächler / 106–111 © architekturphoto / 112–116 top, 117 bottom © H. Helfenstein, Zurich / 116 bottom, 117 top, 120 © Gigon/Guyer Architekten / 119, 121–123 © Lucas Peters Photography / 124, 128, 130 bottom © Christian Richters / 127, 129, 130 top, 131 © Margherita Spiluttini / 132–136, 137 bottom, 138–139, 140 bottom, 141 © Pino Musi – Italy / 137 top, 140 top © Davide Macullo Architetto / 142, 145, 146 bottom, 149–155 © Archive Olgiati / 146 top, 147, 156–161 center, 162–163 top © Christian Richters / 164–167, 170 and 171 top © jeanmichellandecy.com / 168–169 Niklaus Stauss, Zurich / 170 and 171 bottom © Philippe Rahm Architectes / 172–191 © Christian Richters

To stay informed about upcoming TASCHEN titles, please request our magazine at www.taschen.com/magazine or write to TASCHEN, Hohenzollernring 53, D-50672 Cologne, Germany, contact@taschen.com, Fax: +49-221-254919. We will be happy to send you a free copy of our magazine which is filled with information about all of our books.

© 2006 TASCHEN GmbH
Hohenzollernring 53, D–50672 Köln
www.taschen.com

PROJECT MANAGEMENT: Florian Kobler, Cologne
COLLABORATION: Barbara Huttrop, Cologne
PRODUCTION: Thomas Grell, Cologne
DESIGN: Sense/Net, Andy Disl and Birgit Reber, Cologne
GERMAN TRANSLATION: Christiane Court, Frankfurt
FRENCH TRANSLATION: Jacques Bosser, Paris

Printed in Italy
ISBN 3-8228-3973-6

EXTREME ALTITUDE
THE WORLDS GREATEST MOUNTAINS

WHITE STAR PUBLISHERS

CONTENTS

TEXTS
Stefano Ardito

EDITORIAL DIRECTOR
Valeria Manferto De Fabianis

EDITORIAL COORDINATION
Laura Accomazzo

GRAPHIC DESIGN
Paola Piacco

GRAPHIC LAYOUT
Cristina Ansaldi

© 2007 White Star s.p.a.
Via Candido Sassone, 22/24
13100 Vercelli, Italy
www.whitestar.it

TRANSLATION: SARAH PONTING

ISBN: 978-88-544-0279-9

REPRINTS:
1 2 3 4 5 6   11 10 09 08 07

Printed in China

INTRODUCTION

How old is man's love of mountains? Mountaineering, the art of climbing mountains for pleasure, negotiating challenging passages on rock and ice, was born in the summer of 1786, when Jacques Balmat and Michel-Gabriel Paccard, natives of Chamonix and subjects of the King of Sardinia, reached the summit of Mont Blanc. This cold and grueling ascent, bristling with dangers, was officially made in the name of science (Paccard's thermometer recorded 18.5 °F and his barometer an altitude of just over 16,400 ft/4998 m instead of the actual 15,771 ft/4807 m), although the two men acted like true adventurers.

The conquest of the "Roof of Europe" became famous all over the continent, thanks to the writings of Horace-Bénédict de Saussure, the rich and cultured Geneva gentleman who inspired the ascent. Following the return of peace after the French Revolution and the Napoleonic Wars, the Alps and their glaciers became a popular stop for travelers on the Grand Tour. The range linking Nice to Vienna became the playground of Europe for its most enthusiastic supporters – initially British, but subsequently also continental – who are believed to have included Leslie Stephen, one of the first presidents of the British Alpine Club.

However, over the 200 or so years that separate us from Paccard and Balmat's alpenstocks and scientific instruments, many people have wondered whether the ascent of the two brave Chamonix men marks the true birth of mountaineering. Indeed, centuries earlier cultured men such as Petrarch (and perhaps even the Roman Emperor Hadrian) ascended the peaks to reflect on man and the world.

In 1492 a group of French soldiers led by Antoine de Ville conquered the rocky tower of Mont Aiguille, in the Vercors range, overcoming considerable difficulties on the rock face. However, while Petrarch's climbs may have been lacking in technical difficulty, the ascent of the French group lacked a "pure" motive. Indeed, de Ville and his companions had not scaled the sheer rock for pleasure, but in obedience to the orders of King Charles VIII.

Such debates may seem futile, and indeed they are to a certain extent. However, the discovery of the Alps and the other European ranges (the Pyrenees and the Tatras, the Scandinavian and Scottish peaks, the mountains of the Balkans and the Apennines) as extraordinary leisure destinations commenced from Balmat and Paccard's ascent. Today millions of Europeans head for the mountains all year round, equipped with trekking boots, cords or skis. Zermatt, Chamonix, Garmisch-Partenkirchen and Cortina have been transformed from sleepy farming villages into some of Europe's most exclusive resorts.

However, man did not discover the mountains for recreation. During the summer of 1991 the discovery of Ötzi the Iceman, a Bronze-Age man who died 5000 years ago on the ridge that now separates Italy from Austria, made international headlines, bringing to public attention a fact long known to archaeologists. Indeed, man has frequented the Alps since prehistoric times, settling in the high valleys as soon as the retreat of the glaciers of the Quaternary Period had allowed the pastures and woodlands to reach the higher altitudes.

Ötzi's equipment (leather garments and shoes padded with dry grass, a flint dagger and a copper axe, a bow and a quiver with 14 arrows, a bark backpack containing charcoal fragments and a piece of dried ibex meat) demonstrates the skill of our distant ancestors in exploiting natural resources in order to tackle high altitudes in relative safety.

This is also the case for other mountain ranges. As soon as the Earth's climate allowed, the mountain dwellers of Asia

started to till the soil of the high valleys and graze their livestock at altitudes up to 16,500 ft (5029 m), crossing the passes of the Himalaya and Karakoram Mountains with caravans of horses, mules and yaks to enable commerce between the cities of India and China, Tibet and the Central Asian kingdoms.

The scenario was very similar on the other side of the world, in the Andes and the other South American ranges. In 1520, when the conquistador Hernán Cortés sent his soldiers up Popocatépetl, the second highest volcano in Mexico, part of the purpose was to demonstrate European superiority to the natives. Actually, the people of the surrounding valleys had been ascending the 17,930-ft (5465-m) summit from time immemorial to pray. Furthermore, the mummified body of a boy sacrificed to the mountain gods has been found at an altitude of 18,050 ft (5502 m) on Aconcagua.

However, it was not just the Andes that inspired a sense of the divine. For thousands of years, all over the world, men of all religious creeds have identified the great edifices of rock and ice with a stairway leading to heaven. While the God of Israel brought the Ark to rest atop Mount Ararat and commanded Moses to ascend Mount Sinai to receive the Tablets of the Law, the ancient Greeks believed that their gods resided on the summit of Mount Olympus, overlooking the Aegean Sea.

In Asia sacred mountains include the Indonesian volcanoes, Mount Fuji in Japan, and Mount Kinabalu in the Borneo rainforest. Mount Kailas, a pyramid of rock and ice overlooking the Tibetan Plateau, is considered the center of the world by Buddhists, Hindus, Jains and the followers of the ancient Bon religion. Dozens of high Himalayan peaks, including Annapurna and Everest, are also considered sacred. Throughout the Indian subcontinent, as far as torrid Sri Lanka and Kerala, the domes of thousands and thousands of temples rise towards the heavens imitating the distant mountains.

However, during the past century another reason has fueled man's interest in the mountains. Long known to travelers and scholars for their extraordinary flora and fauna, and worshipped as the starting point of the long journey of the rivers to the sea (the Indus, Brahmaputra, Jarnali and Sutlej rivers all rise around Mount Kailas), the world's mountains gradually became more precious as the works of man invaded the hills and plains.

From its beginning in the United States, where John Muir assured the protection of the granite walls of Yosemite, the depths of the Grand Canyon and the Sequoia Forest in the late 19th century, the drive to protect the upper altitudes of our planet has spread to most regions of the world. Although roads, ski runs and antennas continue to advance, today almost all of the world's highest and most beautiful peaks are protected. While Mont Blanc remains a surprising exception, magnificent national parks protect Annapurna, Everest, Kilimanjaro, McKinley, Cerro Torre and Mount Cook.

The purpose of these protected areas is to guard bears, snow leopards and ibex; regulate the flows of climbers and tourists, and extend our knowledge of the world through the work of zoologists, botanists, glaciologists and geologists. They also ensure that our drinking water remains pure and clean. These areas serve to preserve purity, adventure and mystery, just a few hours' journey away from our crowded cities. The protection of the wild mountains is important for all the world's inhabitants.

1 Machapuchare (also known as Fishtail, 22,595 ft/6887 m) viewed from the west, Nepal.

2-3 Mont Maudit (14,649 ft/4465 m) and Mont Blanc (15,771 ft/4807 m), Italy – France.

4-5 Mt. Fitzroy (right, 11,289 ft/3441 m) and Lake Viedma, Argentina.

6 Mount Everest (29,029 ft/8867 m) and the Khumbu Glacier, Nepal-China.

7 Point John (16,020 ft/4483 m), in the Mount Kenya group, Kenya.

9 El Capitan (7569 ft/2307 m) and the Merced River, California, USA.

10 The summit peak of K2 (28,251 ft/8611 m), China – Pakistan.

11 Sassolungo (10,436 ft/3181 m), Trentino-Alto Adige, Italy.

12-13 Everest (left) and Nuptse (25,791 ft/7861 m), China-Nepal.

14-15 Mt. McKinley (20,320 ft/6193 m), Alaska, USA.

EUROPE

The world's most famous and frequented mountain range rises in the heart of Europe. No other range on Earth is home to such a varied collection of summits as the Alps, where peaks such as Mont Blanc and the Matterhorn, the Tre Cime di Lavaredo and Sassolungo, the Vajolet Towers and Triglav, Piz Badile and the Barre des Écrins rise side by side.

Gneiss, granite, dolomite and limestone alternate every few miles to form extraordinary rock formations over the 750-mile (1200-km) range extending from Nice to Vienna. The peaks and rock faces are flanked by densely populated valleys, thick forests and the gargantuan glaciers (currently retreating, as are glaciers throughout the world) of the Bernese Alps, Monte Rosa and the other Alpine "little Himalayas."

The passes connecting the valleys of France, Italy, Switzerland, Austria, Germany and Slovenia at the foot of the great mountains have been frequented since the dawn of time. However, traces of humankind's presence in the Alps can also be found at higher altitudes. Poachers, smugglers and crystal hunters visited the mountains over the centuries. During the past 200 years each ridge, rock face and snowy gully has witnessed adventures, struggles and in some cases tragedies.

However, the Alps are not Europe's only mountains. From the icy peaks of the Norwegian Alps and the Scottish Highlands to the sun-drenched summits of Mt. Olympus and the Sierra Nevada, other imposing mountain systems cross the continent in all directions. In the south Etna, Vesuvius and the other Italian volcanoes overlook the Mediterranean Sea, while the wildest areas of the Picos de Europa, the Pyrenees, Apennines, Balkans and the Tatras rival the Alps.

Each weekend millions of Europeans travel to the mountains in search of adventure and sports. Paths, ski runs, rock faces and torrents are the ideal place to restore body and soul after a hard week's work. Since Europe is a crowded continent, tedious delay on the outward and homeward journeys is often the price to be paid for this passion.

The great European mountains are not just a playground. Mount Ortles, Triglav, La Meije, Gran Paradiso, the Grossglockner and many other imposing peaks overlook some of Europe's largest and most important protected areas. In sight of the glaciers and rocks, high mountain pastures and forests are home to bear, ibex, chamois, eagles, and vultures. Rare species of flora and fauna also live at the foot of the non-protected massifs, such as Mont Blanc and the Matterhorn. Europe's natural environment still survives around the continent's great peaks.

16 left The solitary pyramid of the Bietschhorn (12,907 ft/3934 m) rises in the Bernese Alps.

16 center A roped party approaches Barre des Écrins (13,459 ft/4105 m), in France.

16 right The solid wall of Trollveggen, in Norway, culminates at 5866 ft (1787 m).

17 During winter the Brenta Dolomites in Trentino become a snowy wonderland.

Ben Nevis

UNITED KINGDOM

In the Alps, not to mention the Himalayas, Ben Nevis would appear little more than a hill. However, despite standing a mere 4406 ft (1343 m), the highest peak of the British Isles is a true mountain, protected to the northeast by an imposing sheer face of volcanic rock, which thousands of walkers reach each summer along a grueling path that commences almost at sea level not far from Fort William.

British mountaineers have been at home among the Scottish peaks and lochs since the 19th century and have

traced dozens of routes of all degrees of difficulty on the faces of Ben Nevis. While the great crests of the mountain (and Tower Ridge in particular) are of medium difficulty, the crevices, precipices and slabs of Carn Dearg, an 850-ft (259-m) spur, are all very or extremely challenging.

Winter transforms Ben Nevis into a very harsh mountain. The alternation of rain from the Atlantic on the Highlands and icy north winds that rapidly transform rain into snow and snow into ice mean that the ridges and rock faces are covered with a thick layer of ice between November and April. Winter climbing on Ben Nevis, practiced since the end of the 19th century when Harold Raeburn opened itineraries that were far more difficult than the contemporary routes on Mont Blanc, still leads the world today.

The first ascents of the mountain's almost perpendicular ice gullies, such as the Zero Gully and the Point Five Gully, were made during the 1950s, while the materials used for vertical ice climbing (rigid crampons and short ice axes with serrated picks) were developed here from the 1960s. In recent years the best ice climbers have concentrated on the rock faces covered with a thin frozen crust, which allows risky progress without the chance to secure oneself.

Since the 1970s, many of the top climbers from Alpine countries have spent their winters in Scotland scaling Ben Nevis' ridges, gullies and icy slabs. However, one does not have to be a mountaineer to appreciate the charm of this windblown spot. While the normal route is crowded on sunny days, the long itinerary that reaches the summit via the little refuge dedicated to Charles Inglis Clark (referred to locally as the CIC Hut) passes through wild and solitary areas. From the peak the view takes in summits, mountain ranges, lochs and valleys with few or no signs of human presence. Indeed, the Highlands around Ben Nevis are one of the last great wildernesses in Europe.

18 top Many winter routes have been opened in the Coire na Ciste corrie in the center of the northeast face of Ben Nevis. The unmistakable silhouette of Tower Ridge rises in the middle of the photograph, above the eddies of snow that lash the summit plateau of the mountain.

18 bottom The gullies surrounding Ben Nevis and Scotland's other highest peaks are solitary and windswept even during the warmest weeks of summer, but conditions become particularly harsh when disturbances from the west and the icy north wind cover them with snow and ice.

18-19 Even in winter the morning light manages to reach Tower Ridge and the Great Tower (top left in the photograph), after which it is named. The rocky buttress of Carn Dearg, on which several extremely difficult routes have been opened, can be seen at the bottom right.

20-21 A mountaineer ascends one of the snow and mixed arêtes of the northwest face of Ben Nevis. From the 1960s special equipment for vertical ice climbing (rigid crampons and short ice axes with serrated picks) was developed to ascend this difficult terrain.

20 bottom The north face of Ben Nevis is reached from the town of Fort William, along the long and winding Allt a'Mhuillin approach, which is often covered with snow even at very low altitudes. The small hut named after Charles Inglis Clark stands at the foot of the rock face.

Naranjo de Bulnes

SPAIN

One of the most spectacular massifs in Europe rises in the heart of Asturias, in northern Spain. Exposed to the rains from the Atlantic, which lies less than 10 miles (16 km) from the peaks, the Picos de Europa form a limestone range perforated with grottoes, cirques (half-crescent or shallow caldron-like depressions), and sinkholes, and scored by giant canyons, such as the Gargantua Divina. Although the landscapes are often Mediterranean, the peaks and valleys are frequently enveloped in sea mists that create serious orientation problems for trekkers.

Protected by one of the most famous national parks in Spain, the Picos are home to the chamois, two species of vulture – the griffon and the bearded vulture – the golden eagle, the peregrine falcon, and the magnificent eagle owl, Europe's mightiest nocturnal predator. Other sources of great scientific interest are the wild ponies, known by the local name of asturcón, and the Pyrenean desman, a shy little insectivore belonging to the talpid family that inhabits the woods.

The Torre Cerredo (8688 ft/2648 m) is the highest summit of the Picos. However, the most elegant and famous mountain of the range is Naranjo di Bulnes (8264 ft/2519 m), which Iberian climbers consider to be the most prestigious peak. The vertical south and west faces of the Naranjo ("Orange"), formed by an extraordinarily solid limestone, are crossed by dozens of complex routes and have long been the training ground of Spanish climbers. Indeed, almost all the best Iberian alpinists have left their mark on these rocks. The list includes the Aragonese Ernesto Navarro and Alberto Rabada, who conquered the west face of the Naranjo in 1962 and met a tragic death a year later on the Eiger; César Pérez de Tudela and his companions, who made the first winter ascent of the west face (1973), and the Murcian brothers José Luis and Miguel Angel Gallego, who climbed the most overhanging part of the west face in 1983 without the use of bolts. Their route, named Sueños de Invierno, required a 69-day stay on the rock face.

The first ascent of the Naranjo, made in 1904 via the difficult northwest face, marked the birth of Iberian mountaineering and was made by Don Pedro Pidal, Marquis of Villaviciosa de Asturias, and the guide Gregorio Pérez. "How embarrassing it would be for me and my fellow countrymen if foreign mountaineers should one day plant their flag on Naranjo de Bulnes, in my favorite chamois hunting ground!" the marquis wrote in his diary before attempting the climb.

26 The snow lingers on the rugged northern side of the Cantabrian Mountains, exposed to the Atlantic Ocean.

27 In the heart of the Picos de Europa range, Naranjo de Bulnes rises 8264 ft (2518 m) and is considered the most prestigious peak by Iberian climbers. The first ascent of the mountain was made in 1904.

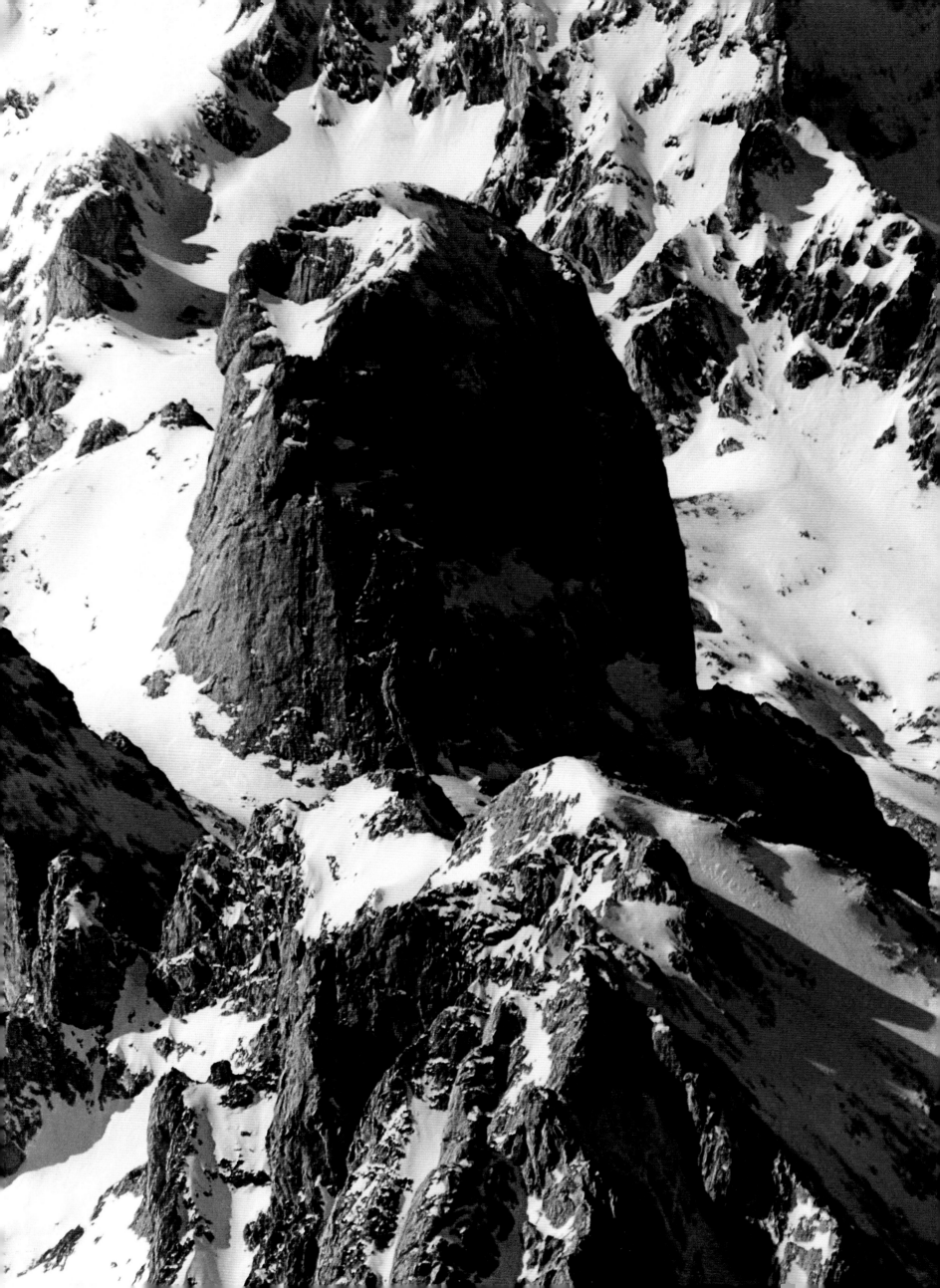

Naranjo de Bulnes

28 top The Picos de Europa rise against the backdrop of Lake Ercina in the National Park named after the range.

28 bottom A fine view of the west face of Naranjo de Bulnes, which rises sheer for 1640 ft (500 m) and was first ascended in 1961 by the Aragonese climbers Rabadá and Navarro.

29 The limestone peak of Naranjo de Bulnes has been much eroded by glaciers that have long since disappeared. The mountain's origins stretch back to the Paleozoic Era, before the Iberian Peninsula collided with the African plate. Its name appears to refer to the orangey color of the rock.

Barre des Écrins and La Meije

FRANCE

One of the wildest ice massifs of the Alps is situated entirely in French territory, between the Rhône Valley and the Italian border. The Oisans wilderness encompasses 50 or so glaciers and dozens of magnificent peaks over 10,000 ft (3048 m). The area, protected by the 354-sq.-mile (917-sq.-km) Écrins National Park since 1973, is home to thousands of chamois, a few hundred ibex and 40 pairs of golden eagles. In recent years the wolf and the bearded vulture have also returned to the massif.

Two of the many interesting peaks for climbers (which include Pelvoux, Aiguille Dibona, Ailefroide and Olan) are in a class of their own. The first of these is the Barre des

Écrins, the southernmost summit above 13,000 ft (3962 m) in the Alps, which towers 13,459 ft (4105 m) above the Glacier Blanc and the deep Vallouise Valley. In 1864, after having made his first ascent of the Barre des Écrins with the guides Michel Croz and Christian Almer, Edward Whymper – the future conqueror of the Matterhorn – observed that nowhere else do mountains assume such daring forms – and also noted the vast panorama that he admired from its summit.

Easy and much frequented in spring by hundreds of alpinist-skiers as far as the Dôme de Neige (13,173 ft/4015 m), the final stretch of the normal route up the Oisans' highest peak is a precarious aerial ridge. The friability of the rock makes the other routes up the mountain impracticable,

30 top Barre des Écrins, the southernmost "four-thousander" in the Alps, has an icy north face and a spectacular rocky west face

overlooking he village of La Bérarde and the Vénéon Valley, which descends towards Bourg-d'Oisans and Grenoble.

30 bottom The imposing north face of Barre des Écrins can be seen in the background (on the right) of this photograph taken from the Refuge des Écrins.

31 The north face of the Barre des Écrins can be seen rising above huge seracs from the normal route of Roche Faurio, which overlooks the Glacier des Écrins from the north.

Barre des Écrins and La Meije

with the exception of the South Pillar, a very difficult climb of over 3280 ft (1000 m).

La Meije is a different story. This huge rocky wall bounds the massif to the north and culminates in the Grand Pic (13,067 ft/3982 m), overlooking the village of La Grave. It is clearly visible from the road that runs between Grenoble and Briançon and was one of the last great Alpine peaks to have been conquered. The ascent was made by an all-French roped party led by Emmanuel Boileau de Castelnau and the guides Pierre Gaspard father and son.

Fifty or so increasingly difficult routes were subsequently opened on the mountain, all in spectacular settings. While the Austrian mountaineers Ludwig Purthscheller and Otto and Emil Zsigmondy made the crossing of the ridges in 1885, and the great Cortina guide Angelo Dibona traced an important route in 1912, the rest of the climbing history of the mountain was written almost exclusively by French alpinists. They include the Parisians Pierre Allain and Raymond Leninger, who conquered the south face of the Grand Pic in 1935 with a particularly elegant route across the extraordinarily imposing rock wall.

32 top The altitude of the Écrins National Park varies from 2625 to 13,458 ft (800 to 4100 m).

32 bottom Winter makes Olan (11,693 ft/3547 m), the mountain that dominates the Valgaudemar, even more fearsome. Its north face was ascended in 1934 by Giusto Gervasutti and Lucien Devies.

32-33 The isolated Champsaur Basin, surrounded by rounded and relatively mild-mannered mountains, marks the southwestern boundary of the Écrins National Park, which covers an area of 226,850 acres (91,800 hectares). This area, renowned for its rich pastures, was the first in the park to have been recolonized by the wolf.

33 bottom The entire La Meije Massif, with the Tabuchet, Meije and Rateau glaciers, provides the backdrop for this photograph taken from the shores of Lake Lérié on the Emparis Plateau. The lake offers one of the finest views of the north face of the Écrins Massif, as can be seen from this evocative picture.

34-35 The imposing south face of La Meije, which rises above the Étançons Glacier, culminates in the Grand Pic (left), Doigt de Dieu and La Meije Orientale. The Refuge du Promontoire, visible in the shade in the lower left of the photograph, serves as a base for around 30 routes, most of which are very difficult.

E
U
R
O
P
E

36 top The Mer de Glace, one of the longest glaciers in the Alps, winds its way towards the Arve Valley and Chamonix. The Dent du Géant, Col du Géant and Mont Blanc stand out against the background. The Mer de Glace flows east to merge with the Leschaux Glacier (left).

36-37 An aerial view shows the great crevasses of the Vallée Blanche, which stretches down from the highest reaches of the massif towards the Mer de Glace and Chamonix. Mont Blanc (left), the snowy Dôme du Goûter and the pointed Aiguille du Midi rise in the background.

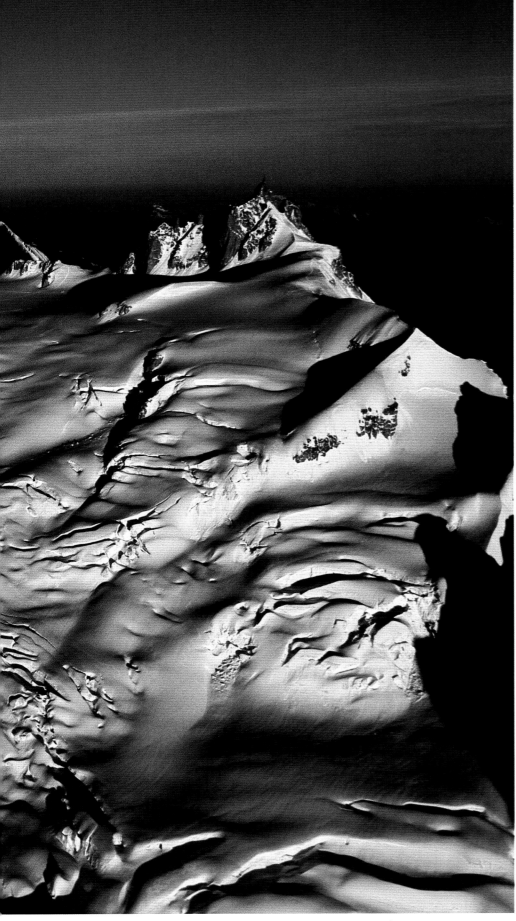

Mont Blanc

ITALY - FRANCE

The allure of the giant lives on. Mont Blanc, situated in the northwestern corner of the Alps at the meeting point of the Italy's Val d'Aosta, France's Haute Savoie, and the Swiss canton of Valais, is the highest and most spectacular mountain in Europe. Granite walls, Himalayan-style glaciers, torrents, spruce forests, chalets and meadows that bear witness to the age-old toil of man form a landscape that has been admired by travelers and alpinists for over two centuries.

Mont Blanc, which forms the roof of the massif of the same name, culminates in a 15,771-ft (4807-m) snow dome that becomes sharper each year due to the thinning of the ice. Another 26 peaks over 4000 m (13,123 ft) surround it; they are celebrated by mountaineers all over the world for the climbs they offer. The Aiguille de Bionnassay, Mont Maudit, Dent du Géant and Grandes Jorasses stand on the ridge that marks the border between France and Italy, while the Aiguille Blanche de Peuterey is entirely in Italian territory and Mont Blanc du Tacul and the Aiguille Verte are completely French. However the concept of borders makes little sense in this natural wilderness, where man often feels an intruder.

The Mont Blanc epic commenced on August 8, 1786, when two men reached the summit for the first time. The crystal hunter Jacques Balmat and the physician Michel-Gabriel Paccard from Chamonix, at the time part of the Kingdom of Sardinia, reached the peak in the late afternoon, after having ascended via the woods of the Montagne de la Côte and the treacherous glaciers of Mont Blanc's north face. Their lack of ropes, crampons and ice axes made their feat truly exceptional.

For historians, Paccard and Balmat's ascent marks the birth of mountaineering. Their route was repeated a year later by Horace-Bénédict de Saussure with 18 guides and porters, and became popular following the Battle of Waterloo and the return of peace to Europe. The systematic conquest of the summits and faces of the massif commenced in the second half of the 19th century, when routes toward Mont Blanc's summit were also opened on the St.-Gervais and Courmayeur sides.

The turning point came in 1865, when the British mountaineers G.S. Matthews, A.W. Moore and F. and H. Walker, guided by Jakob and Melchior Anderegg, scaled the incredibly steep ice slope of the Brenva Spur. Around 1880 rock climbing also made its debut on Mont Blanc, allowing the conquest of the Aiguille du Dru, the Dent du Géant and the Aiguille du Grépon. The main summit was the setting for the ascents of the great snow and rock ridges, commencing with the Peuterey, which was scaled in 1893 by a group led by the guide Emile Rey.

During the interwar years a new generation of climbers trained on the limestone faces of the Dolomites and the Prealps conquered the greatest rock walls of the massif, such as the north face of the Grandes Jorasses and the south ridge of the Aiguille Noire de Peuterey. Other great ice and mixed routes were

opened on Mont Blanc. However the "last problems" of Europe's highest peak had to await the 1960s, when they were solved by the Italian Walter Bonatti (a Lombard by birth, Courmayeur guide by election), the Frenchmen René Desmaison and Pierre Mazeaud and the British climbers Chris Bonington and Don Whillans.

The 1970s saw a change in climbing techniques on both rock and ice. While the Swiss mountaineer Michel Piola and his companions opened extraordinary routes on the granite Aiguilles de Chamonix and Grand Capucin, ice climbers such as Jean-Marc Boivin, Giancarlo Grassi and Patrick Gabarrou discovered dozens of gullies and couloirs on the faces of "old" Mont Blanc.

Although the plans for an international park at the foot of the peaks and glaciers are at a standstill, the chamois and ibex populations are constantly increasing. A network of nature reserves protects the west slope of Mont Blanc and the massifs that crown it. Each year thousands of trekkers complete the path that circles Mont Blanc, which offers extraordinary views of the massif. The allure of the giant manages to bewitch them too.

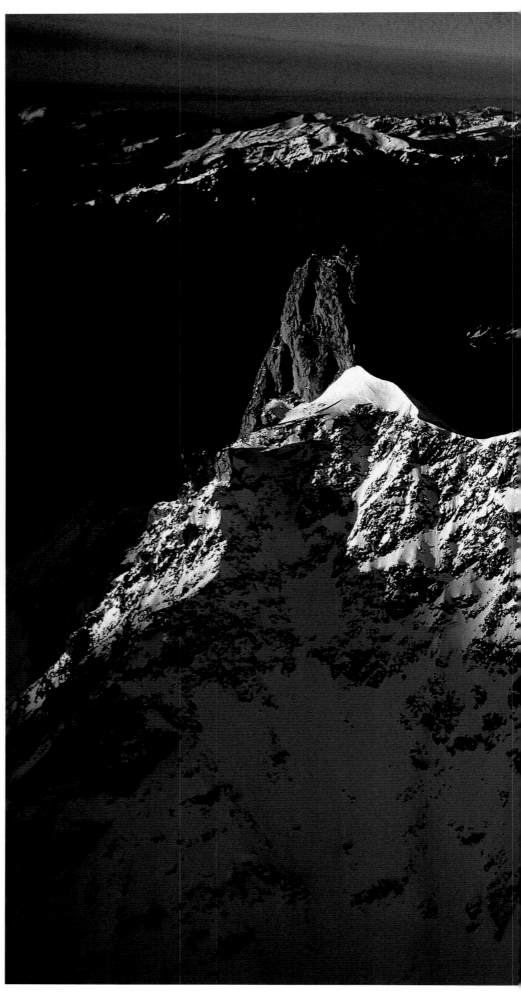

Mont Blanc

38 The Grandes Jorasses culminate in Pointe Walker (13,799 ft/4206 m), flanked by Punta Margherita, Punta Elena, Pointe Croz and Pointe Whymper. The north face drops sharply away beyond the ridge.

38-39 One of the most characteristic granite peaks of Mont Blanc, the Dent du Géant (left in the photograph) stands 13,166 ft (4012 m), rising above the snow ridge at its base. On its right is the Aiguille de Rochefort (13,127 ft/4001 m), while the Aiguille Verte and the Aiguille du Dru are visible in the background.

40-41 The Aiguilles de Chamonix range, encrusted with ice following a winter storm, overlooks the Arve Valley and is home to some of the finest granite peaks in the Alps. In the photograph it is possible to discern (left to right) the Aiguille des Ciseaux, Aiguille du Fou, Dent du Crocodile and Aiguille du Plan.

42-43 Dawn illuminates the east face of the Matterhorn and the ridges of the normal routes. The ice ridges of Dent Blanche can be seen on the right.

43 The huge rock and snow edifice of the Matterhorn culminates in the rocky peak that tapers to form the mountain's aerial summit ridge. On both sides access to the summit is complicated by very steep rocks, which the Italian normal route (left, among sun and shade) ascends by means of grueling fixed ropes and a rope ladder.

The Matterhorn

ITALY - SWITZERLAND

Although Everest is the name that comes to everyone's mind when talking of mountains, the most familiar silhouette is undoubtedly the icy pyramid of the Matterhorn (Cervino in Italian). This 14,692-ft (4478 m) peak separates Zermatt, in Valais, from the pastures of Breuil, in Valtournenche, where the summer and winter resort of Cervinia was established in the 1930s.

Overlooking the Zmutt and Gorner glaciers – visible from the belvederes of the Klein Matterhorn, Testa Grigia and Gornergrat – on the Swiss side, the Matterhorn is a regular pyramid, with four faces separated by the Hörnli, Furggen, Lion and Zmutt ridges. The crumbliness of the rock means that almost all ascents of the summit are made along the ridges.

In August, when the snow has melted to reveal the bare rock, dozens of roped parties reach the aerial ridge of the summit via the Hörnli Ridge, which is the normal route from Zermatt. The greater difficulty of the Lion Ridge, the Italian normal route, which requires an overnight stop at the precariously perched Capanna Carrel refuge, makes it a less popular itinerary. In recent years several landslides have made this route less safe and the Valtournenche guides have had to undertake complex operations to secure new fixed ropes and remove hanging rocks.

Even at a distance of almost a century and a half, the conquest of the Matterhorn remains one of the most famous episodes in the history of international mountaineering. Although Michel Croz, a Chamonix guide, was the first man of the seven-person team to stand on the peak, the leader of these seven who reached the summit on July 14, 1865 was Edward Whymper, a British mountaineer who had already attempted eight ascents during the previous summers. After having attempted the Lion Ridge several times with the Val d'Aosta guide Jean-Antoine Carrel, Whymper finally reached the summit from the Hörnli Ridge. He and Croz were accompanied by Francis Douglas, the Reverend Charles

Hudson, the young Lord Hadow, and the Zermatt guides Peter Taugwalder father and son.

Their descent is tragically famous. Hadow slipped during the steepest stretch, falling onto Croz and knocking him off the mountainside. Hudson and Douglas were dragged down with him. The thin rope that secured Douglas to the Taugwalders and Whymper broke: Croz and the other three British members of the party fell to their death, while Whymper and the two Swiss guides were able to complete their descent. The graves are those who died are in the Zermatt cemetery and are still visited by a ceaseless flow of pilgrims; most also visit the nearby Alpine Museum where the

50-51 The imposing east face of Monte Rosa, which dominates the upper Anzasca Valley and Macugnana, is one of the highest and most spectacular in the Alps. Ascended for the first time in 1872 and descended on skis in 1979, this extraordinary rock face scourged by mighty avalanches continues to command the respect of even expert climbers.

50 bottom The peaks of Lyskamm, Castor and Pollux and Breithorn rise on the boundary ridge between Italy and Switzerland, between Monte Rosa and the Matterhorn, which is clearly visible on the right of the photograph. Rocky Peak Gornergrat, served by a cog railway from Zermatt, offers breathtaking views.

Monte Rosa

In 1872 three other British mountaineers, Richard and William Pendlebury and Charles Taylor, led by Gabriel Spechtenhauser, Ferdinand Imseng and Giovanni Oberto, opened the first route on the east face.

Eight years later the Italian alpinist Damiano Marinelli and the mountain guides Ferdinand Imseng and Battista Pedranzini were killed by an avalanche on the east face. Then in 1893 the Italian Mountaineering Club inaugurated the highest refuge in Europe on Signalkuppe, and named it after Queen Margherita.

In recent years the latest trends in climbing have made their appearance on the massif. In 1979 the Genoese Stefano de Benedetti descended the east face of Monte Rosa on skis; in 1986 the Swiss climbers Erhard Loretan and André Georges made a winter traverse of the entire "Imperial Crown," the series of peaks (including 30 over 4000 m/13,123 ft) that ring Zermatt, in 18 days.

Mountaineering is of course only part of the story on Monte Rosa. While experienced roped parties venture onto the routes already followed in the 19th century, such as the

51 Although less impressive than when seen from the plain to the south (above which it rises to an average height of over 14,400 ft/4390 m), the Monte Rosa massif also offers breathtaking views from high altitudes, from which it appears as a huge plateau isolated from the rest of the range. The unusual conformation of the massif comprises 20 peaks over 13,000 ft (3962 m) high in a relatively small area, making this the region with the highest average altitude in the Alps. Monte Rosa is the second highest mountain in the Alps and the highest in Switzerland.

traverse of Lsykamm and the Signal Ridge, each summer thousands of people climb the Lys Glacier toward the loftiest peaks of the massif.

Although the path toward the Monte Rosa Hut (the historic Bétemps Hut) on the Zermatt face requires the crossing of the level Gornergletscher, the foot of the east face can be reached from Macugnaga by an easy path that crosses the moraine of the Belvedere Glacier. Other easy itineraries, in a wild setting, allow visitors to discover the waterfalls and Alpine pastures of the upper Sesia Valley, where one of the finest regional parks of Piedmont offers protection to eagles, chamois and ibex.

52-53 The north face of the Mönch drops steeply towards Grindelwald, while from the south the mountain resembles a pyramid of ice and snow. The rocky peak of the Eiger can be seen to its right.

52 bottom The setting sun lights up the southwest face (Rottal) of the Jungfrau. The main summit can be seen at the top right, while the Milchstühl face is visible in the center.

53 bottom The north face of the Mönch, the central peak of the trio that also comprises the Jungfrau and the Eiger, has a far more forbidding appearance than the south side of the mountain (as is also true for its two neighbors). The unmistakable shape of the Eisnollen ("Ice Nose"), crossed by a classic ascent route, is visible on the right of the photograph, taken at sunset on a clear winter day.

The Jungfrau, Eiger and Mönch

SWITZERLAND

The Virgin, the Monk and the Ogre dominate the most spectacular valleys of the Bernese Alps. The Jungfrau, Mönch and Eiger stand side-by-side to create the northern bastion of the range that separates Valais from the heart of Switzerland, rising on the horizon in Interlaken and Berne, and dominating the narrow valleys that climb up to the lakes of Brienz and Thun toward Grindelwald, Mürren and Wengen.

The Jungfrau ("Virgin" in German) is the highest of the three, at 13,642 ft (4158 m), and overlooks the Weisse Lutschine Valley with an impressive ice face. Farther east, to the viewer's right, the triangular silhouette of the Mönch ("the Monk," 13,448 ft/4099 m) dominates the Grindenwald with a mixed wall flanked by the rounded ridge of the Eisnollen, the "Ice Nose." However, it is the third peak of the group, the Eiger ("Ogre,") soaring 13,025 ft (3970 m) that has been the most famous mountain of the Bernese Alps for over half a century. Its somber north face, constantly beaten by falling rocks, rises over 6560 ft /2000 m) dominate the Kleine Scheidegg and Grindelwald.

A legend of 1930s European climbing, the Eiger's north face was conquered in 1938 by the Austro-German roped team of Anderl Heckmair, Franz Kasparek, Heinrich Harrer and Ludwig Vörg. Nonetheless, the peak has assumed a rather morbid place in international mountaineering history as a result of the many victims it has claimed. Today the Eiger boasts around 20 routes and the 1938 itinerary is followed by many roped parties each year without any particular problems. Many tourists nonetheless scan the face through powerful binoculars, seeking accidents and rescue operations.

The three peaks overlooking Interlaken and Berne are the most familiar of the Bernese Alps, the "little Himalayas,"

which culminate in the Finsteraarhorn (14,022 ft/4274 m) and the Aletschhorn (13,763 ft/4195 m), and are home to gigantic glaciers such as the Aletsch (the largest in Europe), Fiescher, Oberaar and Unteraar. East of Grindelwald and the Eiger, the picture is completed by magnificent rocky peaks, such as the Schreckhorn and Wetterhorn.

Mountaineering is only part of the picture in this area. In fact, the valleys at the foot of the Bernese Alps have played a very important role in the history of skiing, while magnificent paths (including the 76-mile/122-km Hintere Gasse) wind through pastures and Alpine meadows to reach the highest peaks. The cog railway that ascends to the icy Jungfraujöch saddle (11,401 ft/3475 m) from Grindelwald and Wegen makes it one of the most popular belvederes in the Alps.

54-55 The Jungfrau, crossed by the ridge of the group, stands out on the right of this view, followed by the Jungfraujoch, Eiger and Mönch to the north (far left). The Sphinx meteorological station can be seen on the central col.

55 top The Mönch was ascended for the first time in 1863 by R.S. Macdonald and the alpine guides Anderegg and Almer. The Finsteraarhorn can be seen in the background on the left; the Aletsch Glacier and summit of the Aletschhorn are visible on the right.

55 bottom The Aletsch Glacier, which descends from the Jungfraujoch and the peaks overlooking the Grindelwald and Interlaken towards Valais, is the largest and most spectacular in the Alps. The Aletschhorn group can be seen in the center of the view.

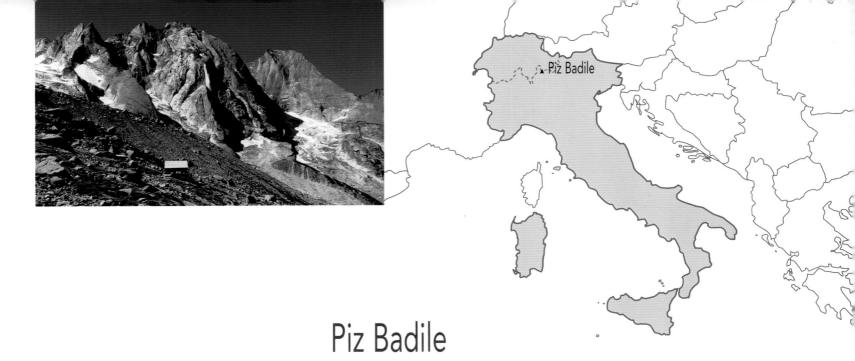

Piz Badile

ITALY - SWITZERLAND

The granite peaks that separate the Bondasca valley in Switzerland from the Masino valley in Italy have transformed many great mountaineers into poets. Gaston Rébuffat, in *Starlight and Storm*, wrote that the Val Bondasca is the most enchanting cirque in the world, while Walter Bonatti, in *My Mountains*, added that the finest mountain landscape that he knew lay just over the Swiss border, on the doorstep of the Engadin valley.

The granite mountains between the Bondasca and Masino valleys are some of the most spectacular in the Alps. Their northern slopes are covered with thick spruce and larch woods that descend toward Promontogno and Bondo, while the Italian side is often bare and rocky. Piz Badile, which reaches a height of 10,853 ft (3308 m), is the best-known peak among mountaineers and is protected by the extraordinary Nordkante (north face) on the Swiss side, flanked by an arête that appears to have been cut by a giant's axe. A series of almost as imposing walls protect Piz Cengalo, which rises to a height of 11,047 ft (3367 m), Cima di Zocca, Punta Allievi and dozens of other summits of the range.

Little known to the thousands of tourists who ascend the mountains by car from Chiavenna toward the Maloja Pass and St. Moritz, and extraordinary when viewed from the historic Sasc Furä and Sciora refuges, Piz Badile and the nearby peaks were discovered by British mountaineers during the 19th century and made mountaineering history during the interwar period. Following the conquest of the hair-raising north ridge in 1923 by the Swiss climbers Walter Risch and Alfred Zürcher, attention shifted to the nearby northeast face, which was scaled in 1937 by Riccardo Cassin, Luigi Esposito and Vittorio Ratti of Lecco and Mario Molteni and Giuseppe Valsecchi of Como. However, Valsecchi and Molteni's deaths from exhaustion during the descent transformed the great victory into a tragedy.

Before and after World War II the foremost Italian mountaineers, including Giusto Gervasutti, Walter Bonatti and Alfonoso Vinci, opened new routes on other peaks of the range. Piz Badile made headlines again in 1968, when three Italian and three Swiss climbers made the first solo ascent via the Cassin route with ten bivouacs en route. Subsequently some very difficult routes, including the Pilastro a Goccia and Via del Fratello, were opened on the Nordkante, considered by mountaineers one of the most prestigious and difficult rock faces in the Alps. Farther down, larches, waterfalls and chamois form an idyllic landscape on the crags around the Sasc Furä hut. Despite the traffic heading for St. Moritz, time seems to stand still in the villages of Promontogno and Bondo.

56 top Piz Cengalo, flanked on the right by the smooth north face of Piz Badile, conquered in 1937, can be admired from the Sciora refuge (center of the photograph).

56 bottom Many of the finest peaks of the Central Alps can be admired in this view looking east from the summit of Piz Badile. Piz Cengalo is visible in the center; Monte Disgrazia can be glimpsed to its right.

57 Despite its fearsome appearance, Piz Badile's many gullies, jags and ledges mean that its normal route, ascended for the first time in 1867, is relatively easy.

58-59 The north face of Piz Badile (right) and Piz Cengalo (11,047 ft/3367 m) form a wild and austere spectacle in this winter view from the upper reaches of the right side of the Bondasca Valley.

Piz Bernina

ITALY - SWITZERLAND

One of the most scenic and photographed ranges in Europe closes off the Engadin valley to the south. The view from Pontresina, St. Moritz, from the railway that climbs the Bernina Pass or from the thick spruce forest surrounding the Hotel Roseg takes in the rocks and ice of Piz Palu, Piz Zupo and Piz Roseg which frame the snow ridges of the Piz Bernina, the easternmost Alpine peak over 4000 m (13,123 ft).

The contrasts between the woods, where it is easy to glimpse deer, the snowy peaks edged with great rocky cornices, and the terrible seracs (ice-pillars) of the *vadrets* (glaciers) of Morteratsch and Roseg explain why this area was nicknamed the "Ballroom of the Alps" over a century ago. While Piz Roseg reaches an altitude of 12,913 ft (3936 m) and Piz Zupo 13,107 ft (3995 m), the summit of Piz Bernina rises to 13,284 ft (4049 m), making it a particularly desirable peak for mountaineers.

Although the massif forms the watershed between Swiss Engadin and Italian Valtellina, the highest peak rises north of the ridge and is consequently entirely in Swiss territory. On the Italian side the rocks and glaciers of the massif slope away more gently toward the upper Valmalenco and manmade Lake Franscia.

The first ascent of Piz Bernina was made by Johann Coaz and his assistants Joan and Lorenz Ragut Tscharner in September 1859, via a difficult route that crossed the Morteratsch Glacier and continued along the rocky East Ridge. Since 1913 the construction of the Capanna Marco and Rosa refuge on the Italian side has led most mountaineers to concentrate on the aerial, but not difficult, rocky Spalla Ridge, which is partly equipped with fixed ropes.

During the century and a half that separates us from Coaz's ascent, Piz Bernina has been explored foot by foot like the other Alpine peaks and numerous difficult routes have been traced on its rock and ice faces. However, the most elegant path and the object of many climbers' dreams is once again the result of the intuition of 19th-century mountaineers.

The first complete ascent of the Biancograt, the sinuous snowy ridge that ascends the mountain on the north, forming the important secondary peak of Piz Alv (13,107 ft/3995 m, was made by the German alpinist Paul Güssfeldt and the Engadin guides Hans Grass and Johann Gross in 1879. Few routes in the Alps are able to match it for elegance and sheer spectacularity.

60 The view from the Corvatsch belvedere encompasses Piz Bernina (left), Piz Scerscen and Piz Roseg. Piz Gemelli, the Sella Pass, Piz Glüschaint and Crasta dal Lej Scrischus can be seen in the background.

60-61 At sunset, Fuorcla Surlej in the Engadin offers a magnificent view of Piz Bernina.

61 bottom Biancograt is an elegant peak even in winter, when the upper reaches of the massif are almost deserted. From this angle it is possible to see the gap that separates snowy Piz Alv (13,107 ft/3995 m) on the right from the rocky peak of Piz Bernina.

62-63 A roped party ascends the snow ridge of Biancograt, which leads to Piz Alv and subsequently to Piz Bernina.

64 The road that climbs from Trafoi up to the Stelvio Pass (9049 feet) was traced between 1820 and 1825 in a forbidding steep-sided valley dominated by Mount Ortles to the south (right).

Mount Ortles

ITALY

One of the most spectacular icy mountains of the Alps stands on the border between Lombardy and the South Tyrol, in sight of the Stelvio Pass and the border with the Swiss canton of Graubünden. Mount Ortles, clearly visible from the upper Venosta Valley and the road to Austria across the Resia Pass, rises to 12,812 ft (3905 m) and is flanked to the south by a range that culminates in the 12,634-ft (3851-m) Gran Zebrù and the 12,365-ft (3769-m) Cevedale. It forms the heart of the Stelvio National Park that covers an area of 520 sq. miles (1347 sq. km), making it the largest in the Italian Alps.

The red deer, ibex, eagles and chamois that inhabit the protected area have recently been joined by the lynx, which has returned to the Martello Valley, and by the bearded vulture, which, once common throughout the Alps, was reintroduced in Austria, France, Italy and Switzerland during the 1990s. The bear,

present in the Brenta Dolomites, returned to Stelvio in 2005.

For many centuries Mount Ortles was the highest peak in the Austro-Hungarian Empire and it is still one of the best-known mountains among German-speaking mountaineers and trekkers. The first ascent, made in 1804 by Josef Pichler, known as Josele, a smuggler and hunter of the Passiria Valley, and Johann Klausner and Johann Leitner, who were both mountaineers of Zillertal Alps region, was greeted with much rejoicing at the Viennese court. The route the three men followed, which Reinhold Messner rediscovered in 2004, crosses rock and ice faces that were extraordinarily difficult for the time.

During the 19th and 20th centuries, several alluring routes were opened on the ridges of Mount Ortles (the Tabaretta, Coston and Solda ridges) and on its steep and treacherous faces. The icy north face, which is the mountain's most difficult, was conquered in 1934 by the German climbers Hans Ertl and Franz Schmid.

64-65 The mighty west face of Mount Ortles (left in the photograph) and the ridge from which Punta Thurwieser (11,982 ft/3652 m), Cime di Campo (11,417 ft/3480 m) and Monte Cristallo (11,266 ft/3434 m) rise form the backdrop for a panoramic stroll along the boundary ridge between Italy and Switzerland.

65 bottom The spectacular north faces of Gran Zebrù (12,634 ft/3851 m), in the center of the photograph, and Monte Zebrù (12,218 ft/3724 m) form the backdrop to the meadows and lakes of the Madritsch Valley. These grassy slopes, carpeted with wild flowers in summer, are home to the Solda ski pistes in winter.

Mount Ortles

An equally surprising, although very different feat, was achieved in 1916 by the Austro-Hungarian mountain troops, who hoisted two 2.75-inch (70-mm) bore cannons up to Mount Ortles' summit.

Today, at dawn on fine summer days, a long line of mountaineers can be seen winding across the rocks of the ridge that connect the Payer refuge to the summit's ice cap.

The mountain's steep slopes can also be admired from the paths and ski runs of Solda, the road that climbs up to the Stelvio and the quiet Alpine village of Trafoi. Reinhold Messner, who is a frequent visitor to Solda, has opened a museum dedicated to the Ortles range in the village and put a few yaks out to pasture in the surrounding meadows, bringing a touch of the Himalayas to Alto Adige.

66 top The Costòn refuge was built in 1892 at an altitude of 8730 ft (2661 m) on a grassy terrace overlooked by Mount Ortles, Monte Zebrù and Gran Zebrù. It is a popular destination for hikers and serves as a base for the

Hintergrat ridge (Cresta del Costòn in Italian) of Mount Ortles and the difficult north face of Gran Zebrù.

66 bottom and 67 Despite its many crevasses and sheer ice walls, the wide, gently sloping northwest face of

Mount Ortles poses no particular difficulties for roped parties ascending the normal route of the highest Tyrolean peak. The sheer and very dangerous north face of the mountain, first scaled in 1934, can be seen in the shadow on the left.

Crozzon di Brenta and Campanile Basso

ITALY

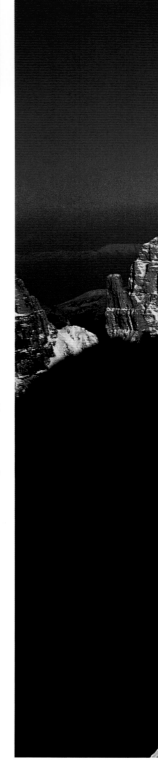

The Dolomites' most famous peak is situated in the Brenta massif, and is only one of the several Dolomite peaks west of the Adige Valley. The Campanile Basso, 9459 ft/2883 m high and defended by perfectly vertical walls and angles, is the symbol of the Trentino mountains. For over a century its elegant form and exceptionally solid rock have made it one of the most popular peaks with mountaineers.

Around the Campanile Basso, the Sfulmini range punctures the skyline with the Campanile Alto, Torre di Brenta and the Brenta Alta, whose North Face is crisscrossed by some of the trickiest routes in the Dolomites. The Brenta Valley separates these dolomitic turrets from the massif's higher range, which culminates in the 10,410-ft (3173-m) peak of Cima Tosa. The imposing rock faces of the nearby Crozzon, whose summit rises 10,285 ft (3135 m), are absolutely breathtaking.

From a geographic point of view, Crozzon di Brenta is a spur of Cima Tosa. However, for mountaineers it is a separate peak, made unmistakable by the north arête, which cuts 2953 ft (900 m) through the sky. "A scene of which I had never seen the like in the Alps," exclaimed the Austrian Paul Preuss, one of the greatest climbers of all times, when he first saw it in 1911.

Over the following days Preuss and his friend Paul Relly made the first ascent of the Crozzon's northeast face, to the left of the arête that Fritz Schneider and Adolf Schulze had conquered six years earlier. However, the feat that made the Austrian mountaineer a legendary figure was his ascent – the first ever – of the east face of the Campanile Basso, a vertical wall of rock rising above a gaping void, which Preuss scaled alone in just two hours without ropes.

A few years earlier Trentino and Tyrolean mountaineers had challenged each other to conquer the Campanile. In 1897 Carlo Garbari, Nino Pooli and Antonio Tavernaro became the first to ascend the mountain and identified many weak points of what is now the normal route, but were forced to accept defeat just a few dozen feet from the peak. Two years later the Tyrolean climbers

Otto Ampferer and Karl Berger followed in their tracks, and subsequently picked the aerial crossing that turned out to be the key to the ascent. "Other men have conquered large islands with flat coasts, ours is small with high, superb edges," Ampferer wrote.

Ever since, the Campanile Basso – like many famous mountains – has been the object of statistics and records. The first winter and nighttime ascents and the thousandth ascent were all accompanied by festivities. A roped party of hundreds of mountaineers ascended the normal route in 1999 to celebrate the centenary of the conquest. Today 20 or so routes zigzag across the mountain's faces. In addition to the normal and Preuss routes, the most popular are the magnificent dihedral scaled in 1908 by Rudolf Fehrmann and Oliver Perry-Smith, with grade-IV+ stretches, and the southwest edge to the shoulder, of grade-V and V+ difficulty, conquered in 1934 by Giorgio Graffer and Antonio Miotto.

A series of local and non-local mountaineers also opened the routes on the Crozzon. In 1929, the Trentino climber Virgilio Neri scaled the snow funnel that separates the peak from the Cima Tosa – and in 1970, the Tyrolean Heini descended it on skis. In 1933, the local mountaineers Bruno Detassis and Enrico Giordani climbed the Via delle Guide, which crosses the sheerest part of the rock face. Thirty-two years later Jean Fréhel and Dominique Leprince-Ringuet scaled the magnificent Northeast Pillar, while Cesare Maestri, another Trentino climber, stunned the public with his solo descent of the Via delle Guide without ropes in 1956.

However, peaks and rock faces are not the only interesting attractions of the Brenta. An unspoiled and untamed massif lies around the finest peaks and the ledges; it is crossed by the Via delle Bocchette, one of the most famous bolted routes in the Alps. Wildlife flourishes in the area: the gullies at the foot of the Crozzon are frequented by chamois, and the forests of the eastern side of the group offer a refuge for the largest bear population of the Italian Alps. Nature continues to reign supreme in the Dolomites.

68 and 68-69 In the clear light of a winter afternoon, the north ridge of Crozzon di Brenta separates the sunny west face of the mountain from the icy northeast face, which at this time of year receives sunlight only during the early part of the morning. The dome of Cima Tosa is visible in the background.

69 bottom The summit plateau of Cima Tosa (the highest peak of the massif at 10,410 ft /3173 m) can be seen in the upper part of the photograph, with the Brenta Alta to the right.

70-71 A bird's-eye view of Crozzon di Brenta (in the foreground) with Cima Tosa and the blue outline of the Campanile Basso beyond.

The Grossglockner

AUSTRIA

The Grossglockner ("Big bellringer"), which is Austria's highest and most spectacular mountain, soars 12,457 ft (3797 m) and separates East Tirol from Carinthia (Kärnten). It is situated in the middle of one of the most beautiful and biologically diverse areas of the Alps and overlooks the Pasterze Glacier. The mountain appears massive when observed from Luckner Haus and the lonely grassy and rocky ridges that separate the valleys of Matrei and Kals in East Tirol, but jagged and spectacular on the Heligenblut side, in Carinthia, where the steep icy gullies of the eastern slope of the mountain plunge toward the Pasterze Glacier's gaping crevasses.

The conquest of the Grossglockner occupies an important place in the early history of mountaineering. In 1800, on order of the Prince-Bishop of Salzburg, a group of "capable vulture hunters" led by Franz Salm reached the rocks and snow of the summit. A famous painting by Johann Pogl, done in 1928 and now housed in the Alpenverein Museum in Innsbruck, commemorates the long-ago feat.

Each year now thousands of mountaineers traverse the aerial ridge that leads to the summit from the Herzog-Johann Hütte via the rocks of the Kleinglockner. The Studl Grat, an elegant rocky ridge that descends toward the Kals slope is another classic and much frequented route with grade-III stretches. However, the retreat of the ice and the many hanging rocks have made the Pallavicini Gully on the side of the Pasterze Glacier less frequented than in the past.

Trekkers from all over Europe throng the paths of the Hohe Tauern National Park at the base of the great mountain and the nearby Gross Venediger (the "Great Venetian"), which covers an area of 687 sq. miles (1780 sq. km) in East Tirol, the area around Salzburg and Carinthia, making it the largest protected area in the Alps.

The park includes woods, high-altitude meadows, forests and dozens of glaciers. Each year it attracts over a million people to whom it offers visitors' centers, films and organized excursions throughout the summer season. In addition to the magnificent bearded vulture, reintroduced to the range during the 1980s, the Hohe Tauern National Park is also home to ibex, red deer, chamois, marmots and all the other examples of the great Alpine fauna. Equally interesting are the glaciers, of which the Pasterze is the largest in the entire Eastern Alps.

---

72 The Kleinglockner and Grossglockner (among the clouds) form the backdrop to the Kodnitzkees Glacier.

73 The spectacular east face of the Grossglockner, furrowed by the Pallavicini Gully, dominates the Pasterze

Glacier, which is the largest in the Austrian Alps, covering an area of almost 8 sq. miles (21 sq. km).

74-75 The light of a winter sunset illuminates the Brennkogel massif (9902 ft/3018 m).

Tre Cime di Lavaredo

ITALY

One of the most famous images of the Dolomites awaits those who climb up to the Locatelli Refuge (Dreizinnen Hütte in German) from the Pusteria or Auronzo valleys. Even for those who know nothing about mountaineering, the silhouette of the Tre Cime di Lavaredo (Drei Zinnen in German) is a symbol of adventure and vertical challenge, just like Everest, Cerro Torre and the Matterhorn. The Cima Grande, which reaches a height of 9839 ft (2999 m), has a sheer north face that plummets to the scree below. The Cima Ovest, rising to 9754 ft (2973 m), is wider and its north face is interrupted by huge overhangs.

The Cima Piccola (9373 ft/2857 m) boasts the spectacular Yellow Edge on the Auronzo side, but fades into insignificance if observed from the north. "Words become insufficient in the face of the terrible austerity of those immense, sinister and solitary faces," wrote Dino Buzzati, a great expert on and lover of the Dolomites. The southern side, which is less steep and terrifying than the other, reveals that there are actually more than three peaks (the Cima Piccolissima, the Punta di Frida and Il Mulo can also be seen), and was chosen for the first ascents of the summits in the 19th century.

However, it was the feats of the 1930s, principally on the north faces, that made the Tre Cime renowned among mountaineers and the public at large. The story commenced in 1933, when the Trieste climber Emilio Comici and the brothers Angelo and Giuseppe Dimai of Cortina ascended the north face of the Cima Grande. A month later, Comici scaled the Yellow Edge with Mary Varale and Renato Zanutti. In 1934 the Lecco mountaineers Riccardo Cassini and Vittorio Ratti conquered the north face of the Cima Ovest, which drops sheer for 1150 ft (350 m).

The north faces returned to the limelight in 1958, when the German climbers Dietrich Hasse, Lothar Brandler, Jorg Lehne

76-77 From the shores of Lake Misurina, the Tre Cime di Lavaredo offers a spectacle as famous as its great north faces. In this photograph the Cima Ovest appears on the left and the Cima Grande on the right. In the foreground, lower down, the elongated massif of Sasso di Ladro can be seen.

77 bottom The south faces of the Tre Cime di Lavaredo form the backdrop to the gully – still covered in snow at the beginning of the summer – that ascends from the Fonda Savio refuge towards the heart of the Cadini di Misurina, the jagged massif that separates the Tre Cime from the deep Ansiei Valley that descends towards Auronzo.

Tre Cime di Lavaredo

and Sigi Löw traced a direct route on the Cima Grande. The following year the precipices of the Cima Ovest were the scene of a contest between the Swiss climbers Hugo Weber and Albin Schelbert and the Cortina "Squirrels" Claudio Zardini, Candido Bellodis, Beniamino Franceschi and Albino Michielli. The two groups chased and overtook each other, only just avoiding physical violence.

A few days later a French team, tackled the great overhangs of the Cima Ovest. Following a week of struggle, René Desmaison finally managed to negotiate the 16.5-ft (5-m)

horizontal ledge that interrupts the vertical wall. "We shouted our joy in frenzy; we wanted them to hear us in Cortina," wrote Pierre Mazeaud, who followed him.

The north faces are still very popular today. While decent mountaineers from all over the world tackle the paths opened by Cassin and Comici, the world-class ones free climb the historic routes traced with steps without the use of bolts. In 1999 the Trieste climber Mauro "Bubu" Bole climbed the route of the French team, without touching the bolts, while two years later the Bavarian Alexander Huber opened an itinerary featuring some

78-79 The north faces of the Tre Cime di Lavaredo (left to right: the Cima Piccola, Cima Grande and Cima Ovest) offer one of the most beautiful and views of the Dolomites in all

seasons. The setting sun illuminates the upper part of the north faces, leaving the imposing sheer walls of the Cima Ovest and Cima Grande almost completely in shadow.

grade-XI stretches on the Cima Ovest. "This is the final step on the ladder leading to the perfection of the art of climbing," commented Reinhold Messner.

However, the Tre Cime are not only rock faces. In the Fiscalina and Campodidentro valleys the chalets and perfectly mown meadows of the upper Pusteria Valley give way to the mugo pines and spruce woods of the Dolomiti di Sesto Natural Park, which is the ideal habitat for chamois. For centuries the Landro Valley has linked the German-speaking mountain people of Sesto, San Candido and Dobbiaco with their neighbors in the Veneto valleys.

These mountains became a battlefield between 1915 and 1917. The Lavaredo Pass, Mt. Piana and the gullies of Cima Undici were the scene of clashes between Italy's Alpine troops, infantry and regular troops and the imperial *Landschützen*, and an Italian reflector was installed on the Cima Grande. In July 1915 a rock thrown by a member of the Alpine troops killed Sepp Innerkofler, a Sesto guide who had made many great ascents. War tunnels and walkways, often perfectly restored, still allow the massif and its history to be explored.

80-81 Three miles wide and up to 4000 ft (1219 m) high, the northwest face of Mount Civetta is the most forbidding in the Dolomites. Punta Tissi (9816 ft/2992 m), Pan di Zucchero (8944 ft/2726 m), Torre di Valgrande (8907 ft/2714 m) and Torre d'Alleghe (8691 ft/2649 m) can be seen to the left of the highest peak in the photograph.

80 bottom The Tissi refuge and the nearby grassy peak of Col Reàn are excellent vantage points for admiring one of the most spectacular sunsets in the Dolomites. The central part of the northwest face, crossed by the Solleder-Lettenbauer route, can be seen on the left. Cima De Gasperi (9823 ft/2994 m) and Cima Su Alto (9682 ft/3042 m) rise on the right.

81 top The east face of Mount Civetta, overlooking the Zoldo Valley, has a far less fearsome appearance than the north face, even in winter. The normal route, opened in 1867 by the British mountaineer Francis Fox Tuckett accompanied by the Swiss guides Melchior and Jakob Anderegg, ascends this side of the mountain.

81 bottom The peak of Mount Civetta appears far more elegant when viewed from Palafavèra and the upper Zoldo Valley. The abyss of the northwest face gapes beyond the ridge.

82-83 The Lagazuoi refuge offers spectacular views over the Dolomites. The north faces of Mounts Pelmo (left) and Civetta can be seen in the background beyond Averau, Nuvolau and Croda da Lago.

Mount Civetta

ITALY

The most forbidding wall of the Dolomites is situated at the eastern end of the group. It is formed by the Pale di San Martino and the Marmolada, overlooking the Cordevole Valley between Cenenighe and Alleghe, and dominating the Tissi refuge and the pastures and screes of the Civetta Valley. The northwest face of Civetta, 3281 ft (1000 m) high and 2.5 miles (4.0 km) wide and adorned with a tiny hanging glacier, culminates in the 10,564-ft (3220-m) peak. This face offers some of the most challenging climbs in the Alps. The routes to the nearby peaks of Punta Tissi, Punta Civetta, Pan di Zucchero, Cima De Gaspari and Cima Su Alto are also very difficult. Then, rising at the end of the rock wall are the extraordinary Dolomite formations of the Busazza, Torre Venezia and Torre Trieste.

The first ascent of Civetta was made in 1867 by the British mountaineer Francis Fox Tuckett and the Swiss guides Melchior and Jakob Anderegg, who reached the summit via the scree slopes and easy rock faces overlooking the Zoldo Valley. However, the Northwest Face and its giant satellites have witnessed the passage of many of the most famous names of Dolomite mountaineering. In 1925 the two Bavarians Emil Solleder and Gustav Lettenbauer opened up the first grade-VI route in history in the heart of the rock wall. "Is it a real spectacle? I'd never seen a rock face like this in the Alps," noted Solleder. The rock falls and storms made his ascent very dramatic.

Solleder's feat drew the best Dolomite climbers to Civetta, starting with the Veneto mountaineers Attilio Tissi, Domenico Rudatis, and Giovanni and Alvise Andrich. In 1931 the Trieste climber Emilio Comici opened up a route to the left of Solleder's one. Other distinguished climbers, among them Riccardo Cassini of Lecco, Celso Gilberti of Trentino, Ettore Castiglioni of Milan and Raffaele Carlesso of Vicenza, concentrated on the Torre Venezia and Torre Trieste.

However, the finest route of all was opened in 1957, when the Austrian climbers Walther Phillipp and Dieter Flamm ascended the great dihedral of the Civetta, which reaches the summit ridge at Punta Tissi, with two bivouacs. Reinhold Messner, who made the first solo ascent, described it as "a fantastic route."

More recently, in 1963, the Friulian climber Ignazio Pussi, the Lombard Giorgio Radaelli and the Bavarian Toni Hiebeler made the exceptionally hard first winter ascent of the Solleder route. The same feat was repeated, this time solo, in 1999 by the Lecco mountaineer Marco Anghileri. A leisurely stroll through the Civetta Valley, between the Vazzolèr, Tissi and Sonino refuges, enables mountain lovers to read this story like the pages of a great book of rock.

The Marmolada

Empire and the Kingdom of Italy led the armies of the two powers to carve a maze of emplacements, dugouts, connecting tunnels and trenches in the rock and ice. Following World War II, the Marmolada was brutally defaced in the name of tourism.

The slopes of the glacier became home to several summer ski pistes, while a huge cableway was built between Malga Ciapèla, the rocky crest of Punta Serauta, and the 10,856-ft (3309-m) peak of Punta Rocca. In recent years the charm of this magnificent mountain has been further reduced by the increasingly marked retreat of the glacier, which is uncovering the rocky slabs that descend toward the Fedaia Pass.

86 The sharp summit ridge of the Marmolada separates the sheer south face from the ice slopes, crossed by dozens of summer ski runs. Punta Ombretta looms in the foreground, while Punta Rocca (with the cable car station) and Punta Penia are visible in the background.

87 top The sharp rocky pyramid of Col Ombert dominates the refuge of the San Nicolò Pass, which stands on a wide grassy col at an altitude of 7671 ft (2338 m). This photograph was taken on the southern edge of the Marmolada massif, overlooking the San Nicolò and Fassa valleys.

87 bottom The sheer limestone walls of the Gran Vernel (10,531 ft/3210 m) and Piccolo Vernel (10,164 ft/3098 m), illuminated here by the warm light of sunset, dominate Alba, Penia, Canazei and the other towns of the upper Fassa Valley.

The Marmolada

88 top The ridge that joins Punta Ombretta (left) to Punta Rocca reveals the asymmetric face of the Marmolada. To the north modest rocky ramparts descend towards the slopes of the glacier covered with the winter snow. On the opposite side – invisible in this photograph – the south face falls sheer to the ground.

88 center The wide glacial indentation between Punta Penia (right) and Punta Rocca is crossed by the mountain's normal route. In winter the thick blanket of snow conceals the extent to which the glacier has retreated and thinned.

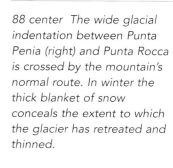

88 bottom Each year the cable car that ascends from Malga Ciapèla – the subject of fierce criticism for its environmental impact – carries tens of thousands of tourists to the summit ridge of the Marmolada, not far from Punta Rocca (10,856 ft/3309 m), the second highest peak of the massif.

88-89 The normal route of Punta Penia, inaugurated in 1864 by the Viennese climber Paul Grohmann and the Ampezzo guides Angelo and Fulgenzio Dimai, ascends the wide icy gully visible to the left of the rocky triangle in the center of the photograph.

89 bottom Very popular in summer with climbers following the normal route, the Via Ferrata of the west ridge and the difficult climbing routes on the south face, during winter the cross and small hut on the summit of Punta Penia become solitary and remote.

90-91 The imposing limestone massif of Triglav (Tricorno in Italian), culminating at 9396 feet, is the symbol of the young Republic of Slovenia. Situated in the heart of the national park of the same name, which covers an area of over 310 square miles, it is one of the most visited mountains in Europe and the world.

90 bottom Although the most difficult and famous climbing routes have been opened on the boundary range, and in particular on Piccolo Mangart di Coritenza, Triglav's faces and ridges are crossed by dozens of routes. The north face, over 3280 ft (1000 m) high, was conquered in 1890 by Ivan Berginc.

91 The rainwater of the Julian Alps returns to the surface in crystal-clear springs. The sources of the Isonzo River (known as the Soca in Slovenian, rise in the Trenta Valley, between Jalovec and Triglav, before heading south towards Kobarid (Caporetto), the Italian border and the Adriatic Sea.

Triglav

SLOVENIA

Only one of the world's national flags bears the stylized image of a mountain. The decision to make Triglav the emblem of the young Republic of Slovenia is a very telling sign of the importance of mountains in a country in which a twentieth of the population enjoys trekking or mountaineering, in which mountains are part of the school curriculum, and skiing boasts a long and important tradition.

Rising 9396 ft (2864 m), Triglav (Tricorno in Italian) is the highest peak of the Julian Alps, the imposing limestone range that overlooks the Friuli plain to the south and the wooded ridges of the Carnic Alps, and the Austrian region of Carinthia (Kärnten) beyond, to the north. The great mountain is surrounded by the 313-sq.-mile (811-sq.-km) Triglav National Park, which is home to one of the largest European bear populations as well as ibex, eagles, red deer and other examples of large alpine fauna.

Westward, the Julian Alps continue with the Slovenian peaks of Jalovec and Razor and the Italian Jof di Montasio and Jof Fuart. The border ridge is marked by the summits of Veunza and Mangart, where since the 1930s mountaineers have opened some of the most difficult climbing routes of the Eastern Alps. The route opened single-handedly by the Trieste climber Enzo Cozzolino on Piccolo Mangart di Coritenza (Mali Koritniski Mangart) in 1970 and repeated by the Vicenza climber Renato Casarotto on a solo winter climb 12 years later is one of the first grade-VII itineraries in the Alps.

The summit of Triglav, scaled in 1778 by four mountaineers from Bohinj, is reached by thousands of Slovenian and European climbing enthusiasts each summer, by means of an easy route with a few via ferrata stretches. However, "the roof of Slovenia" also has a respectable and forbidding north face,

almost 3300 ft (1005 m) high, which the Trenta Valley mountaineer Ivac Berginc scaled for the first time in 1890.

Today the bolted route that connects Triglav's most famous refuges (Aljazev Dom and Triglavski Dom) coasts the face on the left, allowing the mountain's wild beauty to be admired. The slabs and spurs of the central part of the wall, on the other hand, are crossed by extremely difficult routes. Most of these were opened by alpinists such as Francek Knez and Tomo Cesen, who have also achieved great feats in Patagonia and the Himalayas.

Along with the bears, forests and crowds of climbers that ascend the path to the summit, the vertical edge of the Sphinx is one of the most beautiful and best-known images of Triglav.

92-93 The position of Triglav and the other peaks of the Julian Alps is exposed to the full force of the icy northeast winds, making the climate of these mountains much colder than their altitude would suggest. Winter ascents of the range have always been exceptionally grueling.

Triglav

93 From November until late May Triglav's summits are covered with a thick blanket of snow. The Slovenian national passion for mountaineering is also evident in the winter, when skiers born in these valleys often triumph in downhill, cross country and ski jump events.

Etna

ITALY

The highest volcano of the Mediterranean region overlooks Catania, the Taormina coast, and the wooded ridges of the Nebrodi Mountains, which reach inland toward the heart of Sicily. However, Etna, with its plume of smoke can also be seen from Reggio Calabria and the Aspromonte massif in mainland Italy. When the wind blows from the Ionian Sea, the airplanes landing at Catania fly around the volcano, offering extraordinary views of its craters.

Etna was already famous in the ancient world, and was studied by Empedocles, the philosopher of Acragas, who observed the violent eruption of 475 BC and subsequently climbed the volcano to view it at close quarters. According to legend, the Roman emperor Hadrian also ascended to the craters. The traditional Sicilian name of the volcano, Mongibello, recalls the island's centuries under Islamic rule, for *jebel* means "mountain" in Arabic. In 1787 Goethe scaled Etna, stopping at the Monti Rossi double cone. The geologist Déodat de Dolomieu leaned over the "crater lit from inside by a strange white light."

The volcano has erupted 140 times since 475 BC, with a large eruption every 20 years on average. In 1669, despite numerous processions and prayers, molten lava destroyed Catania and reached the sea. The great Italian writer Leonardo Sciascia explained the familiarity and diffidence of the islanders toward the volcano: "It's like a huge house cat that snores quietly; every now and then, it wakes, yawns, stretches lazily and with a swipe of its paw destroys a valley here or there, wiping out towns, vineyards and gardens." Etna is a living mountain that changes from day to day. Its highest mouth is currently the northeast one, at 10,892 ft (3320 m). The old central crater is dormant, while lazy spirals of smoke rise from the Bocca Nuova. The southeast crater, at the center of the most recent eruptions, awakes every two or three days, spurting lava and hurling "bombs," incandescent masses weighing up to 220 lbs (100 kg) that can travel distances up to 330 ft (100 m).

Most visitors to Etna, which is now protected by Sicily's finest regional park, ascend the volcano by off-road vehicle to a height of around 1000 ft (305 m). However, trekkers accompanied by guides may continue up as far as the craters, or walk right around the volcano in three days. During winter skiers can enjoy the Zafferana and Linguaglossa pistes or traverse the volcano. The clear winter air makes it possible to see Calabria and the Lipari Islands.

94 The Monti Rossi cinder cones, formed by a violent eruption during the 17th century, open near the road that ascends Mount Etna from Zafferana Etnea to the Sapienza refuge.

94-95 and 95 bottom The summit of Etna dominates the lava terrace of the volcano's south face. Here, during periods of intense activity, chasms and small secondary craters open, spewing out lava. The northeast crater (10,892 ft/3320 m) is currently the highest point of Mount Etna.

96-97 Etna's recent activity is concentrated on the Bocca Nuova and the southeast crater. However, the cinder cones that open in the upper part of the volcano also emit lava flows, spurts and "bombs."

98-99 The lava flowing out of Etna's craters and cinder cones is one of the most exciting natural spectacles in Europe, which has continued ceaselessly for around 600,000 years.

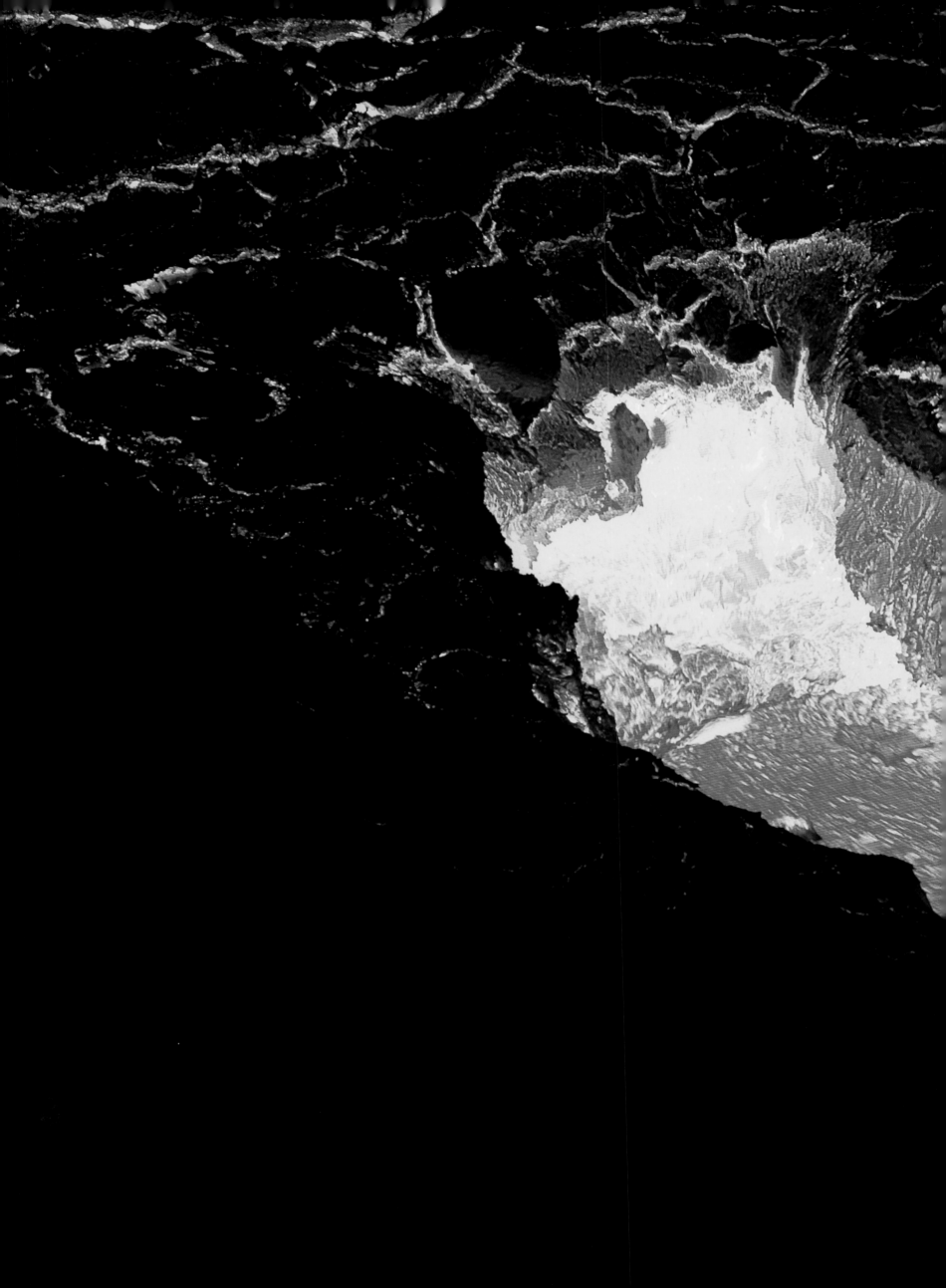

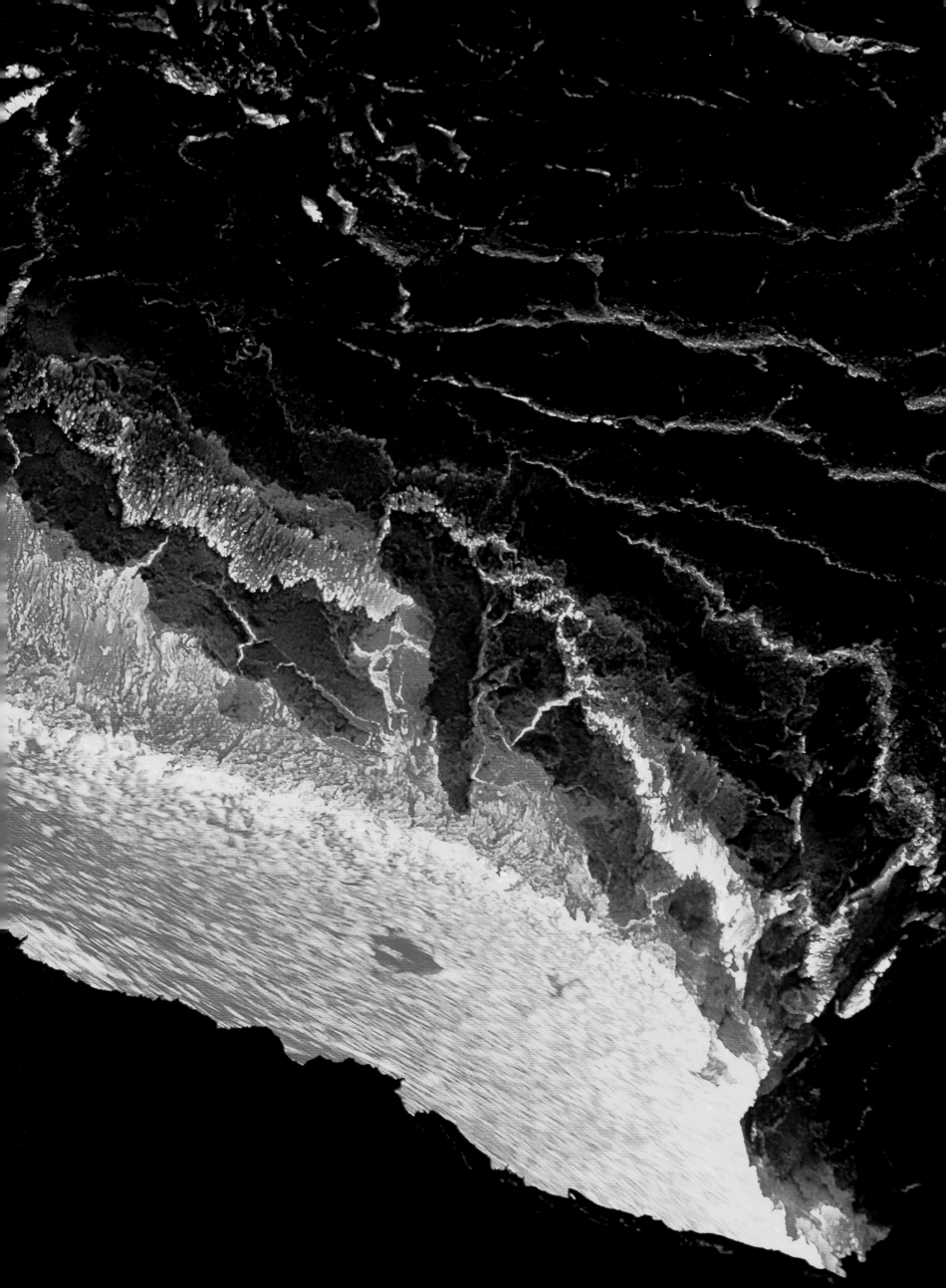

100-101 During winter the west face of Mount Olympus – far less interesting than the east one for mountaineers and trekkers – is a favorite spot for ski-touring enthusiasts. However, the plans for new ski lifts in the area have long been cause for concern for Greek and international environmentalists.

Mount Olympus
GREECE

The "Mountain of Zeus" overlooks the Aegean Sea and the ruins of Dion, one of the most important cities of ancient Macedonia. The lofty and imposing Olympus massif is scored by wild gullies and culminates in the 9570-ft (2917-m) Mytikas, the highest peak in Greece and the Balkans. Defended by spectacular limestone rock faces, the main peak is flanked by Skolio (9550 ft/2911 m), Stefani (or "Throne of Zeus," 9544 ft/2909 m) and Skala (9403 ft/2866 m).

Steep and wild on the seaward side, where the rocky Kazania cirque is situated, the massif slopes more gently to the west, where the little ski resort of Vryssopoulos lies. Its proximity to the coast road and the Aegean routes led the ancient Greeks to consider Olympus (whose name means "The Luminous One," due to the shimmering appearance of the snowy peaks during winter) the home of Zeus and the other gods, who achieved their decisive victory over the Titans here.

The handsome, although often crumbly, limestone walls have been attracting European climbers to the massif for almost a century. In 1913 the first ascent of Mytikas was made by the Swiss mountaineers D. Baud-Bovy and F. Boissonnas, accompanied by the Greek K. Kakalos, via the easy rocks of today's normal route. In 1934 the Trieste climber Emilio Comici, who had achieved great feats in the Dolomites, scaled the northeast face of Stefani.

However, the systematic exploration of the rocks of the Olympus massif was performed by Yorgos Mikhailidis, who opened some 15 new routes during the 1950s and 1960s, often as part of a roped team with Kostas Zolotas, who for many decades ran the busiest refuge of the group. Two of these itineraries, on the west face of the Mytikas have grade-VI stretches.

Mt. Olympus is not all limestone rock faces and mythology. The monotonous side that descends toward Macedonia contrasts with the Aegean slopes, densely covered with

aromatic woods, where the oaks of the lower altitudes gradually give way to conifers and then juniper bushes. The local geology, flora and fauna make the Olympus National Park, covering an area of 172 sq. miles (445 sq. km), one of the most visited in Greece.

Although the rock faces are little frequented, thousands of trekkers from Thessaloniki, Athens and the whole world climb the massif each year from Litochoro to Mytikas and the other highest peaks. In a most successful action for the environment, these trekkers and mountaineers mobilized in the 1990s to block a deplorable project that would have devastated Mt. Olympus by building a Disneyland at its foot, connected to the summits by a cableway.

Mount Olympus

102 top The Skala (9403 ft/2866 m), Mytikas (9570 ft/2916 m) and Stefani (9544 ft/2909 m) peaks dominate the wild Kanzania ("Caldron") cirque, which opens on the side of the mountain overlooking the village of Litochoro and the Aegean Sea.

102 bottom Over thousands of years erosion has carved pinnacles out of the sides of the steep valleys that rise towards the peaks of Mount Olympus from Litochoro. The rock of the massif is crumbly, also along the climbing routes of the Mytikas and Stefani peaks.

102-103 Stefani, standing at 9544 ft (2909 m), is the third highest peak of Mount Olympus, after Mytikas and Skolio. The first mountaineer to open a route on the mountain's vertical west face, scored by parallel clefts, was the Trieste climber Emilio Comici, in 1934.

AFRICA

When we think of Africa, we imagine settings and landscapes quite different from mountains, such as the savannas of the Masai Mara and the Serengeti, the sands of the Kalahari and the Sahara, and the rainforests of the Congo. We envisage spectacular and untamed worlds, inhabited by elephants and lions, or where even today people travel by camel or dugout canoe. Completing our picture are the remains of man's earliest ancestors, the ancient civilizations of Egypt, Islamic North Africa and Coptic Ethiopia, the kaleidoscope of ethnic groups and the myriad problems that the cities and nations of the Black Continent face today.

However, Africa is also a mountainous land. From the ridges of the Atlas Mountains separating the Mediterranean shores from the Sahara to Table Mountain overlooking Cape Town, the continent boasts an extraordinary variety of ranges, plateaus, rocky pinnacles and isolated volcanoes. A few of these mountains are famous, but most are practically unknown. However, all are home to extraordinarily fascinating plants and animals and have been the scenes of great adventures of explorers and mountaineers.

Some of the African peaks are close to the great places of man. Mt. Toubkal and the other peaks of the Moroccan Atlas Mountains provide the backdrop to the ancient cities of Marrakech, Meknès and Fès (Fez); Ras Dashen, the highest peak in Ethiopia, rises close to the rock churches of Lalibela; and the rocky peaks of Adwa witnessed the most terrible battle between an African army and European troops in 1896.

The continent's most extraordinary prehistoric rock paintings are found in the Tassili n'Ajjer in Algeria and the Tadrart Acacus in Libya. The pinnacles of the Ahaggar and Air in Niger have provided the backdrop to the nomad civilization of the Tuareg, while the civilizations of the Masai, Kikuyu and the white colonists of the early 20th century all developed at the foot of Mt. Kenya. The glorious history of the Zulus, on the other hand, played out at the base of the Drakensberg Mountains.

Other African peaks are more isolated, surrounded only by untamed nature. Thick rainforests extend around the Ruwenzori Range, on the border between Uganda and the Democratic Republic of Congo, and the nearby Virunga volcanoes that are home to Africa's last mountain gorillas. Tibesti is the highest massif in the Sahara and can be reached only by interminable journeys from Libya or Chad, offering visitors a barren vista of red-hot rocks under a baking sun.

Other deserts that alternate sand with rocks provide the backdrop to Spitzkoppe, the highest mountain in Namibia, and South Africa's Cedarberg Range, while the truncated cone of Kilimanjaro, the continent's highest peak, rises high above the elephants, antelopes and lions of Kenya's Amboseli National Park. It is images like these that continue to make Africa a legend.

104 left The highest point of Ol Doinyo Lengai, the only active volcano in East Africa, in Tanzania, reaches 9468 ft (2886 m).

104 center The east face of Garet El Djenoun, in Algeria, has two huge pinnacles that reach a height of 7644 ft (2330 m).

104 right Mount Baker rises 15,892 ft (4844 m) above the Buyuku Valley in the Ruwenzori Mountains National Park.

105 About 15,100 ft (4603 m) below Kilimanjaro (19,340 ft/5894 m), the Tanzanian savanna is the realm of wildlife.

Garet el Djenoun
ALGERIA

The Sahara is not all sand dunes and oases. Extending from the Atlantic to the Red Sea and from the Mediterranean to the Sahel, the world's largest desert also comprises some surprising rocky massifs. In Niger the sandstone towers of the Aïr massif rise not far from Agadez and the sands of the Sahara's Ténéré region. Mali is home to the pinnacles of Hombori, while the volcanic Tibesti massif between Libya and Chad is home to the great desert's highest peaks. Other rocky summits rise in Libya, in Mauritania and in Egypt between the Nile and the Red Sea.

The most interesting mountains of all are to be found in the "Great South" of Algeria. In the Tassili n'Ajjer region, on the border with Libya, thousands of rock paintings dating back to 8000 BC illustrate the culture of the Sahara's peoples and the evolution of the desert's climate and fauna. Farther north, near Tamanrasset, the granite peaks of the Ahaggar have represented a challenge for European climbers for decades.

Mt. Tahat, the highest point in Algeria at 9,573 ft (2918 m), can be easily scaled, but the faces and jagged arêtes of the Tehoulaig, Saouinan, Ilamane and Daouda offer very refined climbs in one of Africa's most evocative settings. Assekrem, another easy peak, is home to the hermitage built in 1905 by Father Charles-Eugène de Foucauld, where the ascetic (a former soldier) was killed in 1916 by a group of Libyan rebels.

The Sahara's most famous and feared summit is situated a little north of the Ahaggar, in the Tefedest massif. It is known as Garet el Djenoun, the "Mountain of the Spirits," and reaches an altitude of 7644 ft (2330 m). Surrounded by scree and dunes, and flanked by the monolithic Takouba and the imposing bulk of In Acoulmou, Garet el Djenoun boasts

several very difficult routes opened by French and Spanish mountaineers. However, the most famous line remains the complicated normal route, traced in 1935 by the Chamonix climber Roger Frison-Roche and Captain Raymond Coche. The ascent alternates between slabs and smooth crevices and ledges inhabited by mouflon. In total isolation, excited and parched, the two French mountaineers tackled an exposed chimney, a crumbling slab and a ledge where a wild olive tree grows before reaching the plateau of the summit. "We sailed in the heart of Atlantis, aboard the most monstrous vessel that our imagination was able to dream up," commented Frison-Roche in his *Carnets Sahariens*.

Garet el Djenoun

106-107 The steep north face of Garet El Djenoun dominates the sand, rocks and acacias of Oued Ariaret, at the foot of the Tefedest massif, one of the most spectacular in the Algerian Sahara.

107 bottom The mountain, whose Arabic name means "Mountain of the Spirits," reaches an altitude of 7644 ft (2330 m).

108-109 The clear light of dawn underscores the elegance of the Ahaggar range, the most spectacular in the Algerian Sahara, which rises a few miles from the caravan town of Tamanrasset. The peak furrowed with clefts and pillars in the middle of the photograph is South Tezoulag, on which many difficult routes have been opened.

Nyiragongo

DEMOCRATIC REPUBLIC OF CONGO

One of the most active volcanoes in the world overlooks Goma and Lake Kivu in the Democratic Republic of Congo. Nyiragongo, which rises to 11,385 ft (3470 m), belongs to the Virunga range of volcanoes that extends along the borders of Congo, Rwanda and Uganda. The range culminates in the 14,787-ft (4507-m) summit of Karisimbi and also includes Mikeno, Sabinyo, Visoke, Muhavura and Mgahinga Nyamulagira, standing lower than the others, has devastated the region with its violent eruptions. This region has long attracted volcanologists.

"A brief moment of calm followed each tremor of rage. Brown or blue smoke rose in thick spirals, while a deafening rumble, similar to that of a monstrous dog, shook the entire volcano. However, there was no time for one's nerves to relax, for a new, sudden quake, another explosion, the resumption of the incandescence and the commencement of a new barrage were nigh. The lava bombs rose with a buzz." This was how the French volcanologist Haroun Tazieff described the eruption of Kituro, a pyroclastic cone that had opened just a few weeks earlier between Nyamulagira and Nyiragongo. *Cratères en Feu* (1951), the book that recounts his African explorations, is a classic of volcanology and adventure.

In Kinyarwanda, one of the commonest languages in the region, the term Virunga ("fiery place," or "saucepan") is used to describe all peaks of volcanic origin. It was thus inevitable that the entire volcanic region north of Lake Kivu should end up being called by this name. Imposing Nyiragongo has long attracted visitors. When access to Congo is not prevented by civil wars and conflicts, it is possible to follow the path in a five-hour ascent through the lava slopes and fumaroles to reach an impressive

110-111 A fearsome cloud of smoke rising from the crater of Nyiragongo during the 2003 eruption. The volcano, which reaches a height of 11,385 ft (3470 m), overlooks the town of Goma and the Virunga National Park.

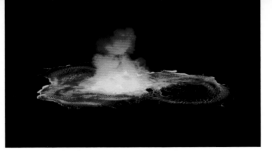

Nyiragongo

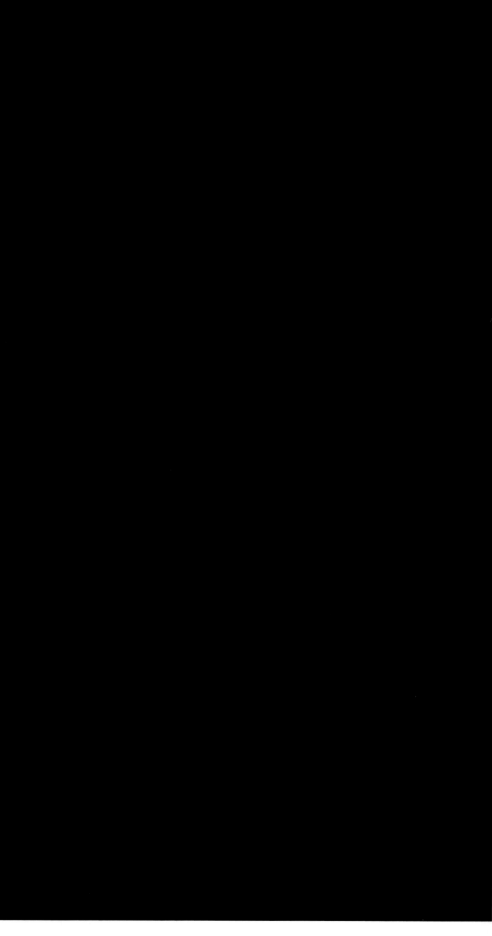

caldera 1640 ft (500 m) across, which is defended by 650-ft (198-m) walls and illuminated by incandescent lava flows. Following decades of tranquility, the volcano erupted in 1996 and again in 2001, threatening Goma and the surrounding towns.

While volcanic activity is the main attraction of Nyamulagira and Nyiragongo, the easternmost volcanoes of the Virunga range are extinct and covered with thick forests. This is the habitat of the mountain gorilla, which the American zoologist Dian Fossey struggled to protect and for which she was killed. Conservation projects for the species have long existed in all three countries of the area. Today the best spot for those wishing to observe these animals is the Bwindi Reserve in Uganda. A close encounter with mountain gorillas is as moving an experience as the sight of the lava flows of Nyiragongo.

112 top During eruptions an awe-inspiring lake of incandescent lava forms in Nyiragongo's huge caldera, over 1600 ft (487 m) across and about 650 ft (198 m) deep.

112 bottom While the uppermost layer of lava slowly starts to solidify, cracks reveal the molten rock that continues to flow beneath the surface. This photograph was taken in January 2002, during one of Nyiragongo's most active periods.

112-113 The lava that erupts from the bottom of the crater illuminates the caldera and the entire upper area of Nyiragongo.

Similar spectacles are also offered by Nyamulagira, another volcano that stands 10,046 ft (3062 m) high and lies within a day and a half's walking distance from the road between Goma and Beni.

Ruwenzori Range

The Ruwenzori Range

UGANDA - DEMOCRATIC REPUBLIC OF CONGO

A pantheon of European crowned heads reigns over Africa's wildest massif. The old border between the British and Belgian colonies, which now separates Uganda from the Democratic Republic of Congo, is marked by the Ruwenzori Range, the third largest on the continent in terms of height. It culminates in Margherita Peak (16,795 ft/5119 m), a pyramid of rock and ice dedicated to the Italian queen who fell in love with Monte Rosa. Not far away, and a few feet lower down, other wind-eroded summits of rock and ice commemorate Britain's Queen Alexandra and Belgium's King Albert. Several secondary peaks overlooking the misty Mokubu and Bukuju valleys are dedicated to members of the House of Savoy, such as Umberto, Vittorio Emanuele, Yolanda and Elena. One recalls Luigi Amedeo of Savoy, the Duke of the Abruzzi, who first climbed the Ruwenzori Range.

The first white man to see the mountains was British-American explorer Henry Morton Stanley during his 1888 expedition. He wrote "[M]y eyes were directed by a boy to a mountain said to be covered with salt, and I saw a peculiar shaped cloud of a most beautiful silver colour, which assumed the proportions and appearance of a vast mountain covered with snow…. [T]hen as the sight descended to the gap between the eastern and western plateaus, I became for the first time conscious that what I gazed on was not the image or semblance of a vast mountain, but the solid substance of a real one, with its summit covered with snow." The legend of the "Mountains of the Moon" recounted by Ptolemy was thus proved true.

Other travelers discovered that the Ruwenzori is a complex range comprising 6 different massifs and 25 peaks over 4000 m (13,123 ft), and described the dense, fairy-tale vegetation that completely covers all its slopes. Luigi Amedeo reached the range in 1906, and scaled Margherita Peak with the Courmayeur guides Joseph and Laurent Pétigax, César Ollier and Joseph Brocherel. The expedition conquered all the highest peaks of the massif and the famed photographer Vittorio Sella took some magnificent photographs of the summits, forests and glaciers.

Over the subsequent decades other mountaineers climbed the most difficult faces and some basic refuges were built on the two sides of the Ruwenzori Range. However, the hostile climate, difficult and muddy paths, coups d'état and wars that have shaken Uganda and the Democratic Republic of Congo (the latter was renamed Zaïre for a few decades) have prevented the massif from becoming a popular mountaineering destination like Kilimanjaro or Mt. Kenya. Protected by the Virunga National Park on the Congolese side, and the Ruwenzori Mountains National Park on the Ugandan one, Africa's third largest massif remains an exceptional destination for adventure lovers.

114 The west side of the Ruwenzori Range is steeper than the one that slopes down towards Uganda, and can be reached from the town of Beni in the Democratic Republic of Congo. Four days of climbing, first in the forest and then amid Senecio and Lobelia plants, are necessary in order to reach the foot of Margherita Peak and Alexandra Peak.

114-115 A huge flat basin is home to Lake Bujuku, at the head of the valley of the same name, at an altitude of around 13,000 ft (3962 m). The rocky east face of Mount Stanley can be seen in the background, partially covered by cloud.

115 bottom The most picturesque of the many lakes of the Ugandan side of the Ruwenzori Range is undoubtedly Lake Kitandara, which lies west of the Freshfield Pass at an altitude of around 14,000 ft (4267 m). Sella Peak (15,282 ft/4658 m) and the other summits of Mount Luigi di Savoia are visible in the background.

The Ruwenzori Range

116 top and 117 Alexandra Peak (16,762 ft/5109 m) is the second highest summit of the Ruwenzori Range, but has lost much of its ice cover during the past few decades. Today little remains of the elegant snow ridge crossed in 1906 by the

Duke of Abruzzi and the Courmayeur guides who accompanied him.

116 bottom At the foot of the highest summits of the Ruwenzori Range, the icy Stanley Plateau is crossed by

the roped parties that make their way up to Margherita Peak and Alexandra Peak from the Elena Hut. The summits of Mount Speke, culminating in Vittorio Emanuele Peak (16,122 ft/4913 m), are visible among the clouds.

Ol Doinyo Lengai

TANZANIA

A very special volcano rises just south of the border between Tanzania and Kenya. Ol Doinyo Lengai, which is sacred to the Masai, who consider it the "Mountain of God," is situated in the Rift Valley northwest of the town of Arusha. This town is the starting point for ascents of Kilimanjaro and visits to the Serengeti Park, Lake Manyara, the Ngorongoro Crater and the other great natural attractions of northern Tanzania.

Ol Doinyo Lengai is the only active volcano in East Africa. It is considerably lower than the surrounding peaks (its summit is 9468 ft/2886 m, almost 10,000 ft/3048 m lower than Kilimanjaro). It culminates in two nearby craters, but what makes it special is its lava. Indeed, it is the only known volcano to erupt natrocarbonatite lava, which is much cooler (950 °F in comparison to ca. 2012 °F

of basalt lava) and more fluid than other kinds of lava. It reaches the surface through small rootless spatter cones up to 50 ft high that volcanologists call *hornitos* ("little horns"), which sometimes hurl lapilli (rounded or angular fragments or lava) into the air.

The natrocarbonatite lava of Ol Doinyo Lengai is not incandescent during the day, when it generally resembles an oil slick. If the gas content is particularly low it may even resemble water. Indeed, in the past many visitors referred to having seen mudslides. At night the lava assumes an orange hue, but it is far less bright than that of other volcanoes. The newly solidified lava is black and contains crystals that glimmer in the sun. Contact with humidity causes the color to change rapidly to white owing to chemical reactions. Indeed, when it rains the transformation is practically instant.

Since the 1980s a growing number of visitors have observed the volcano's activity and volcanologists have recently been joined by an ever-increasing flow of tourists. The volcano alternates periods of calm with explosive outbursts, which may rapidly become dangerous. While the ascent to the crater is particularly difficult (it is necessary to ascend 5577 ft (1700 m) from the Masai village of Engare Sero on sandy terrain in torrid conditions), the sandy areas around the craters allow comfortable camping.

Fortunately, the hostile environment of the crater does not discourage wildlife, and the summit is home to poisonous snakes (especially cobras), small antelopes and birds of prey, and the sandy soil often bears the tracks of leopards.

118 The steep lava and sand slopes of Ol Doinyo Lengai dominate the desolate plateau near the Masai village of Engare Sero.

119 The lava of Ol Doinyo Lengai is cooler and more fluid than that erupted by other volcanoes. It is not incandescent during the day and may even

look like water when the gas content is particularly low. Sometimes the lava from the two craters resembles mudflows.

120-121 The twin craters of Ol Doinyo Lengai alternate calm periods with explosive outbursts, which can rapidly become dangerous.

122-123 The north face of Mount Kenya, which dominates the upper Mackinder Valley, is the most famous and photographed of the mountain. Batian (17,058 ft/5199 m, left), Nelion and jagged Point John are silhouetted against the sky.

122 bottom Like the other great African mountains, the landscape of Mount Kenya above the tree line is characterized by Senecio (in this photograph) and Lobelia plants.

123 Dozens of emerald-green lakes and pools, known as tarns, lie among the moraine overlooked by Batian, Nelion and the nearby peaks. This aerial photograph shows Emerald Tarn, at the top of the Nanyuki Valley.

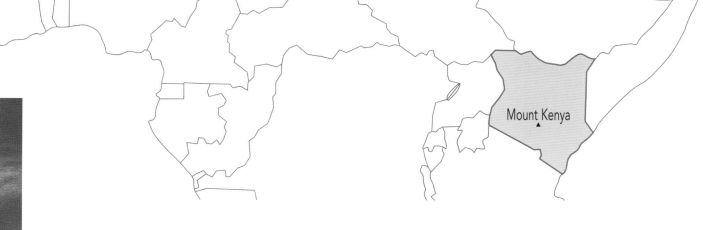

Mount Kenya

KENYA

The "Matterhorn of Africa" stands just a few miles from the equator, overlooking the most fertile plateau of the country to which it has given its name and protected by one of the most beautiful and surprising parks of the entire continent. Mt. Kenya is sacred to the Masai (who call it Ol-Donyo-Oibor, meaning "white mountain"), Samburu and Kikuyu (who refer to it as Kere-Nyaga) and culminates in the rocky twin peaks of Batian and Nelion, 17,058 and 17,022 ft (5199 and 5188 m) above sea level respectively. The exposed Gate of Mists gap lies between the two peaks.

At the foot of the eastern wall of Nelion, which according to the mountaineer and writer Felice Benuzzi, is "the same shining yellow as the houses of old Rome in the autumn, before sunset tinges them vermilion," is the easy Point Lenana. It was formed by broken rocks and snow, reaches a height of 16,355 ft (4985 m), and is the favorite destination of trekkers visiting Africa's second highest massif. The dizziest peaks are surrounded by minor ones, such as Sendeyo, Tereri and Point John, and rapidly retreating glaciers (the largest of which is the Lewis Glacier).

At about 13,000 ft (3962 m) above sea level, amid lakes and moraine, the vegetation is made up of *Senecio* and *Lobelia*, the huge succulents that inhabit all African mountains, flanked by delicate *Helichrysum* and countless varieties of native flora. Lower down, the forest of Mt. Kenya arouses wonder in those who cross it, with its tree heaths, mosses, yellowwoods and towering macarangas in which colobus monkeys shriek and leap.

The skies are home to eagles, vultures and the rare Mackinder's eagle owl. Buffalo, elephants and leopards are still numerous in the forest, which is also the hiding place of shy little forest antelopes, such as the duiker and the bushbuck. However, the easiest animal to spot is the hyrax, a mammal that resembles a marmot in form and size, but is actually a close relative of the elephant.

The Mt. Kenya massif was sighted and described by European explorers in the second half of the 19th century, but only became accessible when the railway from Mombasa to Nairobi linked the interior with the coast. In 1885 the Scottish explorer Joseph Thomson described a "a gleaming snow-white peak with sparkling facets, which scintillated with the superb beauty of a colossal diamond." Two years later Count Samuel Teleki de Szek, a Hungarian, ascended the mountain to a height of 15,420 ft (4700 m), and in 1893 the British geologist John Walter Gregory discovered that it was actually the remains of an ancient volcano.

The first ascent of Batian was made in 1899 by the English geographer Halford Mackinder and the Courmayeur mountain guides César Ollier and Joseph Brocherel, who scaled grade-IV rock passages and the extremely challenging ice slope, named the Diamond Glacier for its hardness. For some obscure reason referred Mackinder invariably referred to his guides as "Swiss guides."

Over the following decades many of the greatest European mountaineers tackled Mt. Kenya's rock faces and glaciers. However, the greatest adventure of all was not merely a mountaineering challenge. In January 1943 three Italian prisoners of war, Felice Benuzzi, Giovanni Balletto and Vincenzo Barsotti, escaped from a British prisoner-of-war camp near Nanyuki, and headed toward the mountain through the myriad

dangers of the forest, tackling the rock faces of Batian with ropes they made from the hemp try unstrung from their camp beds and ice axes and crampons they made from scrap metal. Their sole source of information on Mt. Kenya was a tin of meat with a stylized picture of it on its label.

The three Italian prisoners failed the ascent of Batian, but climbed Point Lenana and planted an Italian flag there before descending and giving themselves up to the British. After the war, Felice Benuzzi's book (entitled *Fuga sul Kenya* in Italian and *No Picnic on Mount Kenya* in English), deservedly became a bestseller. Few books about mountains and climbing recount such romantic, desperate and authentic adventures.

Mount Kenya

124 top Mount Kenya is one of the most popular tourist destinations in Africa and is ascended by hundreds of climbers each year.

124 center Admiring the view from the eastern part of the massif, where Point Lenana rises, Nelion appears as a solitary peak, hiding Batian.

124 bottom Point Lenana (16,355 ft/4985 m) can be reached by an easy walk up the slopes of the Lewis Glacier from the Austrian Hut.

124-125 The Diamond Couloir rises between Batian (left) and Nelion. It was ascended for the first time in 1973, by Phil Snyder and Thumbi Mathenge.

126 bottom and 127 bottom For over a century mountaineers reaching the summit ridge of Kilimanjaro were greeted by the ice cliffs on the north rim of the crater. The first ascent was made in 1887 by the German geographer Hans Meyer and the Austrian mountaineer Ludwig Purtscheller.

127 top Impressive glaciers cover the south face of Kilimanjaro, viewed from the Machame route that crosses the wild Barranco Valley. At least five days of walking are required for the ascent and descent of Africa's highest mountain.

128-129 A spectacular aerial view of Kilimanjaro taken several years ago shows the ice cliffs on the crater rim as they were before their retreat. Uhuru Peak (19,340 ft/5895 m), the mountain's summit, is visible on the left.

Kilimanjaro

TANZANIA

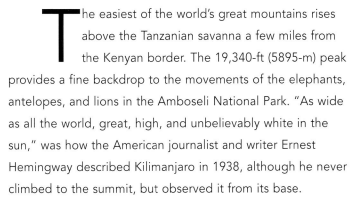

The easiest of the world's great mountains rises above the Tanzanian savanna a few miles from the Kenyan border. The 19,340-ft (5895-m) peak provides a fine backdrop to the movements of the elephants, antelopes, and lions in the Amboseli National Park. "As wide as all the world, great, high, and unbelievably white in the sun," was how the American journalist and writer Ernest Hemingway described Kilimanjaro in 1938, although he never climbed to the summit, but observed it from its base.

Although Ptolemy had written of "a great snowy mountain" in the heart of Africa and in 1519 the Spaniard Fernandes de Encisto mentioned the "Olympus of Ethiopia, west of Mombasa, which is very high, in a land brimming with gold and wild animals," Europe knew nothing more of the continent's highest volcano until 1848, when it was sighted by the Swiss missionary Johann Rebmann.

In 1886 Queen Victoria granted Kilimanjaro to her nephew, the future Kaiser Wilhelm II, and a year later the German geographer Hans Meyer and the Austrian mountaineer Ludwig Purtscheller reached the highest peak, which they named Kaiser Wilhelm Spitze. At the end of 1961, when Tanzania won its independence, the peak was renamed Uhuru, meaning "freedom" in Swahili.

Today Kilimanjaro, with the Kibo cone and the bizarre rocky pinnacles of the Mawenzi, is protected by a magnificent national park and attracts thousands of trekkers from all over the world each year. The Marangu route, which is the most popular, commences in a magnificent forest of yellowwoods and macarangas, passing among various *Helichrysum* species and spectacular giant heathers, before continuing through the lunar landscape of the Saddle. A sleepless night at an altitude of 15,420 ft (4700 m) at the Kibo Hut is the prelude to the tiring scramble up loose volcanic scree toward the edge of the crater and the summit.

Although the Kibo summit is still an extraordinary balcony overlooking Africa, little now remains of the ice cliffs that once distinguished the edge of the crater, where the frozen body of a leopard was found in the 1920s and which is regularly frequented by ravens and African hunting dogs. However, the Heim and Decken glaciers are still impressive and crisscrossed with great crevasses. They descend the southeast face of the Kibo, which is furrowed with routes opened by some of the world's best mountaineers. Those following the Machame path can admire these spectacular glaciers while crossing the Barranco Valley, the wildest and most solitary of Kilimanjaro's valleys.

ASIA

The world's highest and most challenging mountains rise in the heart of Asia. Between the Indus and the Brahmaputra, from Tibet to the torrid Indian plains, the Karakoram and Himalaya ranges extend for over 1200 miles (1930 km) and are home to the 150 highest mountains in the world, and all 14 of the planet's peaks over 26,250 ft (8000 m). At the top of the list is Mt. Everest, long stated to be the world's highest peak at 29,029 ft (8867 m), but recently reassessed to 29,035 ft (8850 m).

The Himalayas (correctly but less commonly called "the Himalaya") are also home to Kanchenjunga, Lhotse, Makalu, Dhaulagiri, Annapurna, Nanga Parbat, Manaslu, Cho Oyu and Gosainthan. To the northwest the Karakoram Range culminates in the 28,251-ft (8611-m) peak of K2 (also known as Mt. Godwin-Austen), flanked by Broad Peak, Gasherbrum I and Gasherbrum II.

In order to include all the peaks over 23,000 ft (7000 m), we must extend our scope beyond the Himalaya and Karakoram ranges and include the Hindu Kush (which culminates in Trich Mir's 25,230-ft (7690-m) summit), the Tien Shan range (Peak Pobeda, 24,406 ft/7439 m) and the Pamirs, whose highest summit is Kongur (25,324 ft/7718 m), in China. The western Pamirs include Ismail Samani Peak (24,590 ft/7495 m) and the other highest mountains of the former Soviet Union.

The great mountains of Asia have been the scene of many of the most dramatic and famous stories in the history of mountaineering. In 1921 a British expedition made the first attempt climb Mt. Everest, while in 1950 the French climbers Maurice Herzog and Louis Lachenal became the first men to set foot on the summit of an "8000er" (26,250 m); this was Annapurna (26,545 ft/8091 m). In 1953 Edmund Hillary and Tenzing Norgay conquered Everest, the following year Italian climbers reached the summit of K2, and in 1986 Reinhold Messner became the first man to scale all the world's "8000ers."

However, these conquests are interspersed with terrible tragedies, such as the huge avalanches that swept away the 1934 and 1938 expeditions to Nanga Parbat and the accidents and snowstorms that caused the death of 14 climbers on K2 in 1986 and 12 climbers on Everest a decade later.

Mountaineering is only part of the story of the Himalayas: they are also the meeting place of three of the world's great faiths – Islam, Hinduism and Buddhism The great snowy peaks form the backdrop to caravan routes, monasteries and historic cities. Around the mountains and glaciers a network of protected areas is home to the snow leopard and Asiatic black bear, and ungulates such as the argali and the Himalayan thar, which are respectively a type of mountain sheep and a large goat-like animal.

Compared to the Himalayas and neighboring ranges, the continent's other mountains inevitably risk appearing insignificant. However, Asia is home to many other important ranges. Even a brief list must include Mt. Sinai, important to a great faith and looking toward both Africa and Asia, the those of the Middle East, from Ararat to Demavend, and in the farthest east,the volcanoes of the Kamchatka Peninsula. Then there are the Taurus Range in Turkey and the mountains of Japan and Korea – much frequented despite their modest height – and the volcanoes of Indonesia, and Kinabulu in Borneo.

130 left The Great Trango Tower (20,528 ft/6257 m) and the Nameless Tower (20,505 ft /6250 m), in Pakistan.

130 center Gasherbrum IV (26,000 ft/7925 m, China – Pakistan) viewed from the Baltoro Glacier.

130 right Mount Fuji (12,388 ft/3776 m, Japan), an active stratovolcano, viewed from the northeast.

131 Mount Everest (29,029 ft/8848 m, Nepal-China) from the Khumbu Glacier to the southwest.

Mount Sinai

EGYPT

The Sinai Peninsula owes its fame to the Bible. "Then Moses led the people of Israel away from the Red Sea into the Desert of Shur. For three days they walked," recounts the Book of Exodus, the part of the Old Testament that narrates the return of the chosen people from Egypt. In the biblical story, Moses lives in the desert, hears the voice of God, who talks to him through the burning bush, and returns to the peninsula at the head of the Jewish people redeemed from captivity in the Nile Valley. He then ascends the mountain and returns with the Tablets of the Law, only to discover his people worshipping a pagan idol. Following the repentance of the people of Israel and a second ascent, the Jews return to the banks of the River Jordan. For millennia the faithful of the three monotheistic religions (Judaism, Christianity and Islam) have pinpointed the location of these events as the highest mountains of the Sinai Peninsula, at whose foot St. Catherine's Monastery was built in the 5th century AD. Although archaeologists now believe that the facts narrated in the Bible probably took place farther north, mass tourism has discovered the peninsula, its coasts and its peaks. Though flat in the north, where the sandy Sinai desert merges into the Israeli Negev, to the south the peninsula is traversed by complex and spectacular granite and sandstone mountain ranges, in which Bedouin have camped for thousands of years. Although the highest peak is Mt. Catherine (8668 ft/2642 m), the most frequented is Mt. Sinai (7497 ft/2285 m), also known as Mt. Moses. The Sinai Peninsula, which was under Israeli administration from the Six-Day War of 1967 until 1979, when it was returned to Egypt following the Camp David accord, is now one of the Middle East's most popular tourist destinations. Sharm el-Sheikh, at the peninsula's extreme southern tip, has witnessed the construction of an intercontinental airport, dozens of hotels and diving centers that organize dives in the Ras Mohammed Marine Park.

Today Mt. Sinai is crowded with holidaymakers from Sharm el-Sheikh and other nearby resorts. Each night, after having made the coach trip to St. Catherine's Monastery, hundreds of people proceed toward the summit, along a path that is also accessible to mounted visitors and that ends in a steep flight of steps. Although the shrieks of the tourists, camel drivers and sellers of food and drinks make the experience less moving than expected, dawn on the rocks of the mountain remains a magic moment and allows the visitor's gaze to roam across the granite mountains of the Sinai.

132 The first ray of sunlight illuminates the ancient chapel of the Holy Trinity on the peak of Mount Sinai.

133 The path that leads to the top of Mount Sinai (also known as Mount Moses) commences next to Saint Catherine's Monastery, at an altitude of 5151 ft (1570 m).

134-135 A magnificent spectacle for trekkers heading for the Chapel of the Holy Trinity (7382 ft/2250 m), the granite rock faces of Mount Sinai (7497 ft/2285 m) are a challenge to the climbers who visit the peninsula. The area is also home to the peninsula's highest peak: Mount Catherine (8668 ft/2642 m).

Nanga Parbat

PAKISTAN

One of the most beautiful and cruelest mountains in the world overlooks the Pakistani plains and the deep Indus Valley, where in the 1970s the asphalt ribbon of the Karakoram Highway replaced one of the most important Asian caravan routes. Nanga Parbat (26,660 ft/81126 m) marks the western limit of the Himalayas and overlooks the Hindu Kush and Karakoram ranges. Its proximity to the plains means that monsoons strike the mountain with extreme violence.

Nanga Parbat, which is visible from the road but whose full splendor and majesty can best be admired from the airplanes that connect Islamabad with Gilgit and Skardu, is an accessible mountain. Groups of trekkers follow the easy path that leads to the foot of the gargantuan Rupal face. Several valleys are now home to little lodges run by local people, while one of the largest national parks in Pakistan is currently being established around the mountain.

However, Nanga Parbat – the first Himalayan peak that climbers attempted –occupies an important place in mountaineering history. In 1895 the British climber Albert Frederick Mummery reached the summit via the Rupal face, crossed to the Diamir face and then disappeared together with two companions at an altitude above 20,000 ft (6096 m). The subsequent history of Nanga Parbat is mainly written in German. In 1934 an Austro-German expedition led by Willi Merkl and Willo Welzembach reached an altitude of 25,590 ft (7800 m) before a snowstorm killed four climbers and six Sherpas. Then four years later a huge avalanche buried the base camp of another German expedition, killing seven mountaineers and nine high-altitude porters. In 1939 another team was blocked by the breakout of World War II.

The mountaineers included the Austrian Heinrich Harrer, who was later to escape from a prisoner-of-war camp and head to Lhasa on foot.

In 1953, Hermann Buhl, the great Tyrolean alpinist, finally completed the 1930s route with a solo ascent of the long ridge of snow and rock that connects the Silver Saddle to the peak. Three German climbers – Toni Kinshofer, Anderl Mannhardt and Sigi Löw – inaugurated what is now the most popular route of Nanga Parbat on the Diamir face in 1962.

In 1970 the Messner brothers conquered the huge Rupal face and descended the easier but perilous Diamir face without ropes or bivouacs. However, 24-year-old Günther disappeared during the descent. Reinhold climbed back up and searched for him for a whole day, scarcely managing to drag himself back down. Günther's remains were not found until 2005 – and Nanga Parbat's fame as a cruel mountain lives on.

146 The gargantuan Rupal face of Nanga Parbat, sighted for the first time in 1895 by the British climber Albert Frederick Mummery (who subsequently perished on the Diamir face) was first scaled in 1970 by Günther and Reinhold Messner.

147 top and 148-149 Rakhiot Peak, the eastern bastion of Nanga Parbat, was first conquered in 1932 by an Austro-German expedition led by Willy Merkl.

146-147 The awe-inspiring ice face overlooking the Diamir Valley was first scaled in 1962 by the German climbers Toni Kinshofer, Anderl Mannhardt and Sigi Löw. Their route, on which Löw perished during the descent, is now the normal route of Nanga Parbat.

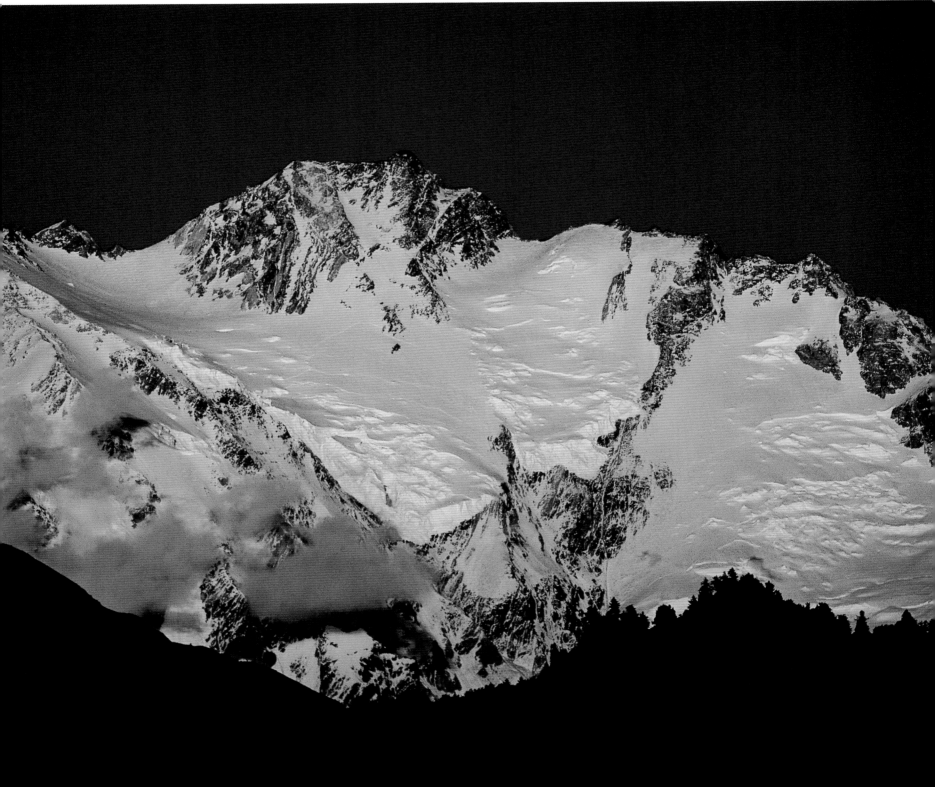

K2

PAKISTAN - CHINA

One of the most difficult and grueling climbs on Earth leads up to the foot of K2, the extraordinary pyramid of rock and ice whose peak marks the highest point of the Karakoram Range: 28,251 ft (8611 m), though several recent measurements state that at 28,268 ft (8616 m), K2 is the second highest mountain in the world, Furthermore, this steep, austere and imposing peak is far more difficult to climb than Everest. Only about 200 mountaineers have ever reached K2's summit, in comparison with the 3000 who set foot on the "roof of the world" between 1953 and 2006. The mountain is best known from the south, where its rock and ice walls tower over the Baltoro Glacier in Pakistan, while the northern side of the mountain overlooks the deserts and fast-running rivers of Sinkiang, in China. Both regions are among the most inhospitable in the world. "A mountain of stunning dimensions. It seems to rise like a perfect cone, but incredibly tall." This was how the Colonel Francis Younghusband of the British Army, the first Westerner to see K2 at close quarters, described it in 1887. Expeditions attempting to reach the summit commenced a few years later. The best route up was identified and the Courmayeur guides of the expedition led by Luigi Amedeo of Savoy, Duke of the Abruzzi, followed it to an altitude of 20,833 ft (6350 m). The route is still known as the Abruzzi Ridge today. The same expedition also included the great photographer Vittorio Sella, who documented the mountain's unrivaled beauty in a series of extraordinary images. Three American expeditions later attempted the conquest of K2, including one in 1939 in which Fritz Wiessener and Pasang Dawa Lama came within 700 ft (213 m) of the summit. Only in 1954 was the peak was finally conquered, when Lino Lacedelli and Achille Compagnoni of the Italian expedition led by the geologist Ardito Desio reached the summit.Unlike Everest, only a small minority of mountaineers attempting K2 has ever managed to reach the peak. Indeed, the second ascent was not achieved until 1977, when a Japanese team accompanied by the Pakistani climber Ashraf Aman succeeded. In 1981 another Japanese expedition reached the summit from the West Ridge and two years later a team of their compatriots ascended the steep and mainly ice-clad north face of the mountain, following a long approach by camel.

150-151 Towering over the border between Pakistan and the Chinese region of Sinkiang, isolated K2 is particularly exposed to bad weather and can prove extremely dangerous for climbers. In the photograph, the summit emerges a few feet above the lenticular clouds that swathe the upper part of the mountain.

151 bottom Broad Peak (left), the 12th highest mountain in the world (26,401 ft/8047 m), dominates the Godwin Austen Glacier, forming a spectacular backdrop for climbers on the Abruzzi Ridge of K2 (right). This photograph was taken from Camp 1 of the Abruzzi Ridge, at a height of 20,013 ft (6100 m).

Five years later, in 1986, a Polish light expedition completed the elegant Magic Line of the south face.

Successes did not come without fatalities. The world's second highest mountain has killed 14 climbers from 7 different countries, including great names such as the Polish mountaineer Tadeusz Piotrowski, the Italian Renato Casarotto and the British Alan Rouse.

In 1990 the Free K2 international expedition cleared the south face of the Abruzzi Ridge of some of the abandoned garbage, tents and fixed ropes. A year later the French climbers Pierre Béghin and Christophe Profit opened another magnificent and very elegant route on the west face of K2, and in 2004 two Italian expeditions returned to the peak on occasion of the 50th anniversary of the first ascent, with Lacedelli (then 76 years old) ascending as far as the base camp on the Baltoro Glacier. Like

Everest, K2 is flanked by magnificent mountains, inclkuding the Gasherbrums, Broad Peak, Masherbrum and the granite Trango Towers, Paiju Peaks and Baltoro Cathedrals. The Central Karakoram National Park, established by the Pakistani government in 2001 (and thus more recent than the Nepalese Sagarmatha National Park), covers an area of 3760 sq. miles (9738 sq. km), flanking the Chinese border for a long stretch. However, just a few miles from K2 the highest war in the world is currently being waged between Pakistan and India on the Conway Saddle, between the Baltoro and Siachen glaciers, at an altitude of around 20,000 ft (6096 m). Military camps and garbage deface these wildernesses, while altitude sickness, frostbite and weapons cause dozens of victims among the ranks of both armies each year. "Men might as well fight on the moon as stand on these heights, gasping for breath, with weapons in hand," commented the American mountaineer and photographer Galen Rowell, who was the first to visit the front.

K2

152 From K2's Abruzzi Ridge the glaciers at the foot of the mountain resemble gargantuan rivers of ice and rock. In the photograph the Savoia Glacier flows from the west (right) into the Godwin Austen Glacier, where the moraine ridge where the expeditions pitch their base camps is clearly visible.

152-153 The classic route leading to the foot of K2 ascends the Baltoro Glacier, much of which is covered in snow when the expeditions reach the mountain in June. In the photograph, a procession of Balti porters on the last leg of the route, between Concordia and the base camp at 16,400 ft (4999 m).

154-155 A tiny tent pitched on an aerial ridge of snow and rock allows full appreciation of the sheerness of the north face of K2, first scaled in 1983 by a Japanese expedition, followed by an Italian team a year later.

155 Approaching the foot of K2 on skis, along the Godwin Austen Glacier, the gigantic pyramidal peak dominates the landscape, revealing its south face and the Abruzzi Ridge, silhouetted against the sky on the left side of the mountain.

K2

156 and 157 The Baltoro Glacier is always visible to climbers on the normal route to the summit. These photographs show climbers in the area around Camp 2, which can be clearly seen in the view on the left, at a height of almost 22,000 ft (6706 m) on the Abruzzi Ridge. This stage of the ascent is accompanied by spectacular views of Broad Peak and the Gasherbrum group (left and right in the large photograph).

ASIA

K2

158-159 *The setting sun illuminates the ice-covered rocks of the southwest face of K2. Even for those ascending via the normal route of the Abruzzi Ridge, the world's second highest mountain is extremely dangerous and difficult to climb. This photograph was taken from the Godwin Austen Glacier.*

160-161 and 160 bottom
Gasherbrum I, (also known as
Hidden Peak), rises to 26,470 ft
(8068 m), making it the highest
summit of the massif. It was first
conquered in 1958 by an
American expedition and
many difficult routes were
subsequently opened on
the mountain.

161 Gasherbrum II, instantly
recognizable by its pyramidal
shape, is 26,360 ft (8034 m) high
and was first scaled in 1956 by
the Austrian climbers Josef Larch,
Fritz Moravec and Hans
Willenpart. It is now one of the
most frequently summited
"eight-thousanders."

162-163 The awe-inspiring west
face of Gasherbrum IV (26,000
ft/7925 m), which dominates
Concordia and the route to the
K2 base camp, is one of the most
difficult of the Karakoram Range.
It was scaled for the first time in
1985 by the Polish climber
Wojciech Kurtyka and the
German mountaineer Robert
Schauer.

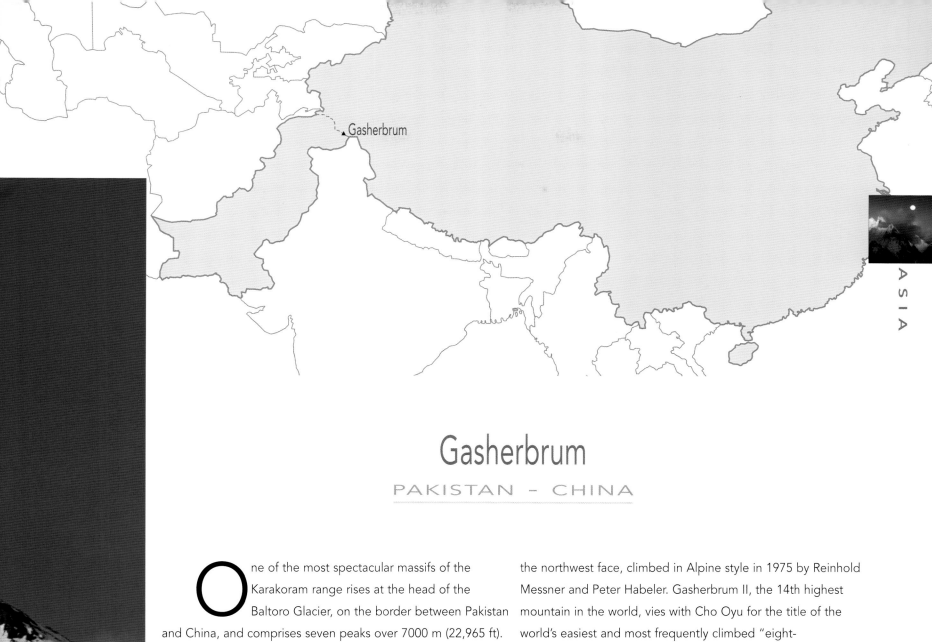

Gasherbrum

PAKISTAN - CHINA

One of the most spectacular massifs of the Karakoram range rises at the head of the Baltoro Glacier, on the border between Pakistan and China, and comprises seven peaks over 7000 m (22,965 ft). Two of these, Gasherbrum I, also known as Hidden Peak (26,470 ft/8068 m) and Gasherbrum II (26,361 ft/8034 m) are among the world's fourteen "eight-thousanders." The name of this extraordinary group is derived from the Balti words *rgasha brum*, meaning "beautiful mountain."

Gasherbrum was discovered at the end of the 19th century by the British explorer William Martin Conway (who named the highest summit Hidden Peak), but climbers did not attempt its peaks until 1934, when Günther Dyhrenfurth led an international expedition, which was accompanied by some movie actors.

The German mountaineer Hans Ertl and Swiss climber André Roche, who had already conquered many Alpine summits, reached 20,341 ft (6200 m) on Hidden Peak before being driven back by the blizzard that killed Merkl, Welzenbach and their companions on Nanga Parbat. Two years later, a French expedition led by Henri de Ségogne reached almost 23,000 ft (7010 m) before severe weather conditions forced them to descend.

Gasherbrum's highest summits were gained during the 1950s, when nylon ropes, warmer and more comfortable clothing, and improved tents allowed for the conquest of all the "eight-thousanders." In 1954, the American mountaineers Andy Kauffman and Pete Schoening finally conquered Hidden Peak, and in 1956 the Austrian climbers Sepp Larch, Fritz Moravec and Hans Willenpart reached the summit of Gasherbrum II.

In the next few years climbers opened several very difficult routes on Hidden Peak. The first was the complicated line on the northwest face, climbed in Alpine style in 1975 by Reinhold Messner and Peter Habeler. Gasherbrum II, the 14th highest mountain in the world, vies with Cho Oyu for the title of the world's easiest and most frequently climbed "eight-thousander."

It was not until the 1990s that the gigantic north faces on the Chinese side of the two summits were reached and attempted – unsuccessfully. However, Gasherbrum III (26,089 ft/7592 m), Gasherbrum V (24,019 ft/7321 m) and Gasherbrum VI (22,976 ft/7003 m) were conquered, one by one.

The massif's most elegant peak is Gasherbrum IV, an extraordinary 26,001-ft (7925-m) pyramid of rock and ice dominating Concordia. In August 1988, Walter Bonatti and Carlo Mauri (who were members of a roped party of the Italian expedition led by Riccardo Cassin) became the first climbers to conquer the peak. The mountain's west face is the steepest and most difficult, but in 1985 the Polish and German duo of Wojciech Kurtyka and Robert Schauer succeeded in scaling it.

Mount Kailas

CHINA

nly one of the most world's most awesome and famous mountains has not yet been conquered by man. Its name is Mt. Kailas (or Kailash), an elegant rocky peak crowned by a jagged cone of snow and ice that soars to a height of 22,028 ft (6714 m) and dominates the desert valleys of western-central Tibet. The first European to set eyes on it was Ippolito Desideri, a Tuscan Jesuit, who traveled in the region in 1715. However, the most moving description was written by Heinrich Harrer, the Austrian mountaineer who was interned by the British in 1939, escaped, crossed the Himalayas on foot and wrote his famous account entitled *Seven Years in Tibet*. "The landscape was dominated by the 25,000-ft peak of Gurla Mandhata; less striking, but far more famous, was the sacred Mt. Kailas, 3000 ft lower, which stands in majestic isolation apart from the Himalaya range. When we first caught sight of it, our Tibetans prostrated themselves and prayed," wrote Harrer, who considered it one of the most beautiful places in the world. Mt. Kailas is considered sacred by the faithful of four religions. Hindus call it Mt. Meru and Buddhists Gang Rimpoche, but both consider it the center of the universe. Followers of the ancient Bon religion, which is still widespread in the most impenetrable areas of Tibet, believe that it is the place where the founder of their sect descended from heaven to Earth. The Jains, on the other hand, believe that the first prophet of their faith rid himself of sin on Mt. Kailas. At the foot of the mountain, 14,950 ft (4557 m) above sea level, Lake Manasarovar attracts pilgrims from all over India, while Tibetan devotees flock to follow the route around the mountain. Indeed, each day between spring and autumn, hundreds of men and women follow the 32-mile (51-km) *kora* path that circles the mountain, crossing the 17,946-ft (5475-m) Drolma La Pass. Instead of walking, some pilgrims even complete the *kora* by making full body prostrations all the way, earning even greater virtue. For all of them the difficulties of the path are compounded by those of the journey to Mt. Kailas, which requires a four-week round trip by truck from some Tibetan regions. In June the Saga Dawa celebrations attract thousands of pilgrims to Tarboche. The religious beliefs of the Tibetans have so far managed to keep Western mountaineers away from the peak, but have not changed the attitude of the Chinese, who grant the Tibetans very few permits to make the pilgrimage. Since 2000 there has been talk of a project for a road around Mt. Kailas, which would not only be an affront to the Tibetan people, but also a colossal eyesore.

168 A Tibetan pilgrim prays in front of the northwest face of Mount Kailas.

169 The dazzling whiteness of a summer snowfall makes the north face of Mount Kailas even more spectacular.

170-171 The setting sun illuminates the austere north face of Mount Kailas. To set foot on the summit of the mountain would be a terrible insult for hundreds of millions of believers who consider it sacred and the center of the universe.

172-173 A magnificent massif with a familiar "alpine" appearance, albeit on a grander scale, Lamjung Himal culminates at 22,920 ft (6986 m) just southeast of Annapurna IV (24,688 ft/7525 m) and Annapurna II (26,040 ft/7937 m).

172 bottom Crumbly conglomerate slopes overlook the course of the Marsyangdi Khola River, which is followed by trekkers on the route around Annapurna.

173 The south face of Annapurna, one of the highest and most awe-inspiring in the Himalayas, greets trekkers on their arrival at the cirque known as the Sanctuary.

Annapurna
NEPAL

One of the highest, most famous and spectacular mountains in the world separates the Pokhara basin and lake in central Nepal from the deep Kali Gandaki Valley and the arid Manang Valley, both inhabited by Tibetan populations. On clear days the peak is visible from the forests, hills and cultivated fields of the lowland Terai region, across the southern border in India. At 26,545 ft (8091 m) Annapurna I is the tenth highest mountain in the Himalayas and the world. Flanked by other elegant peaks, such as Annapurna II, Annapurna III, Gangapurna and Machapuchare, the peak made history in 1950, when a French expedition became the first to reach a summit at over 26,000 ft (7925 m). After having reached the peak by way of the steep and dangerous ice slopes of the northwest face, Maurice Herzog and Louis Lachenal, accompanied by Gaston Rébuffat and Lionel Terray, were forced to make a dramatic descent in a snowstorm. They survived the crevasses, blizzards and avalanches, but suffered terrible frostbite. Twenty years later, in 1970, Dougal Haston and Don Whillans, members of a British expedition led by Chris Bonington, became the first climbers to reach the summit via the south face, a gigantic maze of precariously balanced seracs, sheer rocky walls and gullies traversed by avalanches that dominate the extraordinary cirque known to mountaineers and trekkers as the Sanctuary. This cirque is considered to be one of the most beautiful spots to be found in all the world's mountains. Still later, in 1985, the Tyrolean mountaineers Reinhold Messner and Hans Kammerlander conquered the mountain's narrow, steep and concave north face.

In 1950, while Maurice Herzog and his companions were starting to ascend the peak, the British explorer and mountaineer Harold Tilman ascended the Marsyangdi Khola Valley to Manang and attempted the 26,064-ft (7944-m) peak of Annapurna II. Subsequently, after having crossed the Thorong La Pass, he descended via the Kali Gandaki Valley, inaugurating what is now one of the most popular trekking itineraries in the world.

Although it was conquered before the other great Himalayan peaks, Annapurna remains a dangerous and difficult mountain. Of all the world's summits over 26,000 ft (7925 m), Annapurna has been conquered least frequently and is among those that have accounted for the most fatalities. However, the paths around the foot of the mountain, frequented by almost 50,000 trekkers each year, are neither difficult nor dangerous. Visitors are attracted not only by the elegant peaks (in addition to Annapurna, Machapuchare and the nearby summits rising over 23,000 ft

(7010 m), Dhaulagiri and Manaslu – the seventh and ninth highest mountains in the world – are also visible), but also by the variety of the landscapes, the mosaic of ethnic groups, the austere Buddhist temples and the Hindu shrines brimming with perfumes and sounds. In the forests tropical trees, conifers and bamboo are all found. Eagles and bearded vultures appear frequently overhead, while some lucky visitors even catch a glimpse of the rare snow leopard. Those who wish to walk for a month can complete the circuit around Annapurna, while those with less time must choose between two shorter but equally fascinating itineraries. While the path that leads up to the Sanctuary from Birethanti may be covered in a week, two to three weeks are necessary to ascend from the paddy fields of Besi Sahar to the arid Manang Valley, over the 17,769-ft (5416-m) Thorong La Pass and down toward the Kali Gandaki and lower Mustang through a thoroughly Tibetan landscape, characterized by rock engravings and erosion furrows. The first path is easier,

busier, warmer and more spectacular, while the second, with its continuous changes, is a journey through bygone times in the heart of the Himalayas. The flood of trekkers has made the valleys at the foot of Annapurna the only mountain areas in Nepal where the process of depopulation has been stemmed and even reversed. This is also due to the Annapurna Conservation Area, founded in 1986 and covering an area of 2934 sq. miles (7600 sq. km). It is one of the largest protected areas in Nepal and the Himalayas and its managers successfully reconcile environmental protection with economic development. In addition to reforestation and research on the rarest species of the area, such as the snow leopard and the bearded vulture, the management team also builds fountains and aqueducts, mends bridges and paths and restores monuments and monasteries. However, there is still room for man at the foot of the mountain on which he first ascended higher than 26,000 ft (7925 m).

Annapurna

174 top Annapurna, the tenth highest mountain in the world at 26,545 ft (8090 m), is scaled far less frequently than Everest, the world's highest peak: just 103 people reached the summit between 1950 and 2005.

174 center and bottom The Annapurna massif is 34 miles (55 km) long and comprises 7 peaks over 7200 m (23,622 ft), the altitude adopted to denote the highest mountains in the world.

174-175 *A mountaineer climbs Annapurna's steep northwest ridge. Awe-inspiring icefalls descend towards the Miristi Khola Valley.*

176-177 *Jagged snow ridges and gullies mark the eastern side of the Annapurna Sanctuary, between Gandharba Chuli and Machapuchare.*

178-179 *Dawn illuminates the rocks and ice of Tent Peak (also known as Tharpu Chuli, 18,579 ft/5663 m), which overlooks the Sanctuary and the Annapurna massif.*

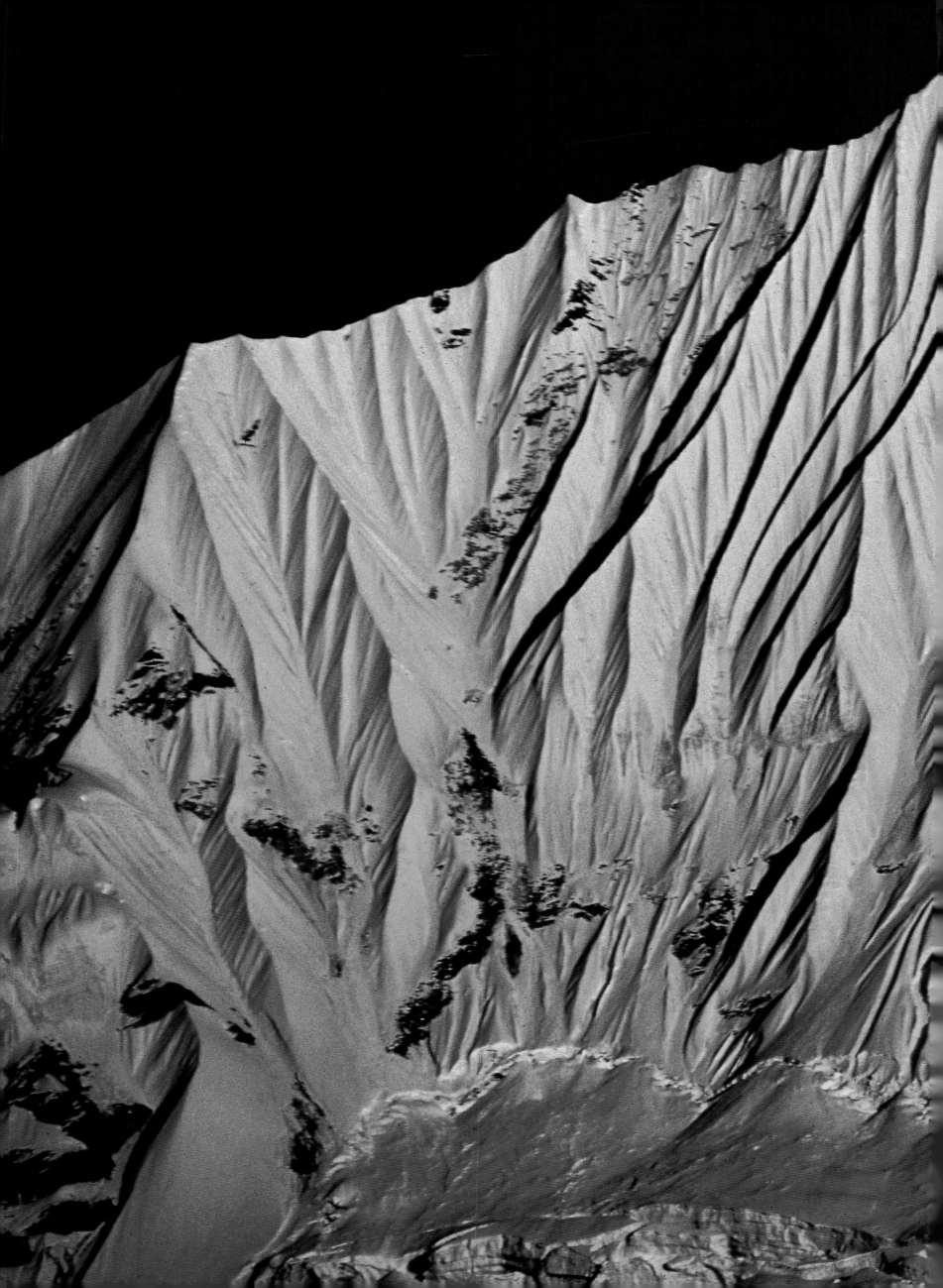

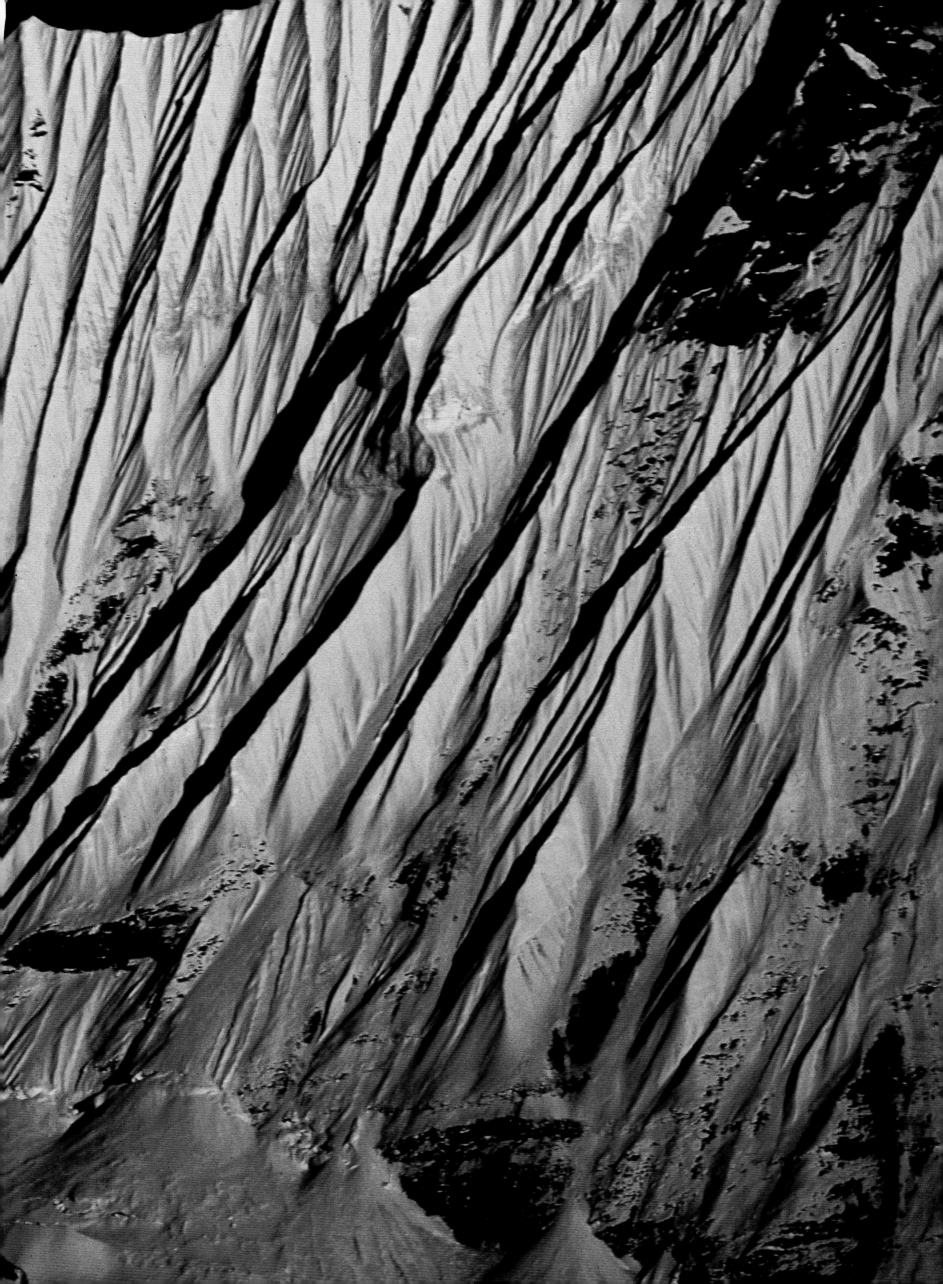

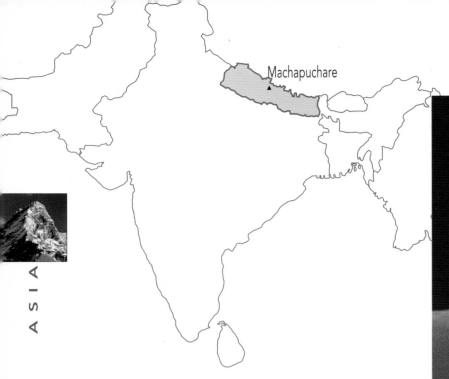

Machapuchare

NEPAL

One of the most photographed mountains of the Himalayas overlooks Nepal's Pokhara Valley and Lake to the south, while its icy rock faces dominate the Modi Khola Valley, densely covered with tropical trees and bamboo. In terms of altitude alone, its 22,595-ft (6887-m) summit makes Machapuchare a secondary peak when compared to Annapurna (26,545 ft/8090m) and the other summits over 23,000 ft (7000+ m) that surround it. However, the elegant shape of this two-pronged peak has made it one of the icons of the Nepalese Himalayas. Every year thousands of walkers follow the magnificent and grueling path that ascends through the fields and villages from Birethanti to Ghandrung toward Chomrong before entering the Modi Khola Valley toward the Sanctuary amphitheater, a highly popular trekking destination. One or two days walking from Chomrong leads to the moraine of the basin and a little group of lodges that offer marvelous views over Annapurna. Machapuchare dominates the landscape in Birethanti, but Annapurna South and the nearby peaks gradually become more impressive, until Machapuchare almost disappears from sight of the walkers struggling through the thick forest. However, the mountain's rocky walls and the ice slopes modeled by avalanches that form its west face regain their majesty in the light of sunset at the Sanctuary. Although the mountain seems to have just one peak when seen from Pokhara, the view from the foot of Annapurna clearly reveals its twin summits, separated by 26 ft (8 m) in height and a snowy saddle, which gave the mountain its name: Machapuchare, which means "Fishtail" in Nepali.However, despite its impressiveness and fame among trekkers, the peak that dominates the Modi Khola Valley is not frequented by mountaineers. Since 1957, the date of the first ascension, the Nepali government and the Gurung mountain people, who consider the peak a sacred abode of the gods, have refused all permits for expeditions. Even the British expedition that made the first ascent had trouble obtaining the necessary authorization. In order to attempt the climb the 1957 mountaineers had to promise to respect the holy nature of the mountain, avoiding the consumption of meat and killing living beings at its foot, nor could they tread on the virgin snow of its summit. It was quite a feat for Wilfrid Noyce and David Cox to stop almost at the top on May 28, 1957, just 150 ft (45 m) from the summit, at the foot of four or five pillars of blue ice resembling a dragon's claws. However, their renouncement of the last few feet was a mark of compliance and respect.

180-181 Machapuchare ("Fishtail"), towers above the wooded heights that separate the Modhi Khola and Mardi Khola Valleys.

181 bottom The setting sun illuminates the ice faces and rocky triangle of the peak of Machapuchare. Despite its relatively modest altitude (22,595 ft/6887 m), this elegant, soaring mountain stands out among all the other peaks that form the eastern boundary of the Annapurna Sanctuary.

182-183 Although its elegant appearance makes it the dream of many climbers, Machapuchare is prohibited to mountaineers. Following the 1957 British expedition, whose roped party headed by Wilfrid Noyce and David Cox had to stop 150 ft (45 m) from the summit, the Nepali government has refused to authorize any other expedition. Viewed from the city of Pokhara, to the south of the range, Machapuchare is the most prominent peak, far more visible than those of Annapurna.

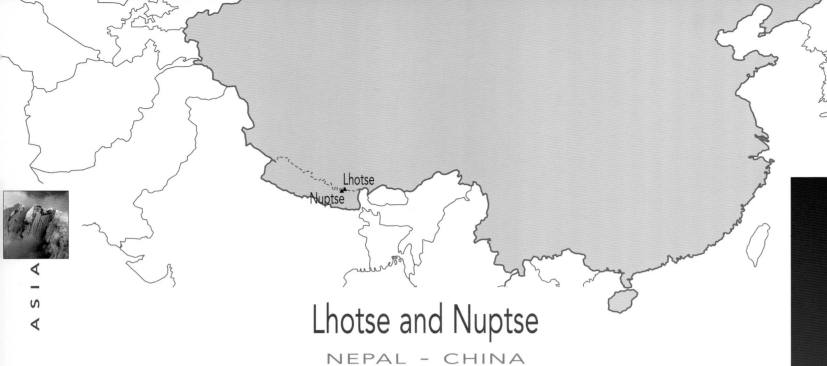

Lhotse and Nuptse

NEPAL - CHINA

Mount Everest is not a lone giant: alongside the world's highest and most famous peak, other gigantic mountains form one of the most spectacular massifs of the Himalayas. Their simple names denote the cardinal points of the compass in Tibetan and the Sherpa dialect.

Lhotse (*Lho-tse*, meaning "South Peak"), at 27,890 ft (8500 m), the fourth highest mountain in the world, is flanked by the wild and breathtaking Lhotse Shar ("Southeast Peak," 27,552 ft/8397 m)), followed by a series of elegant "seven-thousanders" (7000 m/22,965 ft) such as Shartse and Peak 38 farther east.

Another spectacular and imposing sight is the snow ridge of Nuptse ("West Peak," 25,791 ft/7861 m). The ridge overlooks the last-day stretch completed by trekkers who ascend from Namche Bazaar and Lobuche toward Kala Pattar and the Nepal's Everest base camp, and also closes the Western Cwm with a huge wall of snow and ice. The cwm is crossed by climbers heading for the South Col and the highest peak in the world.

These three extraordinary mountains are somewhat underrated owing to their proximity to Everest. However, their ridges and faces are crossed by some of the most dangerous and demanding routes in the Himalayas, and several of these walls still remain to be conquered.

The route the Swiss climbers Fritz Luchsinger and Ernst Reiss opened in 1956 for the first ascent of Lhotse symbolizes this mountain's close bond with Everest. The route largely coincides with the normal advance from Nepalese territory toward Everest, via the Khumbu Icefall, the Western Cwm and the west face of Lhotse.

The climb toward Lhotse's summit, which is still often followed today, breaks away from the route to Everest when it starts to cut across toward the South Col, reaching the peak via steep snowy slopes and difficult mixed passages. The Tyrolean mountaineer Reinhold Messner followed this route in October 1986, when he became the first man to conquer all fourteen of the world's "eight-thousanders" (8000 m/26,246 ft).

It is impossible to underestimate Lhotse's immense east face, which rises from the Tibetan valley of Kangshung between Everest, Chomo Lonzo and Makalu. The mountain's south face is also extraordinary, in terms of both beauty and size. It dominates the Chukhung Valley and the busy path that joins Namche Bazaar to Tengboche Monastery and in the 1980s became one of the most famous "last problems" of the Himalayas. However, a Russian expedition succeeded in climbing the face in 2001.

Since 1975, many of the greatest modern climbers have attempted Lhotse's south face. In 1986 the Polish mountaineer Jerzy Kukuczka (the second man to ascend all fourteen "eight-thousanders" after Reinhold Messner) lost his life on the face, but in 1990 the Slovenian solo climber Tomo Cesen achieved the first ascent. However, three months later a Soviet team that reached the peak by a different route accused Cesen of not having completed the ascent, giving rise to a fierce dispute destined to last for years.

Few people recall the first ascent of the Lhotse's south face, which was made in 1984 by a Czech expedition that opened a route on the right of the face toward the 27,552-ft (8398-m) summit of Lhotse Shar which, along with Kanchenjunga's Yalung Kang summit, is one of the most spectacular "eight-thousanders" not included in the official list.

Similarly, the first ascent of Nuptse via the south face, which the British climbers Dennis Davis, Chris Bonington, Les Brown and Jim Swallow, and Tashi and Pemba Sherpa made in 1961 is certainly not one of the most famous Himalayan conquests. The steep modern routes on ice and rock opened on Nuptse's northeastern face by American and Italian roped parties are far more popular.

However, there are still many routes to be opened on the peaks that flank Everest to the south and east. The traverse of the ridge edged with giant cornices that connects Lhotse to Lhotse Shar, or the even more delicate and wild one that reaches it from Nuptse, continuing toward the South Col and Everest, are among the greatest goals of Himalayan mountaineers for the coming years. Many important chapters in the mountaineering history of these peaks are still waiting to be written.

192-193 From Kala Pattar, the classic viewpoint of the Khumbu Valley, the peak of Lhotse appears framed between Everest (left) and Nuptse. The normal route ascends the steep sunlit slopes. The South Col can be seen between Everest and Lhotse, while the Khumbu Icefall is visible at the bottom.

193 bottom Viewed here from the snowy cornices along Everest's northwest ridge, Lhotse rises in the bottom left part of the photograph. Standing 27,890 ft (8501 m), it is the fourth highest mountain in the world.

194-195 Nuptse (25,791 ft/7861 m), with its distinctive "hump" can be seen on the left of the photograph, closing off the head of the Khumbu Valley, known as the Western Cwm, to the south. The mountain's name is Tibetan for "West Peak" and refers to its position in the Lhotse-Nuptse massif.

196-197 Lhotse's rock faces and ice cornices, flushed with the warm light of sunset, offer an extraordinary spectacle to those admiring the "eight-thousanders" of the Khumbu region.

Ama Dablam

NEPAL

Sunsets at Tengboche (Thyangboche) are among the most beautiful in the world. When the shadows lengthen around the monastery, monks and novices interrupt their prayers to go outside and warm themselves in the last sunrays, mingling with trekkers from all over the world. Then, as the sun leaves the walls and the pinnacles of Nepal's most photographed Buddhist monastery, the air at 12,000 ft (3657 m) becomes chilly, and the mountains offer an extraordinary spectacle.

Before disappearing, the sun inflames the south face of Lhotse and the summit of Everest that looms behind it. However, before doing so, it illuminates the extraordinary peaks that rise over 19,685 ft (6000 m) above the south side of the Dudh Kosi Valley. Kangtega and Thamserku are adorned with lacy caps of ice and snow, as is Kusum Kangguru, which overlooks the town of Lukla. However, it is Ama Dablam, an elegant peak that soars to a height of 22,493 ft (6856 m) and dominates the landscape with a magnificent ice face.

"Thyangboche must be one of the most beautiful place in the world," remarked John Hunt, the leader of the British expedition that saw Edmund Hillary and Tenzing Norgay reach the summit of Everest in 1953. Hunt described the monastery as having a strangely medieval appearance and serving as an unrivaled platform for contemplating the finest mountain view he had ever seen.

After having conquered Everest, Hillary returned to the land of the Sherpas many times, first as the leader of exploratory and mountaineering expeditions, and subsequently to present the inhabitants of the Khumbu with schools, bridges, airports, hospitals and the Sagarmatha National Park. In 1959 the most famous New Zealand mountaineer of all times also promoted an expedition to seek the yeti. Four members of the team – British climbers Mike Ward and Mike Gill, American Barry Bishop and New Zealand mountaineer Wally Romanes – made the first ascent of Ama Dablam via an aerial ridge of ice protected by gigantic cornices.

Over the years, often having to overcome considerable difficulties, mountaineers have scaled the peak's ridges and faces. However, most climbers concentrate on the normal route, which during the 1990s became one of the most popular destinations for commercial expeditions.

Ama Dablam's beauty and its peak's high but not towering altitude attract many mountaineers on their first Himalayan trip, although its cornices and the ridge's vertical drops drive back those with insufficient technical experience. The moraine at the foot of Ama Dablam is marked with the tracks of the snow leopard, which in recent years has returned to the valleys of the highest national park in the world.

198-199 The northwest face of Ama Dablam (22,349 ft/6812 m) can be seen from the top of the Khumbu Glacier during the approach to the Everest Base Camp. The ascent via this face is more difficult than the normal route on the southwest ridge, which was scaled for the first time in 1961.

200-201 Rising above the village and monastery of Periche, the most famous and photographed face of Ama Dablam can be admired from the southwest. The 1961 route, opened by Barry Bishop, Mike Gill, Wally Romanes and Mike Ward during an expedition led by Sir Edmund Hillary, runs along the right edge of the hanging glacier that descends the summit peak and is visible as a vertical white band. The mountain, known as the "Jewel of the Khumbu" for its impressiveness and elegance, constitutes a practically constant landmark for trekkers in the Khumbu Valley.

202-203 An aerial view of Makalu. The French expedition that made the first ascent of the summit in 1955 climbed the sunny slopes of the east face, visible on the right of the photograph.

202 bottom Five routes have been opened on the breathtaking north face of Kanchenjunga.

203 The high ice wall of the southeast face of Kanchenjunga overlooks the Indian state of Sikkim. Following the attempts made during the interwar period, only a handful of Indian expeditions have obtained permission to scale the world's third highest mountain from this side.

204-205 The remoteness of Kanchenjunga and Makalu from the Nepalese plain means that mountaineers and trekkers wishing to reach them must walk for over two weeks.

206-207 A photograph taken at dawn from the Kharta Valley in Tibet, explored in 1920 and 1921 by the first mountaineers heading for Everest, reveals the awesome grandeur of the north faces of Makalu (left), Lhotse and the highest peak in the world.

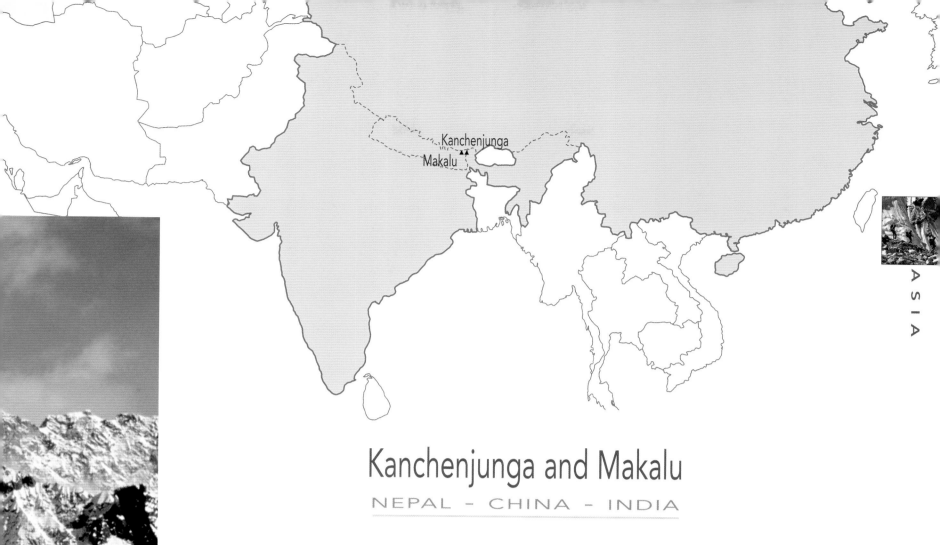

Kanchenjunga and Makalu

NEPAL - CHINA - INDIA

The third and fifth highest mountains in the world rise imposingly east of Everest and are visible from Nepal's Terai plain on clear days. The sight of 28,169-ft (8586-m) Kanchenjunga and 27,766-ft (8463-m) Makalu on the horizon beyond the buffalo at pasture constitutes one of the most evocative natural scenes in the world. The trekking trails to the two mountains commence from this plain and offer demanding and spectacular alternatives to the classic routes to Annapurna and Everest. While Makalu, like Everest, rises on the border with Tibet, Kanchenjunga stands to the south of the Himalayan watershed and separates Nepal from Sikkim, which became part of India in 1962. The sight of the peak from the Darjeeling tea plantations has thrilled generations of travelers and led to the belief, held for a few years, that it was the highest mountain in the world. The impressiveness of Kanchenjunga and its proximity to Darjeeling meant that it attracted the attention of mountaineers from a very early date. In 1899 an expedition led by Douglas Freshfield traveled right around it, illicitly entering Nepal; later, between 1929 and 1931, three German expeditions led by Paul Bauer and Gunther Oskar Dyrenfurth attempted to scale it from the Sikkim side. Kanchenjunga was finally conquered in 1955, when George Band, Joe Brown, Norman Hardie and Tony Streather of a small British expedition reached the summit. Although the ascent was made from the Nepalese side, the British respected the request of the Sikkimese *chogyal* (temporal and spiritual ruler), stopping a few feet short of the peak, which is considered sacred by the local people. In 1977 an Indian expedition climbed the east face of the mountain and subsequently Kanchenjunga became a challenge for the

best alpinists in the world. The many expeditions include the first alpine-style ascent by Doug Scott, Pete Boardman and Joe Tasker (1979), the first ascent of the north face by a Japanese party led by M. Konishi (1980) and the crossing of the five summits by a Russian expedition (1995).

In comparison to the mountaineering history of Kanchenjunga, that of Makalu is very short. The first serious attempt at its ascent was successfully made by a French expedition in 1955. Jean Couzy and Lionel Terray were joined on the summit by the other French mountaineers and a Sherpa. The subsequent history of Makalu has centered on its west face, which is one of the most difficult in the Himalayas. Six routes (the most famous of which is the West Pillar, conquered in 1971 by a French team) have been opened over the years, although the central part of the face has yet to be scaled. Makalu and Kanchenjunga still offer many challenges.

208-209 and 208 bottom
Mount Fuji, known as Fuji-san in
Japanese, in a snowy winter view.
Due to its vicinity to the Pacific
Ocean, it is often subject to
blizzards during this season.

209 Although Mount Fuji is one
of the most photographed and
climbed mountains in the world,
the origin of its name is
uncertain. Suggested meanings
include "Without Equal,"
"Immortal" and "Never-ending."

210-211 While considered a
"quiet" volcano, characterized by
gentle slopes, Mount Fuji
nonetheless has its share of
dangers, partly due to its
considerable height of 12,388 feet
(3776 m). The volcano is several
hundred thousand years old, but
its present form dates back to just
10,000 years ago.

Mount Fuji

JAPAN

The snowy form of Mt. Fuji (also known as Fujiyama or Fuji-san) is one of the most famous images of Japan. The imposing volcano (12,388 ft/3761 m), which rises about 60 miles (96 km) southwest of Tokyo and can be seen from the city center on clear days, is a recurrent theme in Japanese art and literature and one of the most visited mountains on Earth. Indeed, every year up to 300,000 people – a third of whom are foreigners – make the ascent. Mt. Fuji, which is flanked by the five lakes of Kawaguchi, Sai, Yamanaka, Motosu e Shoji, and the more distant Lake Ashi, is part of the Fuji-Hakone-Izu National Park. The Aokigahara Forest extends at its foot, with caves containing ice formations even at the height of summer. The mountain is a stratovolcano that last erupted in 1707; geologists still consider it active but with a low probability of eruption. The various phases of volcanic activity have modified the shape of the mountain several times over the last few hundreds of thousands of years; in fact the "new Mt. Fuji" was formed around 10,000 years ago. The volcano has been sacred since ancient times and was probably ascended for the first time in AD 663 by an unknown monk. For centuries women were not allowed to climb it. The Samurai used the modern-day city of Gotemba, at the base of the mountain, as a training ground and this tradition has in some way been preserved by the military bases of the Japanese Self-Defense Forces and the U.S. Marine Corps that now stand at the foot of Mt. Fuji. The official season for the ascent of the volcano is from the beginning of June to the end of August. During this period, when the snow completely disappears from the mountain, it is possible to choose between four different paths and stay at the refuges and hotels situated on the slopes of the volcano up to an altitude of 11,155 ft (3400 m). Visitors may also travel by bus to an altitude of 7,546 ft (2300 m) to join the path.

The ascent route is dotted with temples and religious symbols and is considered sacred and symbolic by the majority of Japanese Shintoists and Buddhists. The summit is home to a shrine and a small lake. A torii (sacred gateway) stands a few feet from the highest point. The ice, wind and frost mean that ascents of Mt. Fuji out of season are reserved for mountaineers, and may be impossible on stormy days. Indeed, every winter many fatal accidents occur on the mountain.

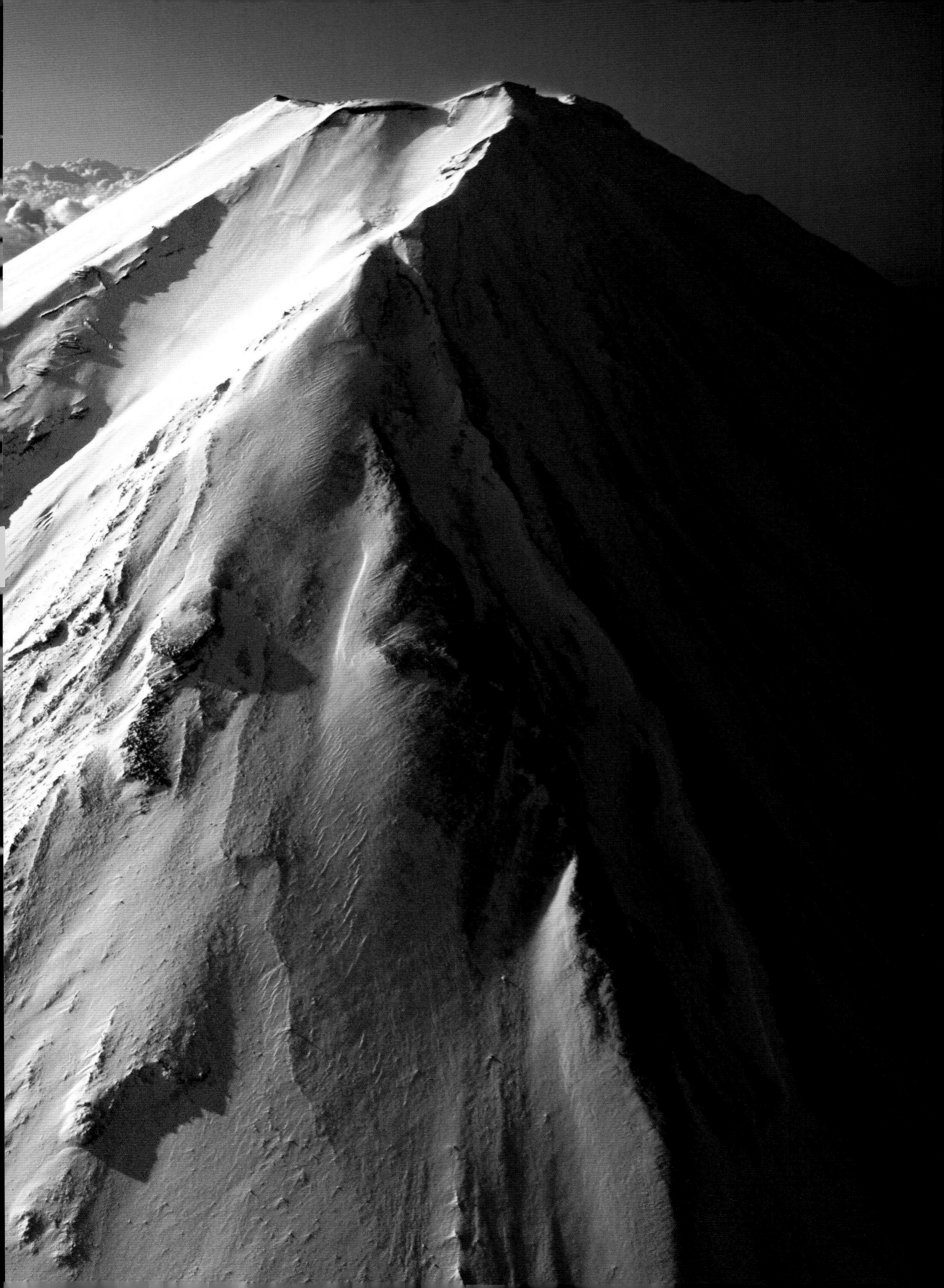

212-213 The imposing granite dome of Kinabalu, the highest mountain in Borneo, Malaysia and the whole of Asia east of the Himalayas, rises above the forests of Sabah just a few miles from the South China Sea. It is considered a sacred mountain by the Kadazan, who inhabit its slopes.

Kinabalu

Kinabalu
MALAYSIA

A huge, magnificent rocky mountain dominates the northern coast of Sabah, the state of the Malaysian federation that forms the northeastern corner of Borneo. Kinabalu is an enormous granite dome crowned with elegant and jagged peaks culminating in the 13,455-ft (4101-m) summit of Low's Peak and a series of slightly lower ones, such as the bizarre lopsided St. John's Peak (13,422 ft/4091 m) and the Victoria Peak massif (13,432 ft/4094 m), which is tinged with a magnificent red at dawn. Kinabulu, which is sacred to the Kadazan people who inhabit its slopes, is now protected by one of the most interesting national parks in Malaysia. The lower areas are covered with impenetrable and sultry tropical rainforest, which rings with the shrieks of monkeys, while the vegetation above 10,000 ft (3048 m) resembles that of the great African mountains, with giant heathers, mosses and lichens. Higher still these plants are give way to an austere mineral world: an ocean of smooth granite slabs where a seemingly endless fixed rope guides trekkers toward the little refuge of Sayat Sayat and the massif's highest peak, which is usually reached before dawn. Although the rock is very solid, only a few climbing itineraries have been traced on the Donkey's Ears and the towers west of Low's Peak.

The 30,000 trekkers (mainly Asians) who climb the mountain each year make Kinabalu – Asia's highest peak east of the Himalayas – one of the most frequented summits in the world. The forest, rocks and shadow of the mountain that lengthens toward the South China Sea at dawn make this a very memorable climb. The fog and sudden showers that assail the path mean that even the most expert climbers must proceed with caution.

The first person to experience Kinabalu's treacherous climate was the British botanist Hugh Low, a friend of James Brooke, the "White Rajah" who ruled nearby Sarawak. In 1851, Low reached the coast of Kota Beludu aboard a *prahu* sailboat from the island of Labuan, and battled his way through the jungle to the foot of the mountain, where he commenced an endless climb through rocks, heathers and rhododendrons. On the summit Low and his guides were enveloped by a thick fog and left a note in what they described as a bottle of excellent Madeira drained to Her Majesty Queen Victoria's health. The group carried back 79 species of plants (ferns, heathers and orchids) hitherto unknown to botanists.

Kinabalu

214-215 Each year around 30,000 trekkers, mainly Asian, climb towards the summit of Kinabalu, making it one of the most desirable and popular mountains in the world. Normally climbers set out from the Laban Rata Resthouse in the middle of the night, in order to reach the easy rocks of the summit just before dawn.

215 right Visible on clear days from the coastal town of Kota Kinabalu, Borneo's highest mountain was first ascended in 1851 by the British botanist Hugh Low, a friend of James Brooke, the "White Rajah." Low returned from the summit with 79 species of plants (ferns, heathers and orchids) hitherto unknown to science.

OCEANIA AND ANTARCTICA

The most inhospitable range in the world rises in the heart of Antarctica, midway between the Antarctic Peninsula and the South Pole. The Ellsworth Mountains culminate in the Vinson Massif, at 16,066 ft (4897 m) the highest point on the White Continent, but the masssif's Sentinel Range is also home to dozens of other mountains over 13,000 feet (3960), protected by imposing glaciers and in some cases rock faces. The great difficulties involved in reaching them mean that most of these mountains have never been scaled.

Many other mountain ranges interrupt Antarctica's icy terrain. The region has a little-known distinction: its ice-cap makes Antarctica the continent with the highest average altitude. Its vicinity to the Ross Sea, the Ice Shelf of the same name, and the largest and oldest scientific bases means that Antarctica's most famous and most frequently climbed peak is Mt. Erebus, a 12,448-ft (3794-m) volcano, visibile from both New Zealand's Scott Base and the United States' McMurdo Base.

In pride of place in the Queen Maud Mountains, between the Ross Sea and the South Pole, is Mt. Nansen, rising to 13,350 ft (4070 m). The Antarctic Peninsula, which can be relatively easily reached from both Argentina and Chile, is the continent's most-visited and best-known sector, and is home to many handsome peaks overlooking the sea. The region became the birthplace of Antarctic climbing in 1905 when the Italian alpine guide Pierre Dayné and the French climber J. Jabert scaled the 4642-ft (1415-m) Savoia Peak.

However, the Earth's far south is home to lands other than Antarctica. Between the continent and the Atlantic Ocean, just north of 60° south, and thus outside the scope of the Antarctic Treaty, the British possession of South Georgia. The island group is home to imposing glaciers and fine peaks. Despite its modest altitude of 9626 ft (2934 m), Mt. Paget compares favorably to other higher and more famous mountains.

Mt. Cook, the highest peak of New Zealand's Southern Alps, rises to just 12,349 ft (3764 m) but its ridges and faces, isolation and elegance allow it to bear comparison with much higher European, North American and Asian mountains. Discovered by the British and their Alpine guides, New Zealand's mountains have been the training ground of many of the world's leading mountaineers.

The highest mountain of Oceania, Puncak Jaya, reaches a height of 16,023 ft (4883 m). It dominates the forests of Irian Jaya, the Indonesian part of the island of New Guinea, and is almost always swathed in clouds. Australia has only modest peaks, the highest of which is Mt. Kosciusko at 7316 ft (2230 m). However, the island continent's impressive deserts are overlooked by pinnacles and rock faces – such as those of Mt. Arapiles – renowned among the world's best climbers.

216 The view north from the summit of Vinson Massif (16,066 ft/4897 m), the highest mountain in Antarctica, encompasses

Mount Tyree and Mount Shinn, the second and third highest peaks of the Sentinel range and the White Continent.

217 This aerial photograph shows the south face of Mount Cook, New Zealand's highest peak. Although the summit is just

12,349 feet high, it is nonetheless comparable to the "four-thousanders" of the Alps and many Alaskan peaks.

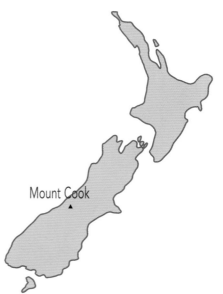

Mount Cook

Mount Cook

NEW ZEALAND

An extraordinary mountain rises in the land of the kiwi. Despite its modest height of just 12,349 ft (3764 m), the massive and remote peak of Mt. Cook – known by the Maori as Aorangi, or "cloud-piercer" – is the highest and most beautiful in the Southern Alps and the whole of New Zealand. Ever since the times of Edmund Hillary, generations of climbers have trained here in preparation for scaling the world's great mountain ranges.In 1770, Captain Cook, who was the first European to lay eyes on the Southern Alps (albeit from the sea), described them as wonderfully high with snow-covered peaks and valleys, and admitted to admiring them even though they were evidently useless for sheep farming. Ninety years later, the Victorian novelist Samuel Butler (who spent some years in New Zealand as a successful sheep-breeder) wrote that he did not believe that any man could ever reach the summits.

While Cook's remark regarding sheep – which are more numerous than people on South Island – proved to be correct, Butler's observation was refuted in 1894, when the globetrotting Monte Rosa guide Matthias Zurbriggen (who was also the first man to conquer Aconcagua) systematically started to ascend the finest summits of the Southern Alps. Before Zurbriggen and his Irish client Edward Fitzgerald could conquer Mt. Cook, the New Zealand climbers J. Clarke, G. Graham and T. Fyfe beat them to the summit.

However, the Monte Rosa guide soon made up for it by opening a new route and making the first solo ascent of Mt. Cook. In 1913 the Australian mountaineer Freda du Faur, accompanied by the guides P. Graham and D. Thompson, made the first crossing of the Summit Ridge, the hair-raising ribbon of snow and ice that connects the three summits of Mt. Cook. In 1949 the south ridge was ascended by Edmund Hillary, Harry Ayres, R. Adams and M. Sullivan, while in 1962 J. MacKinnon, J.S. Milne, R.J. Stewart and P.J. Strang conquered the Caroline Face, the huge southeast wall that has been likened to the north face of the Eiger.In recent decades modern climbing has also reached New Zealand and Mt. Cook. Leading names include Bill Denz, who made the first solo ascent of the Caroline Face during the early 1970s and put up several complex new routes. Modern routes include David and Goliath, a steep and dangerous itinerary on ice on the south face, inaugurated in 1991 by Paul Aubrey and P. Axford. However, it isn't necessary to be a mountaineer in order to see Mt. Cook. Indeed, the foot of the mountain, which is home to several hotels, can be reached by airplane. Visitors can get closer still by taking another flight aboard a small aircraft or by scrambling up the endless moraine slopes. The heavy rain clouds coming in from the Pacific mean that the ridges, icefalls and gullies are often so deeply coated with snow as to resemble the Himalayas or the Andes.

218 top This suggestive picture of the east face of Mount Cook shows the Zurbriggen Ridge and the buttress of Bowie Ridge.

218 bottom Some of the most challenging ice routes of the Southern Alps have been opened on the steep south face of Low Peak.

219 Three peaks rise from Mount Cook's narrow and fairly exposed summit crest. The northernmost of these is the highest (12,349 ft/3764 m).

220-221 Dawn illuminates the east face of Mount Cook and the snowy pyramid of Mount Tasman (11,476 ft/3498 m) to its right.

222-223 A sharp snow ridge forms the summit of Mount Cook.

Vinson Massif
ANTARCTICA

Antarctica's highest and most visited mountain rises in the Sentinel Range, 720 miles (1160 km) from the South Pole. From an altitude of 16,066 ft (4870 m), the Vinson Massif overlooks the desolate glacial expanse of the Antarctic ice cap to the east. In height it is only 52 ft (16 m) higher than Mt. Tyree, the White Continent's second highest point. The ice-cap is not unbroken. The rock, which in some areas emerges through the thick layer of ice, is of metamorphic origin with alternating yellow and darker bands.

The Vinson Massif was scaled for the first time in 1966 by ten members of the American Antarctic Mountaineering Expedition, but it became famous during the mid-1980s when the Seven Summits (the highest peak of each of the seven continents) became the goal of many mountaineers. In fact, with his ascent of the Vinson Massif in 1985, the Canadian climber Patrick Morrow became the first man to complete the conquest of the Seven Summits.

While not considered technically difficult, the Vinson Massif is certainly not accessible to everyone. Although a private organization has been offering a fully equipped base camp on Branscomb Glacier connected by small aircraft to Patriot Hills base and Chile since the 1980s, the costs of the expeditions are prohibitive for many, forcing almost all of them to seek major sponsors. So far approximately 500 people have conquered the Vinson Massif. During breaks between commercial expeditions, the guides have opened more challenging routes on the west face and on the Branscomb Ridge that climbs toward the south peak.

The normal route, followed by most climbers, is a long trek up huge and gently sloping ice slopes, which become steeper only on the summit face and the ridge that leads to the summit itself. Most climbers take about a week to reach the summit; many of them use skis for much of the route.

Although the altitude can certainly not be considered low, the real problem posed by the Vinson Massif is the climate. The ever-present wind can rise rapidly to speeds of over 90 mph (145 km/hr), forcing climbers to take shelter in tents, igloos or holes in the ice.

Although solar radiation is extremely high during the summer, the temperature can drop from -15° to -40° F (-26° to -40° C) in the space of a few minutes, putting a severe strain on mountaineers' stamina. Furthermore, the clouds of snow raised by the wind can make orientation very difficult. Adventure in Antarctica remains a struggle for survival, just as it was during in the day of Shackleton, Amundsen and Scott.

224-225 Before touching down on the Branscomb Glacier the aircraft flying towards Vinson Massif offers magnificent views over the surrounding peaks (here looking south, towards the Pole), the most spectacular in Antarctica, which rise over 600 miles (966 km) from the South Pole.

225 bottom The sheer vastness of Antarctica's ice plateaus can be fully appreciated from the small aircraft that connects the Patriot Hills base with the Vinson Massif base camp, revealing isolated peaks and entire mountain ranges.

*226 top A group of climbers
crosses a snow plateau during
the descent from Vinson Massif
(16,066 ft/4897 m). The first
ascent of the mountain was
made in 1966 by ten members of
the American Antarctic
Mountaineering Expedition.*

*226 bottom Roaring gales from
the South Pole deposit an icy
crust on even the lowest rocky*

*outcrops, making the summit
ridge of Vinson Massif uniformly
white.*

*226-227 The descent from
Vinson Massif alternates stretches
on fairly steep terrain with the
crossing of vast icy plateaus
swept by violent winds, in a
setting that conjures up images
of Shackleton, Amundsen, Scott
and the other Antarctic explorers.*

NORTH AMERICA

Although much of the continent is flat, North America, from Alaska to Yucatán, offers nature lovers and climbing enthusiasts a great variety of peaks, landscapes and adventures. The glaciers of Mt. McKinley and Mt. Logan, the great walls of the Yosemite and the sandstone towers of the Utah deserts, the plumes of smoke and glaciers of the perilous volcanoes that loom over the states of Oregon and Washington and Mexico's central valley are full of challenges. Likewise the rocks, forests and volcanoes continue in Central America, with the canyons and fiery mountains of Mexico's Chiapas highlands, Guatemala and Costa Rica, are full of reward for the adventurous.

The Rocky Mountains are the linchpin of the North American ranges, stretching for 3000 miles (4825 km) from Alaska toward California, comprising thousands of peaks and hundreds of glaciers, and separating the Far West of the continent from the Great Plains of Canada and the United States. The highest peaks are in the north, in the ranges of Alaska and the Yukon, where the environment and climate of Mt. McKinley and the other highest peaks are similar to those of the Himalayas.

Other magnificent mountains, much more accessible to trekkers, mountaineers and skiers, rise on the border between the United States and Canada and continue south as far as Colorado. West of these mountains lie the ranges of British Columbia (including the splendid granite peaks of the Bugaboos) and the Californian Sierras, world famous for their granite walls and sequoia forests.

Although much lower, the ranges closer to the Atlantic seaboard (the Adirondacks in New York State and the Great Smoky Mountains on the border between North Carolina and Tennessee) offer surprisingly wild vistas to those who, judging them from their position on a map, consider them too near to the great conurbations of the East Coast.

During recent decades expert climbers have been attracted to the granite faces of Baffin Island and the rock and ice peaks of Greenland. However, North America's mountains are not just for a small elite. From north to south and from to east to west, the summits and ranges of the continent are at the center of an unparalleled network of protected areas.

From Popo-Ixta to Denali trekkers, climbers, off-piste skiers or simply those wishing to relax in breathtaking surroundings are spoilt for choice with the Kluane, Jasper, Banff, Cascades, Yosemite, Rocky Mountains and hundreds of other parks. The paths, lined with bristlecone pines and sequoias, afford glimpses of moose, grizzlies, pumas, bison and many other extraordinary species. After all, the name "America" is synonymous with nature.

228 left Mt. McKinley, in the heart of Alaska, reaches an altitude of 20,320 ft (6193 m).

228 center The granite range of the Tetons culminates at a height of 13,766 ft (4196 m).

228 right Popocatépetl's lava slopes form the backdrop to the churches of Puebla.

229 The sun flushes the northwest face of Half Dome, in the Yosemite Valley.

230-231 Pyramidal Mt. McKinley, known to the Athabascan Indians as Denali ("The High One"), forms the backdrop to the mighty Ruth Glacier. Today the name Denali is used to denote the magnificent national park covering an area of 9310 sq. miles (24,113 sq. km) that protects the massif.

231 Climbers attempting Mt. McKinley reach the Kahiltna Glacier and base camp aboard the small airplanes that fly back and forth from Talkeetna, the nearest town to the mountain. Traffic of these aircraft becomes very intense during May and June, which are the best months for climbing.

Mount McKinley

USA

The highest mountain in North America rises in Alaska, in one the world's most spectacular national parks. On a summer day it is easy to sight eagles, mountain goats, moose and caribou, and perhaps even a mother grizzly loping through the grass accompanied by her cubs, beneath the icy walls of Mt. McKinley (20,320 ft./6193 m), known to the Athabascan Indians as Denali ("The High One").

Established in 1917 as the McKinley National Park, and rechristened in 1980 with the native name of the mountain, the Denali National Park and Preserve, covering an area of 9310 sq. miles (24,113 sq. km), has long been Alaska's most famous natural attraction. Each summer hundreds of visitors get in line to travel on the park buses at the entrance to the protected area at Wonder Lake.

Earlier in the year, between May and June, several hundred mountaineers board the small aircraft that ply between Talkeetna and the flat Kahiltna Glacier at the foot of the peak's southern slope to attempt the normal route that follows the mountain's

western spur. The high altitude, bitterly cold temperatures that can reach -40° F (-40° C), and violent winds that often blow mean that only a few of them manage to reach the summit.

The "official" story of Mt. McKinley, which was already well known to the Athabascan Indians, commenced in 1794, when the British navigator George Vancouver sighted a splendid snow-covered mountain. However, mountaineering in the far north of the Americas was born in 1897 with the Duke of the Abruzzi 's expedition to Mount Saint Elias, which of the great mountains on the Canadian-Alaskan border is the closdest to the coast. Five years later the United States Geological Survey ascertained that Mt. McKinley was the highest peak of all.

The earliest climbers reached the mountain in 1903, but the story of the first ascent is tinged with mystery. In 1906 Frederick Cook, accompanied by Ed Barrill, Hershel Parker and Belmore Brown, claimed that he had reached the summit, but was belied by a "photograph of the summit" taken from a peak 650 feet lower down.

Mount McKinley

Subsequently, amid general skepticism, the gold prospectors Pete Anderson, Charley McGonagall and Billy Taylor claimed to have conquered the mountain. The official conquest is attributed to Hudson Stuck, Robert Tatum, Harry Karstens and Walter Harper in 1912. However, the four men found a flagpole left by the prospectors on the north peak.

The remoteness of Mt. McKinley from the civilized world required a month's journey and the mountain was little frequented until the 1950s, when it became possible to reach it by plane. In 1951 a group led by Bradford Washburn ascended the West Buttress, which is today's normal route. Three years later a team from the University of Alaska made the first crossing. In 1961 an expedition of the Ragni di Lecco mountaineering group, led by Riccardo Cassin, conquered the highest buttress of the south face of the mountain, considered the greatest mountaineering "problem" in North America. In 1967 an international team made the first winter ascent, during which the French climber Jacques Batkin fell into a crevasse and died.

Over the past few decades other very difficult routes have been opened on the great faces of the mountain. New routes on the south face have been put up by British climbers Dougal Haston and Doug Scott (1976) and single-handedly by Czech mountaineer Miroslav Smid (1991). However, the greatest feat is that of another Italian, the Vicenza climber Renato Casarotto, who conquered the northeast ridge of Mt. McKinley, which he named "The Ridge of No Return" in 1977.

In the meantime the normal route has become increasingly popular. The hundreds of climbers who now attempt the peak each spring are creating serious pollution problems. Furthermore, despite monitoring by the park, the presence of groups without adequate experience is causing a growing number of accidents. It is true: the West Buttress not particularly difficult from a technical point of view. However, there is no such thing as easy climbing given the altitude and latitude of Mt. McKinley.

232 Mt. McKinley, the highest point in North America, is one of the Seven Summits, the highest peaks of each continent.

233 The ascent of Mt. McKinley is very grueling due to its exceptionally harsh weather conditions. During the coldest part of the year temperatures range from -33 to -69 °F.

234-235 The last of the sun's rays flush the peaks surrounding Mt. McKinley (20,320 ft/6193 m), the highest point in North America. The photograph was taken from a bivouac on the south face of the mountain, on the route opened in 1961 by Riccardo Cassin and the Ragni di Lecco mountaineering group.

Mount Asgard

CANADA

Extraordinary sheer granite rock faces dominate the fjords and glaciers of the Cumberland Peninsula on Baffin Island, in wild northeastern Canada. Spectacular and remote, worn smooth by glaciers over thousands of years, the walls of Mt. Thor, Mt. Asgard, Mt. Overlord and the nearby peaks were discovered during the early decades of the 20th century and not attempted until after World War II. Today they attract thousands of climbers from all over the world, who reach them by a long journey by boat and then on foot from Pangnirtung.

Mt. Asgard is Baffin Island's most elegant and renowned peak. Despite its modest height – the north and highest summit is 6598 ft (2011 m), while the south one is a few feet lower – this two-pronged peak has long been a training ground for roped parties from all over the world. While Mt. Asgard's North Peak was ascended for the first time in 1953 by the Swiss geologists Hans Weber, J. Marmet-Rothlisberger and F. Schwarzenbach, the South Peak was not conquered until 1971. Having gained the summit, the Canadian climbers G. Lee, R. Wood and P. Koch were then forced to make a dramatic ascent in a snowstorm.

The following year four internationally renowned mountaineers – the Britons Doug Scott, Paul Nunn and Paul Braithwaite and the American Dennis Hennek – climbed the North Peak's 3940-ft (1200-m) east spur, after having reached the base of Mt. Asgard on foot. Three years later the American Charlie Porter, a veteran of numerous ascents of the walls of the Yosemite Valley, single-handedly opened a route of 40 rope lengths on the North Peak's north face. These two extraordinary ascents made Mt. Asgard famous among climbers worldwide.

Following a pause of a decade, climbers commenced the systematic exploration of the faces of Mt. Asgard during the 1990s, when Canadian, American, Spanish, British and Italian roped parties opened dozens of advanced routes comparable in difficulty to those of the Californian big walls, but located in one of the wildest and most isolated settings in the Americas.

Indeed, despite their modest height and frequently sunny faces, the isolation of the peaks and the need to transport heavy loads make each ascent a challenging experience in the wilderness. As helicopters are not allowed to approach the mountains in the Auyuittuq National Park, climbers heading for Mt. Asgard must walk almost 30 miles (48 km) to Summit Lake and the base camps, carrying their food and equipment on their backs. The lack of any real path and the many fords to be negotiated make this a grueling and often dangerous journey.

236 Two climbers approach the awe-inspiring faces of Mt. Asgard.

237 The morning sun illuminates the faces of Mt. Asgard's South Peak (foreground) and North Peak.

238-239 The unmistakable forked silhouette of Mt. Asgard, with its sheer granite walls, dominates the glaciers of the Auyuittuq National Park, on Canada's Baffin Island.

Mount Logan

CANADA

The vast and wild Saint Elias Range, scoured by storms from the Pacific Ocean, is home to the largest glaciers in North America. One of the longest and most tortuous, the Seward Glacier, descends the southern slope of Mt. Logan in the Yukon. At 19,524 ft (5851 m), this peak is the highest point in the whole of Canada. It is an enormous, isolated and remote mountain.

The nearest town lies over 150 miles (240 km) from its foot, and half of the approach is over glaciers. The Mt. Logan massif rises in the Kluane National Park, which covers an area of

850 sq. miles (2200 sq. km) and is home to grizzly bear, moose mountain goats and the rare white bighorn.

While Mt. McKinley in Alaska attracts nature lovers and climbers from all over the world, Mt. Logan remains a solitary mountain, visited by just a few dozen groups each year. A flight of over 60 miles (96 km), completely over glaciers, from Haines Junction (the small settlement inhabited by the park's rangers) is necessary in order to reach its foot. The first ascent of Mt. Logan played a very important role in the development of Canadian climbing.

Promoted and headed by Albert MacCarthy, famed for his extraordinary stamina, the expedition set out in the heart of winter, when the snow-covered glaciers are easier to traverse on sleds. For two months MacCarthy and his five companions transported food, fuel and equipment toward Mt. Logan with the aid of three sleds pulled by dogs and two by horses. In the spring the mountaineers labored for another month to reach King Col at the base of the most technical part of the climb.

Although the subsequent difficulties were never excessive, the distance, high altitude and bad weather tried the mountaineers to the limit. Finally, on June 23rd, six men crossed the summit plateau and reached the peak. Upon their return, the British *Alpine Journal* reported that never before had any mountaineering expedition experienced such great suffering.

Following World War II the possibility of using small aircraft able to land on the Seward Glacier made Mt. Logan a little less remote. However, no technological invention has been able to reduce the size and height of the mountain, nor quell the ferocity of the Pacific storms that assail it. All the great feats that have taken place on the mountain, from the first ascent of Hummingbird Ridge by a Californian expedition (1965) and the four routes opened on the huge south face between 1959 and 1979 to the first winter ascent in 1986, are comparable to the hardest Himalayan ascents.

240 top and 241 Ice faces and crests make Mt. Logan and the other peaks of the Saint Elias Range a wild and spectacular world.

240 bottom The north face of Mt. Logan is one of the most remote and least frequented of the mountain.

Mount Logan

242-243 The last rays of the setting sun light the peaks and summit plateau of Mt. Logan (19,524 ft/5951 m), the highest mountain in Canada, which rises in the middle of the wild and spectacular Kluane National Park. The area is normally reached by two small aircraft that land on the Seward Glacier.

Mount Robson

CANADA

The highest and most impressive face in the Rocky Mountains overlooks one of the greenest and most spectacular valleys of British Colombia. The lower part is composed of crumbly rock shaped by erosion but is is crowned by a magnificent ice cap with crevasses and huge precariously balanced cornices. The mountain, standing 12,972 ft (3954 m) high, gives its name to the Mt. Robson Provincial Park, whose eastern border adjoins the Jasper National Park in Alberta, with its many peaks, forests and glaciers. A short distance to the south, the Banff and Yoho national parks and the Mt. Assiniboine Provincial Park are home to other incredibly evocative peaks that have been famous since the early days of mountaineering in the Rockies.

Although Mt. Robson can be glimpsed from the road running along the valley floor, it is a remote mountain.

Trekkers wishing to climb up toward Berg Lake, into which the finest glacier of the massif plunges, must walk for eight hours along an endless path with views of Kinney Lake and many spectacular waterfalls. Deer, mountain goats, moose, black bears and grizzlies can be encountered along this path and on the other routes of the park. As was the case with other peaks in western Canada, the ascent of Mt. Robson was not attempted until after 1886, the year in which the rail link from the Great Plains to Vancouver was completed and the first train crossed the Rocky Mountains. In addition to transporting goods, the Canadian Pacific Railway also aimed to develop tourism. In order to do so, it built hotels and invited to Canada mountaineering celebrities, such as Edward Whymper and Norman Collie, and leading Swiss and Austrian Alpine guides. It was, however, a Canadian – the Reverend George Kinney – who made the first serious attempts at climbing Mt. Robson and claimed to have reached the summit in 1909. After the admission that Kinney's ascent had been a hoax, the Canadian climbers Albert MacCarthy and William Foster, who subsequently also conquered Mt. Logan, reached the summit in 1913 together with the Austrian guide Conrad Kain, negotiating huge and challenging seracs and steep ice slopes that obliged Kain to cut over 600 steps. Due to the crumbliness of the rock, almost all the most important routes opened over the subsequent decades on Mt. Robson are on ice, commencing with the endless Emperor Ridge and the nearby and almost vertical Emperor Face. The Southwest Ridge is an even longer route, with a large proportion of rock, rising almost 10,000 ft (3048 m) before reaching the summit.

244 The rock and ice tower known as The Helmet rises among the crevasses and seracs of the Berg Glacier at the foot of Mt. Robson's north face. Some of the most classic climbing routes depart from Helmet Col.

244-245 The twin Berg and Mist Glaciers descend from the 12,972-ft (3954-m) summit of Mt. Robson to Berg Lake, at an altitude of 5423 ft (1653 m). Emperor Ridge is on the right, while the Emperor Face is visible to its left.

245 bottom The crumbly, eroded west face of Mt. Robson is crowned by a magnificent ice cap and overlooks the Yellowhead Highway linking Jasper with Valemount.

246-247 A closer look, again from the Berg Lake side, reveals the snowy cornices and rocky towers of the Emperor Ridge and the ice-streaked rock of the Emperor Face.

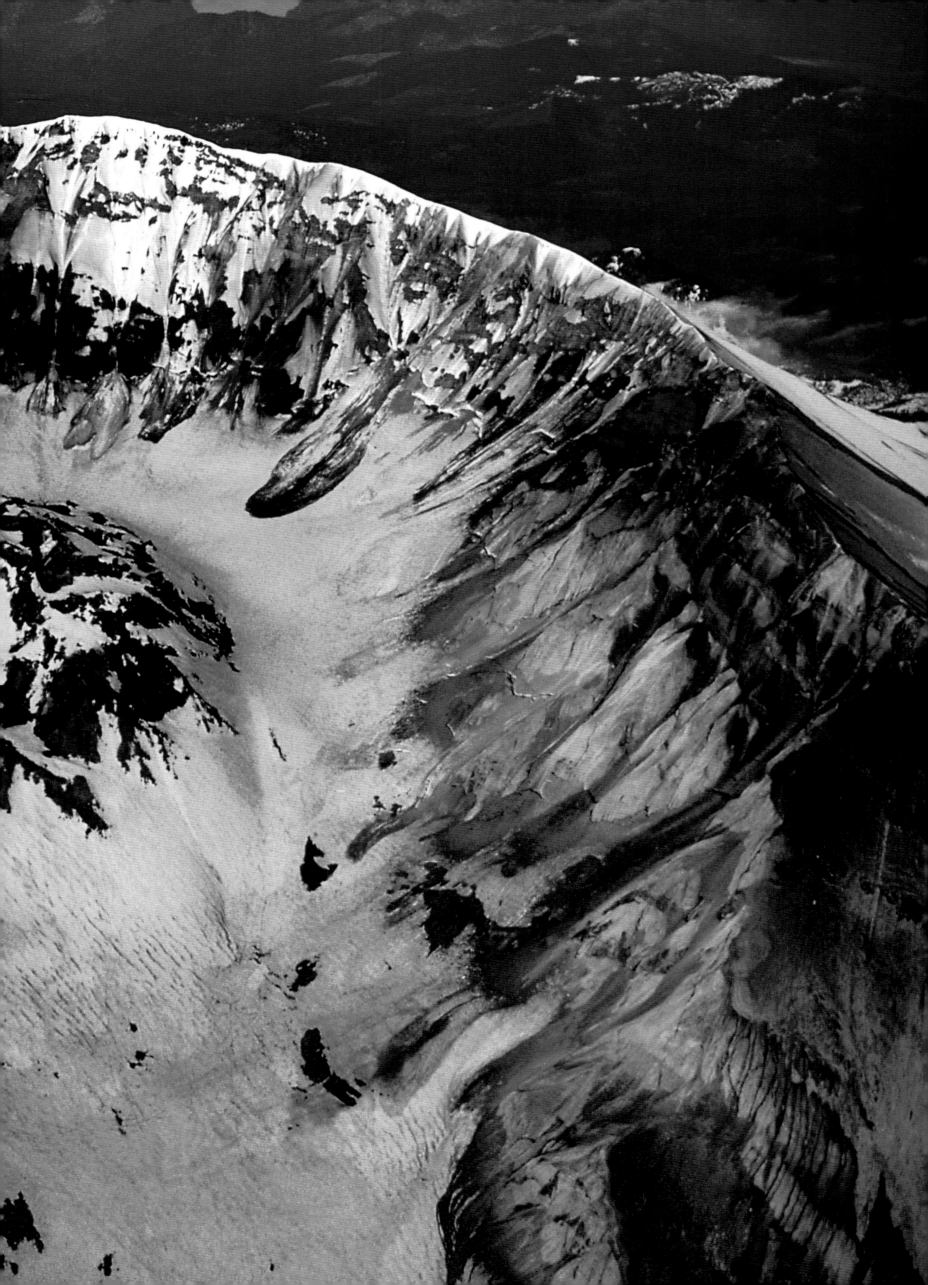

254-255 A ridge of rock, snow and detritus joins Middle Teton, in the foreground of the photograph, to the sharp rocky triangle of Grand Teton, the highest and most elegant peak of the range. The photograph was taken in late spring, when numerous trekkers and climbers prepare to return to the massif.

254 bottom At 13,766 ft (4196 m), Grand Teton is the highest peak of the range and also the most coveted by climbers.

255 The Grand Teton National Park, which protects the mountains, lake and meadows of Jackson Hole, is one of the most scenic in the Rockies and the United States.

256-257 During winter the pastures and forests of Jackson Hole are buried under a thick blanket of snow, and the ice-covered peaks of the Tetons become much more solitary and remote than in summer. The photograph shows awe-inspiring Grand Teton flanked by Middle Teton (left) and Mount Owen.

Grand Teton

USA

One of North America's most alpine landscapes greets visitors to the Jackson Hole valley in Wyoming, just south of Yellowstone's forests and hot springs. A band of lakes surrounded by thick conifer forests separates the pastures of Jackson Hole from the granite peaks of the Tetons (the name, given to the range by a French trapper, means "big heads"), which include imposing Mt. Owen, Middle Teton and Teewinot. However, by far the most elegant summit in the range is Grand Teton, which looms over all the peaks of the area from a height of 13,766 ft (4196 m).

Although Yellowstone is the world's most famous national park, American nature lovers consider the Grand Teton National Park one of the most scenic in the Rockies and the United States. Dotted with lakes, waterfalls, forests and valleys carved by ancient glaciers, it is home to black and grizzly bear, moose, and an amazing variety of birds of prey, while huge herds of deer can often be sighted at the foot of the mountains. Much dispute surrounds the first ascent of Grand Teton. In 1872 the surveyors James Stevenson and Nathaniel Langford announced that they had conquered the peak. However, in 1898 William Owen reached the summit and disputed the ascent allegedly made 26 years earlier, due to the inaccurate accounts of the mountaineers and to the absence of rock cairns, which the surveyors of the period used to build atop even much lower peaks. Surprisingly, Grand Teton was not climbed during the quarter of a century that followed Owen's feat. During the 1920s, as the normal route became popular, a new generation of climbers started to put up new routes on the mountains ridges and faces. Much of the merit for this goes to Robert Underhill, who ascended the long east ridge in 1929 (with K. Henderson), and followed this with ascents of the south and north ridges in 1931. A plethora of routes were opened on Grand Teton during the 1930s and the mountaineers who ascended them include such famous names as Paul Petxoldt, Willy Unsoeld and Jack Durrance, who were members of the great American expeditions to K2 and Everest during the years immediately preceding and following World War II.

Today, on fine days, roped parties of amateurs led by alpine guides line the Grand Teton normal route, which comprises a grade-III stretch. Only a handful of climbers attempt the endless and challenging ridges, or the modern routes on rock and ice that now cover every corner of the mountain. Wild and spectacular scenery extends in all directions.

El Capitan and Half Dome

USA

The sheerest and most difficult walls of granite in the world overlook the Yosemite Valley in the heart of one of America's most famous national parks. Renowned among travelers for its waterfalls, forests, lakes and bears, the most visited valley of the High Sierras – the granite range that separates California from the Nevada deserts – has been attracting the world's best climbers for half a century. Worn smooth by glaciers over thousands of years, the rocks of El Capitan, Half Dome, Cathedral Spires and other neighboring formations offer a breathtaking spectacle to the tourists on the valley floor traveling alongside the Merced River by car, bicycle or bus, and to the trekkers who throng the park's paths. However, to climbers, Yosemite means smooth slabs, crevices and challenges of days and days in an austere and vertical world of stone.

John Muir discovered the Yosemite and the High Sierras at the age of just over 30 and dedicated the rest of his life to showing the world its beauty during the second half of the 19th century. Scottish-born, Muir was a tireless walker and a lover of the wilderness, who became a writer and a militant conservationist. After having made the first ascents of several peaks of the valley (including Cathedral Peak in 1869), he made the natural wilderness of the West famous throughout America and the world, fighting to save rocks, animals and forests from the increasingly invasive presence of man. He was largely responsible for the foundation of the Yosemite National Park in 1890.

Climbers started tackling the granite of the Sierras at the beginning of the 1930s and immediately discovered that the walls of the Yosemite Valley were particularly challenging. It took Jules Eichorn, Dick Leonard and Bestor Robinson two years of attempts, with bolts and carabiners sent specially from Bavaria, before they managed to conquer the Higher Cathedral Spire, the first summit in the valley to be reached by man, in 1934.

Following World War, II John Salathe – a Swiss climber who moved to the United States to develop and manufacture steel bolts suitable for the crevices of Yosemite (the European ones, made of soft iron, bent on this very hard rock) – made the first ascents of Lost Arrow, the finest pinnacle of the valley, followed by the sheer wall of Half Dome. In 1957 Royal Robbins, Jerry Gallwas and Mike Sherrick reached the summit of the peak in five days via the sheer northwest face.

258 Though torrid at the height of summer, the Merced River Valley becomes cold and inhospitable in winter. The ice and snow that cover the ledges and fill the clefts make it impossible to climb El Capitan (the upper part of the wall can be seen in the photograph) and the nearby rock faces.

259 Many climbing routes that are now classics have been opened on the northwest face of Half Dome since 1957. While most of the Tis-sa-ack route, opened in 1969 by Royal Robbins and Don Peterson, is scaled by aid climbing, much of the classic route of the face is ascended by free climbing.

SOUTH AMERICA

The longest mountain range on Earth stretches between the Caribbean Sea and Tierra del Fuego. The Andean cordillera extends for 5500 miles (8050 km) from Venezuela to Chile, forming the watershed between the valleys that descend toward the Pacific Ocean and those that descend toward from the Amazon Basin and the Argentine pampas. Second in height only to the great mountains of Asia (Aconcagua, 22,835 ft/6960 m), is the highest peak of "the rest of the world"), this extraordinary range is even more varied and surprising than the Himalayas.

The succession of great Andean peaks commences with the Sierra de Santa Marta in Colombia, whose summits and glaciers are surrounded by tropical rainforest. Farther east, in Venezuela, the Sierra de Mérida overlooks the Caribbean's blue waters, then on the border between Venezuela, Guyana and Brazil stand the bizarrely shaped rocky *tepuis*, surrounded by the Amazonian rainforest. One of these mountains, Ayuantepui, is the source of the Angel Falls, the world's highest waterfall, whose waters plunge 3212 ft (979 m).

Ecuador, in contrast, is the home of fiery mountains. Cotopaxi, Cayambe, Antisana, Tungurahua, Illiniza and other volcanoes down whose steep slopes glaciers flow, flank Chimborazo. At 20,702 ft (6310 m), Chimborazo, was long believed to be the highest mountain in the world. Although many of Ecuador's volcanoes have often been climbed, they are not without danger: they are active and periodically cover the fertile valleys at their feet with lava.

Ice is the main attraction in the highlands between Peru and Bolivia, where the Cordillera Blanca, Cordillera de Huayhuash and the isolated massifs overlooking Lake Titicaca and La Paz are home to the continent's finest and most frequented ice peaks. Elegant summits such as Alpamayo, Yerupaja, Chopicalqui, Huandoy and Illimani, the king of the Bolivian cordilleras, surround the 22,205 ft (6768 m) summit of Mt. Huascarán, the roof of the Cordillera Blanca.

The easy-to-climb solitary volcanoes on the Bolivian-Chilean precede the highest part of the Andes, which culminates in Aconcagua. Extremely steep on the south face, which is one of the highest and most dangerous in the world, the Americas' tallest peak is renowned for its easy normal route that allows even fit and well-acclimatized trekkers to reach an altitude of almost 23,000 ft (7010 m)

The most handsome Andean rock peaks are situated much farther south; most of them are not even half as high as Aconcagua. Mt. Fitzroy, Cerro Torre and the Torres del Paine are renowned among climbers worldwide and rise from the flat landscape of the pampas and its lakes with granite pinnacles over 3300 ft (1006 m) high. Rare birds and pumas live at the foot of these mountains, while condors soar above and storms from the Pacific Ocean regularly scour the rocks and valleys. The wilderness of the Antarctic awaits the traveler beyond Cape Horn.

266 left Chimborazo (20,702 ft/6310 m) can be seen behind Cotopaxi, which rises to a height of 19,347 ft (5897 m).

266 center Overlooking the fjords of the Pacific coast, the three peaks of Torres del Paine are the most famous in Patagonia.

266 right The light of the setting sun illuminates the crumbly reddish rock of the west face of Aconcagua (22,835 ft/6960 m)).

267 Cerro Torre, considered by many climbers the world's most beautiful granite peak, reaches a height of 10,262 ft (3128 m).

Cotopaxi and Chimborazo

ECUADOR

Which is the highest mountain in the world? At the end of the 18th century, when researchers and explorers began to probe the high altitudes, Europeans were still unaware aware that the great Asian ranges were home to the highest peaks in the world. The summits of the Andes, on the other hand, had already been discovered. In 1744 a French scientific expedition measured the height of Chimborazo as 20,702 ft (6310 m) and made the first attempt at scaling it. In 1802 the German naturalist Alexander von Humboldt attempted the climb, reaching an altitude of 19,286 ft (5878 m), accompanied by the French botantist Aimé de Bonpland and the Ecuadorian Carlos Montúfar. Von Humboldt coined the term "The Avenue of Volcanoes" for the central valley of Ecuador, which is lined by 20 or so fiery mountains, including Cotopaxi (19,347 ft/5897 m), Cayambe, Antisana and Illiniza. Even El Libertador himself, Simón Bolívar, visited the foot of Chimborazo in 1822. Glaciers, scoured by avalanches and rent by great crevasses, make these mountains the realm of expert mountaineers. In fact, fifty years passed before first ascents were made: in 1879, the renowned climbers Edward Whymper and the Matterhorn mountain guides Jean-Antoine and Louis Carrel conquered Chimborazo and another eight volcanic peaks. However, seven years earlier the German climber Wilhelm Reiss and the Colombian mountaineer Angel M. Escobar had made the first ascent of Cotopaxi.

The Ecuadorian volcanic peaks do not attract only mountaineers. They offer extraordinary scenery to visitors to the central valley and to Quito, the nation's capital city. However, their eruptions have often caused serious damage. The lava flows of Cotopaxi have repeatedly invested Latacunga, but sudden reawakening of Tungurahua, for decades considered to pose no danger, caused extensive damage in the Baños area in 1998-99. The grasslands at the foot of Cotopaxi, protected by a national park, are home to herds of vicuña (a llama-like animal) and dozens of rare species of birds. Condors are frequently seen, while pumas are far less common. Chimborazo offers similar sights and is protected by a wildlife reserve. Above the snowline, access to both mountains is limited to mountaineers only, and each year they arrive in their hundreds equipped with ropes, ice axes, ice screws and crampons. Many achieve the feat of reaching a summit, though others are defeated by the high altitude and crevasses. Few of these climbers are aware that Alexander von Humboldt was right at least in part in an assertion he made: due to the flattening of the globe at its poles, Chimborazo's peak is the point on the Earth's crust farthest from the center of the planet, despite being 8327 ft (2538 m) lower than Mt. Everest.

268 Chimborazo was believed to be the highest mountain in the world for over a century, due to its gargantuan proportions. Attempted in 1802 by Alexander von Humboldt, Aimé de Bonpland and Carlos Montúfar, the mountain was conquered in 1879 by the British climber Edward Whymper with the Valle d'Aosta guides Jean-Antoine and Louis Carrel.

268-269 Although lower than Chimborazo (19,347 ft/5897 m compared with 20,702 ft/6310 m) Cotopaxi is the most elegant of Ecuador's great volcanoes.

269 bottom The route that ascends to the crater of Cotopaxi from the José Ribas refuge zigzags among walls of ice and gaping crevasses, which are usually easily visible and thus not particularly dangerous.

270-271 Whereas Chimborazo is an extinct volcano, Cotopaxi is still active and dangerous. On several occasions lava flows have spewed out of its small crater, next to the snow summit ridge, destroying the town of Latacunga, 22 miles (35 km) from the mountain.

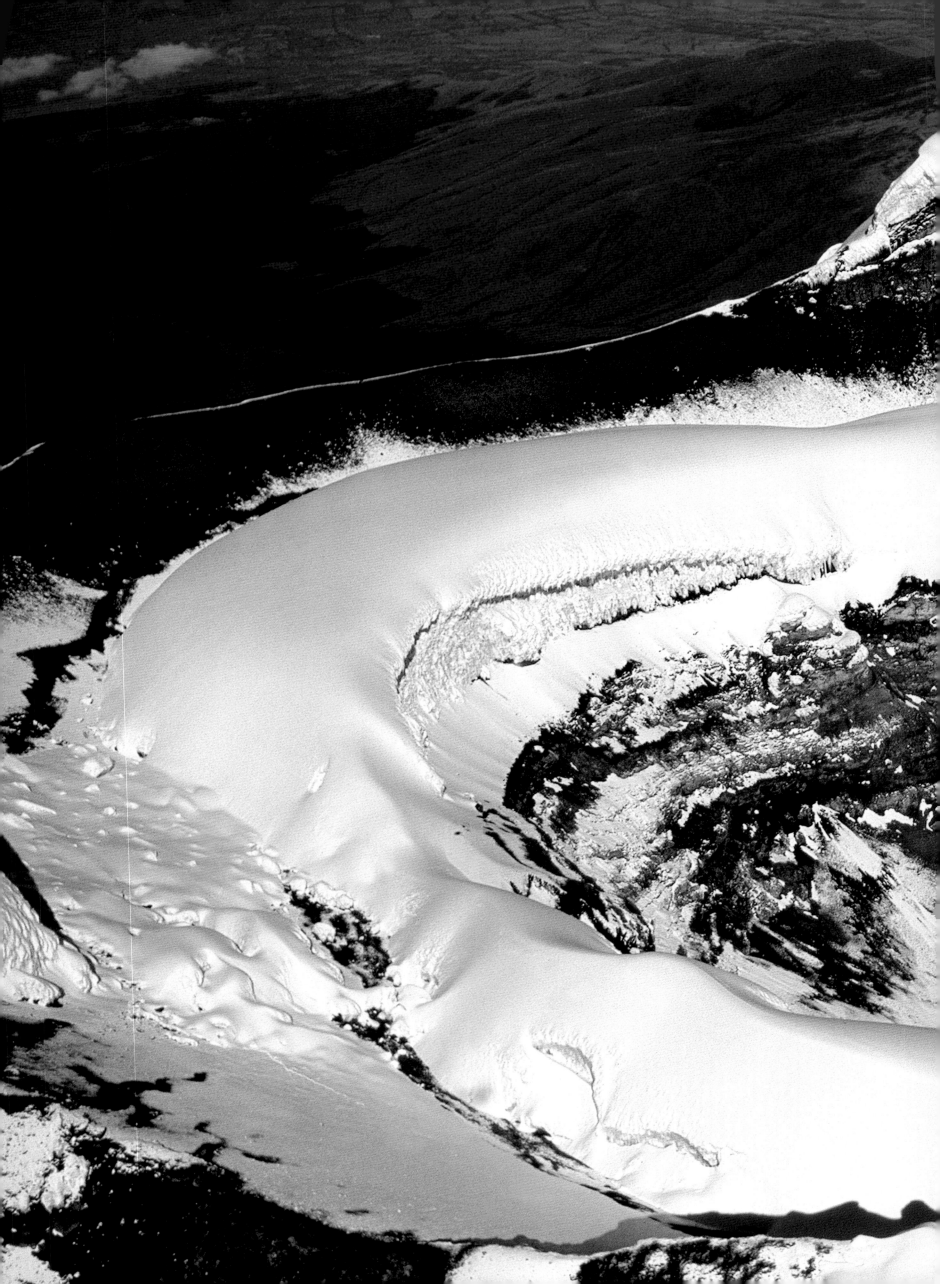

Huascarán and Alpamayo

PERÙ

The peaks of the Cordillera Blanca, among the most spectacular in the Andes, overlook the Callejón de Huaylas Valley and the city of Huaraz in northern Peru. Stately Mt. Huascarán (22,205 ft/6768 m), the fourth highest mountain in the Americas, is flanked by splendid ice peaks, including Chacraraju, Chopicalqui and Huandoy. However, the title of the most elegant peak of the range must go to Alpamayo, which rises 19,511 ft (5947 m), but is hidden to viewers on the valley floor by Nevado Santa Cruz. The Huascarán National Park covers an area of 1313 sq. miles (3400 sq. km) and is the largest in Peru. It is home to 663 glaciers, 33 archaeological sites, 112 species of birds, 10 species of mammals and 779 species of plants. The latter include *Puya raimondii*, a giant bromeliad that grows at altitudes between 12,500 and 13,800 ft (3810 and 4206 m), can reach a height of 40 ft (12 m) and produces a spike comprised of 20,000 flowers. However, in these mountains nature does not just mean great biodiversity and breathtaking landscapes. On several occasions huge avalanches originating on the highest peaks have reached the valley floor and its villages. In one tragic incident, on May 31, 1970 the little town of Yungay was buried and most of its inhabitants killed.

The Cordillera Blanca's mountaineering history commences with an remarkable figure. In 1908 Annie Peck, an American traveler, suffragette and early feminist from Rhode Island, ascended the 21,831-ft (6654-m) peak of Huascarán Norte with the Valaisian mountain guides Peter Taugwalder and Gabriel Zumtaugwald. The conquest of the highest summit had to await 1932 and an expedition organized by the German and Austrian Alpine Club in which Philip Borchers led E. Schneider, E. Hein, H. Hoerlin, W. Bernard, B. Lukas and E. Kinzl in the ascent of several peaks of the range, including Huascarán Sur.

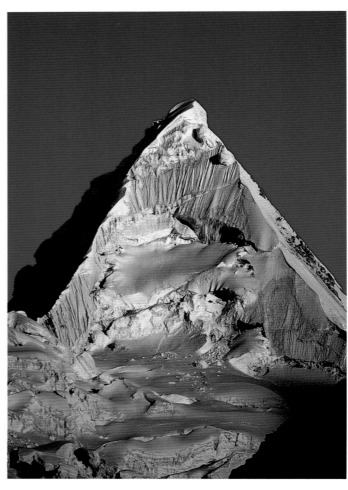

The cartographer Erwin Schneider drew a map of the Cordillera Blanca that is still used today.

Interest in the great Peruvian peaks increased following World War II, when travel to South America became accessible. The first mountaineer to fall in love with the icy mountains of the Cordillera was the Frenchman Lionel Terray, who conquered Huantsán, Taulliraju and Chacraraju Oeste between 1952 and 1956. In 1966, another French expedition, with R. Paragot, R. Jacob, C. Jaccoux and D. Leprince-Ringuet, scaled the north face of Huascarán Norte.

---

272 and 273 Although its altitude of 19,511 ft (5947) does not make it one of the Andean "giants," Alpamayo is ranked among the most beautiful

mountains in the world, as shown by these two views (left: the mountain seen from northwest; right: the famous southwest face).

274-275 The soaring, crumbly north face of Huascarán Norte is crowned by dangerous ice ledges and is one of the most difficult of the Cordillera Blanca.

Its first ascent, made in 1977 by the Vicenza climber Renato Casarotto, is one of the greatest feats of solo climbing of all times.

Five years later an American team climbed the Huascarán Sur's perilous east face. However, these climbers' feats pale besides that of Renato Casarotto, who single-handedly opened a direct route on the north face of Huascarán Norte in 16 days in 1977. A year later the French climber and physician Nicolas Jaeger camped on the main summit of Huascarán for 55 days as part of a physiological research project.

Three years earlier, in 1975, an expedition of the Ragni di Lecco mountaineering group led by Casimiro Ferrari and including Angelo Zoia, Danilo Borgonovo, Pino Negri,

Giuseppe Castelnuovo and Alessandro Liati scaled the southwest face of Alpamayo. The elegant rock wall, and the relative ease of their route have made it one of the most popular in the Andes. In recent years some of the best Slovenian alpinists, including Tomo Cesen and Pavle Kozjek, have left their mark on the faces of Alpamayo and Huascarán, while another trio of Slovenian climbers, B. Lozar, T. Petac and M. Kovac, have opened a new and dangerous route on Huascarán's Ancash face, with five bivouacs. However, mountaineering in the Cordillera Blanca is not just a leisure

activity. Since the beginning of the 1990s, the combined work of the members of the Salesian order and Italian Alpine climbing instructors in the Mato Grosso Project has led to the construction of three refuges (Ishinca, Huascarán and Peru), the establishment of a climbing school and the professional training of mountain guides. A hospital has also been built in Chacas, on the valley floor. Much of the revenue from the refuges is used to build houses for the poor and elderly inhabitants of the villages. These projects enable the climbers and trekkers who visit the Cordillera to help the local people.

Huascarán and Alpamayo

276-277 Slightly lower than its southern neighbor, Huascarán Norte rises 21,831 ft (6654 m) above sea level. It was first scaled in 1908 by the Rhode Island climber Annie Peck, accompanied by the Swiss mountain guides Peter Taugwalder and Gabriel Zumtaugwald.

Illimani

BOLIVIA

The king of the Bolivian mountains rises to a height of 20,741 feet on the horizon of the capital, La Paz. It is one of Latin America's most frequented and elegant great ice and snow peaks. Illimani is an imposing mountain with a complex topography. It belongs to the Bolivian Cordillera Oriental, beyond which the plateau that forms the central part of the country begins to drop eastward in the direction of the Amazon Basin.

The massif is crowned by a snowy ridge that is clearly visible from the capital, protected on the western side by steep slopes of snow and ice. The summit ridge culminates in the South Peak, but is also punctuated by the Central Peak (20,873 feet), North Peak (20,932 feet) and Pico del Indio (20,111 feet), long known as Pico Paris, but renamed after the discovery of a fragment of pre-Colombian rope.

The first ascent of Mount Illimani was made by the British mountaineer Sir Martin Conway, who reached the summit in 1898 together with the Valtournenche guides Antoine Maquignaz and Louis Pellissier. The group approached the mountain from the east and reached the summit by climbing the Pico del Indio. The current normal route was opened in 1940 by the German climbers R. Boetcher, F. Fritz and W. Kühn. Ten years later the famous German mountaineer Hans Ertl made the first solo ascent of the main peak and the first ascents of the Central Peak and North Peak (with G. Schröder). The first traverse of the three peaks, in 1958, was also achieved by a German roped party.

Only later did mountaineers of other European nationalities make their contribution to Illimani's climbing history. The list includes the Spanish expedition led by J. Monfort, the Italian group headed by the guide Cosimo Zappelli, and the great French ice climber Patrick Gabarrou who single-handedly opened a difficult route on the south face of the mountain in 1988. However, the greatest expert of the massif is another Frenchman, Alain Mesili, who has opened several new routes, both solo and as part of a roped party.

Although Mount Illimani offers great scope for exploratory climbing, most of the expeditions follow the 1940 route, which commences at the Puente Roto mine and normally requires two bivouacs. It is wise to keep away from the north face, which is home to the wreckage of an airplane that crashed in 1938 and was probably transporting gold, as Bolivian soldiers have opened fire on mountaineers close to the area of the accident on several occasions.

278-279 The sides of Illimani are covered with awe-inspiring glaciers. The South Peak (20,741 ft/6322 m)) rises from the summit ridge, alongside the Central Peak (20,873 ft/6362 m), North Peak (20,932 ft/6380 m) and Pico del Indio (20,111 ft/6130 m).

279 bottom The normal route of Illimani, on the west face of the mountain, is usually ascended in three days, with two intermediate camps. The group of climbers in the photograph has pitched camp within sight of the mountain's highest peak.

Illimani

280-281 In addition to the high altitude, the main obstacles encountered by alpinists heading for the summit of Illimani are walls of ice and huge crevasses. The photograph shows the ice towers a few feet from the normal route of the mountain, which is scaled each year by climbers from all over the world.

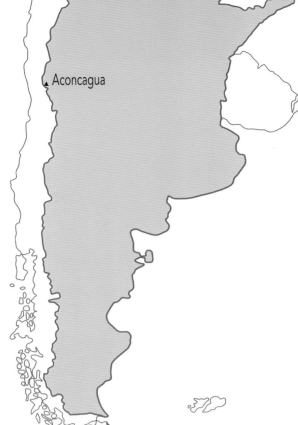

Aconcagua

ARGENTINA

The giant of the Andes is the roof-top of Argentina and the Americas. Standing 22,835 ft (6960 m) high, Aconcagua is the only "almost 23,000-footer" (7000+ m) outside the great Asian ranges and is the highest point on Earth south of the equator and in the Western Hemisphere. Its huge south face, traversed by enormous avalanches, is 1.5 miles (2.4 km) high and over 3 miles (4.8 km) wide, competing with the east face of Everest and the south face of Annapurna as the world's highest and most hostile rock face. However, the straightforward scree slopes of the west face allow thousands of mountaineers to attempt the summit each year. Nonetheless, the altitude and physical fatigue met with in the feat mean that only part of this number succeed. Aconcagua is visible from the road that links the Argentinian city of Mendoza with Santiago in Chile. The revolutionary leader José de San Martín skirted it in 1817, Charles Darwin observed it from afar, and in 1897 Matthias Zurbriggen, the great Monte Rosa guide, conquered it. The south face was not climbed until 1952, when the French mountaineers René Ferlet, Lucien Bérardini, Adrien Dagory, Edmond Denis, Pierre Lesueur, Robert Paragot and Guy Poulet made their successful ascent. Then in 1974 the Tyrolean climber Reinhold Messner single-handedly opened up a 3280-ft (1000-m) variation of the French path. In successive decades French, Argentinian and Slovenian roped parties traced other itineraries – all very difficult.

Aconcagua does not only attract mountaineers. The mountain, protected by a 275- sq.-mile (712-sq.-km) park, is also frequented by pumas and condors, while geese and other migratory birds flock to the Horcones Lagoon, at the park entrance. The flora, influenced by the altitude, includes herbaceous plants, succulents and a great variety of lichens. The Huarpes Inca tribe, driven out of Peru by Pizarro's conquistadors, settled at the foot of the mountain during the mid-16th century. They named it Aconcáhuac, "Stone Sentinel," and left the dramatic traces of their cruel veneration of the peak on its West Ridge.

During the summer of 1985 two mountaineers discovered a mummy at the foot of a sheer rock face at an altitude of 18,050 ft (5502 m). It was a nine-year-old boy, who had either been killed on the spot or bound and left to die. Today such rites seem incredibly cruel. However, for many pre-Columbian Andean populations, sacrificing what was dearest was considered the best way to invoke the protection of the gods.

282-283 The huge south face of Aconcagua, 1.5 miles (2.4 km) high and over 3 miles (4.8 km) wide, is one of the highest and most spectacular in the world.

283 bottom While elegant to admire and to photograph, the penitentes of Aconcagua and the neighboring peaks hinder the progress of trekkers and mountaineers. The ice spikes in the photograph rise on the Horcones Glacier, at the foot of the west face of the mountain.

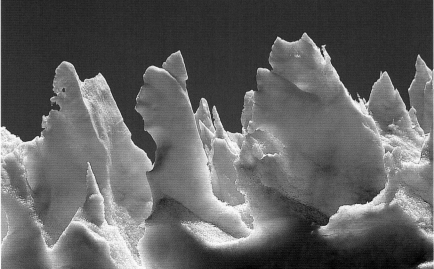

284-285 The sheerest part of the west face of Aconcagua overlooks Plaza de Mulas.

286-287 The steep, crumbly, complex west face of Aconcagua, scored by deep couloirs, has been ascended by several routes, almost all of which were opened by Argentinean roped parties. The very high altitude and difference in height, verging on 5000 ft (1525 m), make these routes very challenging even in the absence of any particular difficulties.

288 top A fantastic world
of rocks, glaciers, southern
beech woods and lakes extends
around Cerro Torre (visible on
the left in the photograph) and
Mount Fitzroy (right) in the heart
of Patagonia.

288-289 The mountaineering
history of Cerro Torre commences
with a mystery: the 1959 ascent
by the Trentino climber Cesare
Maestri and the Tyrolean
mountaineer Toni Egger, which
cost the life of the latter.

Cerro Torre and Fitzroy

ARGENTINA

Two extraordinary granite mountains rise in
Argentinian Patagonia, between the ice of the Hielo
Patagonico Sur, which acts as a barrier to the storms
of the Pacific Ocean, and the arid plateau that reaches east toward
the Atlantic. Mt. Fitzroy (11,289 ft/3441 m) and Cerro Torre (10,262
ft/3128 m) are renowned among climbers worldwide and are
surrounded by a forest of towers and pinnacles, including Cerro
Adela, Torre Egger, Cerro Standhardt, Aguja Poincenot and Cerro
Piergiorgio. On the Atlantic side, the peaks are encircled by a
spectacular landscape in which the Grande, Piedras Blancas and
Marconi glaciers descend toward the arid grasslands and the
perennially windblown great lakes. The area, together with the
Perito Moreno Glacier, is protected by Los Glaciares National Park
and is home to the condor, puma, guanaco (an animal similar to
llama) and rhea (also known as the *nandu*, the rhea is a strange
birds similar to a small ostrich). The paths that lead up toward the
mountains cross fantastic forests composed of species of
Patagonian beech, such as the *lenga* (*Notofagus pumilio*) and the
nire (*Notofagus antarctica*).

Though well known to the Tehuelche Indians, who called it
Chaltén ("the mountain that smokes") this highest Patagonian peak
was first recorded in 1834 by the British naturalist Charles Darwin,
who dedicated it to Robert Fitzroy, the captain of H.M.S *Beagle*,
aboard which he was making his famous voyage around the world.
However, it was the Salesian missionary-naturalist, Father Alberto
Maria De Agostini, who first explored its valleys and glaciers, which
he did during the 1930s.

The earliest colonists to settle the area were from Scandinavia and used horse-drawn carts to reach their *estancias* and ford the dangerous rivers. Some of them, such as the Norwegian Halvorsen and the Dane Andreas Madsen, made an important contributions to the exploration of this wilderness. However, alpinism did not make its debut on the granite Patagonian peaks until 1952, when the French climbers Lionel Terray and Guido Magnone made the first ascent of Mt. Fitzroy.

The attempts at scaling Cerro Torre commenced in 1958, when a Trentino and a Lombard expedition met at the foot of the mountain and chose two different faces for their ascents. In the event, Bruno Detassis, the leader of the Trentino expedition, prohibited his party (including Cesare Maestri) from ascending Cerro Torre, but Walter Bonatti and Carlo Mauri ventured onto the Hielo and tackled the west face, but were forced to give up. In 1950 Maestri returned with the Tyrolean alpinist Toni Egger. After days of struggling against adversities and bad weather, an avalanche caused Toni Egger to fall to his death. Then, at the last double rope, Maestri also fell onto a glacier, where Cesarino Fava found him two days later. When he had recovered, Maestri recounted how he and Egger had reached the summit and how the avalanche had swept away his companion during their descent. The conquest of Cerro Torre was thus recorded in the history books.

However, over the following years the climbing community increasingly questioned the ascent. In 1970 Maestri responded to his detractors by returning to the mountain and developing a new route, along which he secured hundreds of bolts, stopping just below the summit. In 1974 four members of the Ragni di Lecco mountaineering group (Casimiro Ferrari, Mario Conti, Daniele Chaiappa and Pino Negri) reached the summit from the Hielo side. The question of the disputed Maestri-Egger ascent appeared to be solved in 2005 when the Argentinian mountaineer Rolando Garibotti and the Italian climbers Ermanno Salvaterra (who also made the first winter ascent and opened several new routes) and Alessandro Beltrami followed the presumed 1959 itinerary without finding any traces of previous passage.

The controversy surrounding Maestri and Egger's ascent often overshadows the dozens of extraordinary routes on Cerro Torre and Mt. Fitzroy. Even the briefest list must include the Supercanaleta (1965), the Californian Route (1968), Cararotto's route on the North-Northeast Pillar (1978) and El Corazón (1992) on the East Pillar of Mt. Fitzroy; and the Slovenian Route (1986) and Infinito Sud (1995), Ermanno Salvaterra's masterpiece on the Cerro Torre. Each of these routes takes weeks, months or years of toil, for mountaineering on Mt. Fitzroy and Cerro Torre requires great class and willingness to suffer.

Cerro Torre and Fitzroy

290 To the west, in the direction of Chile, the granite pinnacles of Cerro Torre and the nearby peaks dominate the ice plateaus of the Hielo Continental, the largest icefield in the world outside the polar regions.

291 The east face of Cerro Torre, about 3300 ft (1006 m) high, dominates the Torre Glacier and Lagoon. The imposing icy peaks of the Cordón Adela range rise to the south (left) of Cerro Torre.

292-293 The light of dawn make the granite range culminating in Cerro Torre (10,262 ft/3128 m, left), and continuing with Torre Egger (9800 ft/2987 m) and Cerro Standhardt (8694 ft/2650 m), even more spectacular.

Torres del Paine

CHILE

The stiff wind off the Pacific ceaselessly caresses the most beautiful peaks of Chilean Patagonia, which overlook lakes Grey, Sarmiento, Nordenskjöld and Pehoé between the fjords of Puerto Natales and the Argentinian border. "The most superb group of peaks and summits of the Patagonian Cordillera," was how the Salesian father Alberto Maria De Agostini, who was a great Patagonian expert and keen mountaineer, described the Torres del Paine in 1943. Before glimpsing the three granite towers – the South, Central, and North – at the heart of the massif, those approaching from the pampas and the border see the peaks of ice and rock that crown them. The glaciers, gullies and snowy cornices make the Paine Grande and Cerro Bariloche resemble the 6000-m (19,685-foot) peaks of the Peruvian Andes. The bizarre silhouettes of the Cuernos stand out against Lake Pehoé, and it is necessary to climb the valley of the Rio Ascencio, covered with thick southern beech woods, to arrive at the foot of the South Tower (8202 ft/2500-m), Central Tower (8071 ft/2460-m) and North Tower (7415 ft/2260 m) overlooking the sandy plateaus and glaciers. Father De Agostini's writings meant that Italian mountaineers were the first to scale these peaks. In 1957 five Val d'Aosta guides made the first ascent of Paine Grande, while six years later, in 1963, the British climbers Chris Bonington and Don Whillans beat a Trentino and Lombard expedition to the summit of Central Tower, the slenderest of the trio. A few weeks later, Armando Aste, Vasco Taldo, Josve Aiazzi, Carlo Casari and Nando Nusdeo got their own back by conquering the South Tower, which they dedicated to Father De Agostini. Over the following years other great routes were opened by Argentinian, Chilean, New Zealand and American roped parties. The massif is surrounded by an extraordinary landscape, protected by the 700-sq.-mile (1813-sq.-km) Torres del Paine National Park. The Pacific wind blows the icebergs that break away from the Grey Glacier toward the shores of the lake of the same name. In the most sheltered valleys the southern beech woods (known as *lenga* in Argentina and Chile) are fabulous and intricate. The windblown grasslands are home to small herds of guanaco and fast-running, ostrich-like rheas (also known as *nandu*), while the sandy soil bears the tracks of puma and condors glide overhead. As Pablo Neruda wrote, "Anyone who hasn't been in the Chilean forest doesn't know this planet."

294 Blue icebergs float on Lake Grey, one of the many lakes in the Torres del Paine National Park. The lake, fed by the glacier of the same name, extends to the immediate east of the massif.

295 Paine Grande in the far west corner of the massif marks the highest point of the group, at 10,006 ft (3050 m). The frequent storms that hit this remote region mean that the mountain is rarely fully illuminated by the sun.

296-297 The Torres del Paine massif (from left: the South Tower, 8202 ft/2500 m; Central Tower, 8071 ft/2460 m; and North Tower, 7415 ft/2260 m), boasts the finest granite peaks in Chilean Patagonia.

298-299 The faces of the Cuernos del Paine group are formed by granite at the base and dark volcanic rock higher up and dominate the most frequented area of the Torres del Paine National Park.

INDEX